The Walleye War

The Walleye War

The Struggle for Ojibwe Spearfishing and Treaty Rights

LARRY NESPER

University of Nebraska Press : Lincoln and London

⊗

Library of Congress Cataloging-in-Publication Data
Nesper, Larry, 1951–
The Walleye War : the struggle for Ojibwe spearfishing
and treaty rights / Larry Nesper.
p. cm.
Includes bibliographical references and index.
ISBN 0-8032-3344-2 (cloth : alk. paper) – ISBN 0-8032-
8380-6 (pbk. : alk. paper)
1. Ojibwa Indians – Fishing – Wisconsin. 2. Ojibwa
Indians – Legal status, laws, etc. 3. Lac du Flambeau
Reservation (Wis.) 4. Wisconsin – Ethnic relations.
I. Title.
E99.C6 N47 2002 639.2′1′089973–dc21 2001053181

To the memory of Jerry Maulson   And for my parents and daughters

CONTENTS

ILLUSTRATIONS

Preface

My brother Glen graduated from Ripon College with Nick Van Der Puy in 1975. By the late 1970s they had both come to live within a few miles of each other in Eagle River, Wisconsin, forty miles east of Lac du Flambeau. Nick drew me into the spearfishing conflict as a supporter in 1988 and 1989. In the spring of 1989, while standing in solidarity with spearing families on the boat landings, I decided to undertake an ethnographic study of what was unfolding, having returned to graduate school the previous fall. I made seven trips to Lac du Flambeau and other Indian communities in northern Wisconsin between mid-April and mid-July of that year.

I lived at Lac du Flambeau for seven months from February to September of 1991, doing fieldwork on the cultural dimensions of a conflict that was at that point largely over. I began my work by informing Mike Allen, then tribal chairman, of my interest, giving him a copy of my dissertation proposal. As we had become somewhat acquainted during the spearing season of 1989, he agreed that such a study would be worthwhile. I then sought out Tom Maulson, Nick Hockings, Scott Smith, and Gilbert Chapman—whom I had also met in 1989—told them of my interest, provided them with copies of my first published work so they could understand my goals (Nesper 1989b), and secured their support. As I met more of the people who appear in this book, I told them of my interest and intentions. The stories and accounts in the text are their recollections. Accounts that are not specifically identified with tribal members are my own perceptions and memories of events.

I had a great many breakfasts in the Outpost Cafe talking with spearers. In the afternoons, I visited Family Circles, one of the tribal social program offices that sought to involve tribal members more deeply in their culture. It was there that I spoke with Ernie St. Germaine, who would soon become the band's chief judge. I also attended language classes, ceremonies, public events, and meetings, which led to visits with people in their homes. In addition, while my wife, Julie, worked as a home health nurse, I worked as a part-time substitute teacher a day or two a week from February to June in both the elementary school on the reservation and at the high school in Minocqua.

Since 1991 I have returned to Flambeau for numerous visits that now, collectively, exceed my original period of research in 1991. Though it could be said that I conducted informal interviews at Lac du Flambeau over the last twelve years, I prefer to think of them as organic conversations indicative of deepening relationships with people, a number of whom have become my friends.

ON TERMS

I use the native term "Flambeau" throughout this book. It is the most common reference used on the reservation and is accented on the first syllable, like "Rambo," with which it rhymes. The name Lac du Flambeau is said to have originated with the French as a reference to the local natives' use of torches while hunting or fishing on the lakes (Warren 1984:192). Today, Ojibwe people say that Lac du Flambeau is French for the Anishinaabemowin term "Waswaaganing," meaning "Torch Lake." By the time the indigenous people dwelling in the area of these lakes were named by the French after their practice of hunting and fishing at night, they were known by others and to themselves as a kind of "Ojibwe." There are at least three different understandings of the origin of the term "Ojibwe," two that imply relations with non-Ojibwes. According to Warren (1984:35–37), the preeminent nineteenth-century mixed-blood ethnohistorian of the Ojibwes, the name either refers to the moccasin that they wore or to their practice of roasting captives. He noted that "the name does not date that far back." Hickerson (1962:78) suggests and Schenk (1997) argues at length that "Ojibwe" derives chiefly from the Crane clan as the morphology suggests the sound of the Crane's voice as expressed in Anishinaabemowin. The term "Chippewa" is the American version of "Ojibwe" and is used in most official relations between the United States and these people. My occasional use of it will be in contexts where officials or agents of the United States play an important role in defining the particular situation.

Among the neotraditionals at Lac du Flambeau in the 1990s, "Ojibwe" was preferred to "Chippewa." In the same way and to a greater degree, "Waswaaganing" was preferred to "Lac du Flambeau" as it marked both a biculturality and a developed political conscious-ness of colonization. Waswaaganing was usually used with "Anishi-naabeg" instead of "Ojibwe," as Anishinaabe was the most general characterization used by the peoples who have become the historic Ojibwes, Ottawas, and Potawatomis (Day and Trigger 1978:797; Clif-ton 1978:741). "Ojibwe" may also be preferred to "Chippewa" by neotraditionals because it is used in the north (specifically in Canada and Minnesota), which is perceived to be the source and site of more credible and traditional knowledge of cultural matters and also the di-rection from which these people came sometime in the eighteenth century.

I use whites and non-Indians nearly interchangeably, and when foregrounding the conflict between indigenous people and Euro-Americans, I use "Indian" as it is used on the reservation to discuss in-tercultural and interracial matters.

"Tribe" is synonymous with band and, following current usage, re-fers to both the separate governments of the six bands of Lake Supe-rior Chippewa Indians and the reservations as a social totality. The term suggests subethnic units within the larger category of Ojibwe. This usage reflects the reality and importance of different band histo-ries. It also reflects the policy that federal Indian status is determined by blood quantum that is ascertained by each band's tribal council.

ACKNOWLEDGMENTS

The late Jerry Maulson referred to the many different good things that came out of the conflict over spearing as "the flowers of *Voigt*," refer-ring to the name of the court case that began this conflict. They in-cluded marriages, children, attitudes, personal capacities, interests, even institutions like the new elementary school at Lac du Flambeau, the Family Resource Center, and the casino. I will always remain grate-ful for Jerry's friendship, his generosity, his love of dialogue about cul-tural and educational matters, and for everything that he taught me about the community at Lac du Flambeau. I miss him a great deal but am comforted that he lives so fully in the hearts of many people.

I thank my parents for the different kinds of encouragement and support they gave me over the years, and especially my father for his unschooled yet long-standing interest in ethnography. I am very grate-ful to Nick Van Der Puy, fishing guide and a treaty rights activist in the

1980s and early 1990s, for his friendship and hospitality over the years and for encouraging me to support the exercise of treaty rights and write about the courage and vision of the Anishinaabe people. I am also grateful to Julie Seavy, the mother of Molly, our own "flower of *Voigt,*" for her support in accompanying me to Lac du Flambeau in 1991, and to my daughters, Hanna and Emma, for their interest in and enthusiasm for this project that has gone on for more than half their lives.

I thank Gary and Neil Kmiecik for their friendship, hospitality, and for many hours of conversation about cultural, social, and political matters in northern Wisconsin.

I am grateful to Ernie St. Germaine for his friendship and everything he has taught me about Anishinaabe spirituality. I am grateful to Gilbert (Gibby) Chapman; Tom and Laura Maulson; Alex and Alice Maulson; Nick and Charlotte Hockings; Don, Joey, and Scott Smith; Brooks Big John; Vince St. Germaine; Joe, Mike, and Ed Chosa; Wayne Valliere; Robert Martin; Mike Allen; George Brown; Pam Torres; Pat Hrabik; Betty Jo Graveen; Larry Mann; Frank White; Goldie Larsen; Denise Wildcat; Dorothy and Brandon Thoms; Anita Koser; Tinker Schuman; Gregg and Marcus Guthrie; Gail Guthrie Valaskakis; the late Walter Bresette; Betty Martin; James Yellowbank; Eddie Benton-Banai; Nan Andrews; Annamarie Beckel; Glen Nesper; and Jim Jannetta for the many conversations about spearfishing, treaties, conflict, identity, history, and Indian-white relations in the Northwoods over the years.

Raymond Fogelson, Marshall Sahlins, John Comaroff, Terry Straus, John MacAloon, Neil Kmiecik, Gary Kmiecik, and Jim Schlender read the much earlier dissertation version of this account and made many thoughtful suggestions for its improvement. I have returned repeatedly to their comments and their written work for inspiration.

I owe a debt of gratitude to the entire faculty of the anthropology department at the University of Chicago for the Frederick Starr lectureship in 1993 that permitted me to teach a course on Ojibwe culture and history. That course helped me to appreciate the different roots of the conflict over off-reservation spearfishing. Terry Turner, Larry Sullivan, and Tim Buckley read even earlier versions of this and suggested directions to take that I often followed. I thank them all for their insights.

I also thank friends and colleagues with whom I have discussed aspects of the book: Ray Bucko, Bill Balan-Gaubert, Fred Gleach, Sharon

Stephens, Rob Brightman, Jim Zorn, and Eric Lassiter. Esteban Chiriboga, Teresa Story, Paul Shanayda, Charlie Rasmussen, and Annie Thannum helped me with technical matters.

I am grateful to Charles Cleland and Ronald Satz for their critical reading of the manuscript and their encouragement.

Clearly, I have had the benefit of many good teachers. I share credit with them for the strengths of this book, but I assume full responsibility for its shortcomings.

The Walleye War

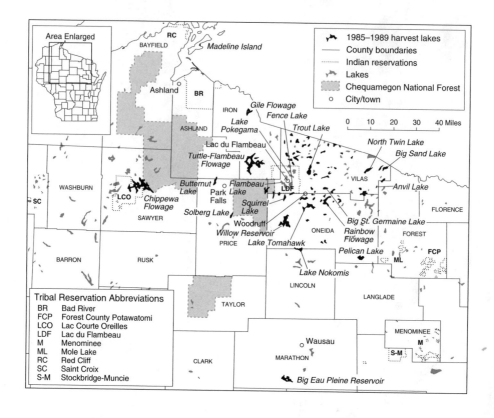

The Ojibwe bands and the lakes they harvested
between 1985 and 1989. After a map prepared
by Esteban Chiriboga, Great Lakes Indian Fish
and Wildlife Commission.

Introduction

1. Tribal member Scott Smith sharpens the tines of his fishing spear. Photo courtesy of the author.

On October 25, 1989, the adult membership of the Lac du Flambeau band of Lake Superior Chippewa Indians voted down tribal council Resolution 369 (89), a proposition that would have leased federally guaranteed treaty rights for off-reservation hunting, fishing, and gathering to the state of Wisconsin for a ten-year period, pending state and federal approval. The community, numbering some twenty-four hundred, would have received a package of social and economic programs, employment opportunities, and per capita cash payments collectively valued at fifty million dollars.

The vote came toward the end of an intense six-year period of conflict between the Flambeau band, its neighboring non-Indian communities, and the state. It was the culmination of a series of events and interactions between the six Wisconsin Chippewa bands that both reorganized their cultural identities and reconfigured the relationships among them, the latter through the emergence of the Great Lakes Indian Fish and Wildlife Commission (GLIFWC), a consortium of eleven tribal governments from Minnesota, Wisconsin, and Michigan.

In 1983, after nine years of litigation, the U.S. Court of Appeals had upheld the Wisconsin bands' rights to hunt, fish, and gather on the lands and lakes of the northern third of the state—the area ceded in the treaties of 1837 and 1842. The court decision upheld the Indian right to use traditional methods to harvest fish. No one had been permitted to spear game fish in Wisconsin for over a century before that decision. The conflict focused on the Lac du Flambeau band's harvesting of spawning walleyed pike, a species of game fish that the state had been cultivating in the northern lakes for over a century.

Many non-Indians in the politically conservative north-central area of Wisconsin saw themselves as dependent on tourism and feared that spearfishing would destroy the economy over time. They were concerned that Ojibwe spearfishing would deplete the fish population and leave little for tourists. Non-Indian groups such as Equal Rights for Everyone, Protect America's Rights and Resources (PARR), and Stop Treaty Abuse/Wisconsin (STA/W) emerged and became allied with national anti-Indian organizations in order to oppose the local Indian exercise of treaty rights. Basing their opposition on the principle that such rights represented a violation of equal justice under the law—as similar groups had done in the Northwest (Cohen et al. 1986) and Michigan (Doherty 1990)—hundreds of non-Indians protested at the lakes where Indian people spearfished. Between 1985 and 1991, hundreds of protesters were arrested for acts of civil disobedience. The state spent millions of dollars on law enforcement, and the social fabric of northern Wisconsin became torn along racial lines through numerous acts of overt hostility and violence between tribal members and non-Indians.

Some Anishinaabe people at the Lac du Flambeau reservation attempted to mold this conflict into a political and social movement, drawing on the local cultural capital they had inherited as well as their relationships with other Indians in the region and beyond. Tribal members helped revive the community's memory of a relationship with the federal government that had been ratified a century and a half earlier and evoked culturally specific and long-contested subsistence practices such as spearfishing and "violating" (hunting out of the state's season). Cultural practices that had retreated to the relative privacy of extended family gatherings over the course of the century became realized once again at the community level. Large feasts and ceremonies bolstered and hardened the resolve of those who were taking the risk of reimagining Lac du Flambeau. Prophecy reemerged and played a key role in this unfolding drama.

In an attempt to buy out the Lac du Flambeau band, the state offered its members effectively the equivalent of over three hundred dollars per fish speared. The offer was meant to quell the social unrest brought about by the bands' spearing of 2 percent of the annual 670,000 walleyed pike taken from the lakes by sportfishers in the ceded territories. The value of the exercise of these rights in monetary terms would have been more than compensated by the proposed per capita payments alone. More interesting still, only a small proportion of tribal members—no more than 15 percent—ever fished off the reservation; half of those fished for only one or two nights, taking a few dozen walleyed pike. An even smaller number of tribal members went off the reservation to gather wild rice in the late summer or hunt deer over a three-month season in the fall.

Juxtaposing the limited exercise of treaty rights with what the state was willing to pay to lease their forbearance, Flambeau's vote to turn the offer down is counterintuitive and begs explanation in cultural and historical terms. The off-reservation exercise of rights and everything it would come to mean point to a distinct and dynamic order of value, system of meaning, and cultural complex at Lac du Flambeau. These values, meanings, and practices are in many ways profoundly different from the ones assumed to have been adopted by these Indian people over the last century.

How did a sense of distinctness remain viable enough, despite all of the changes experienced by the Lac du Flambeau community since the fur trade and treaty period, to motivate sustained practical and political actions of such consequence? How does an indigenous system of meaning endure and transform even as the individuals who transmit it revalue and appropriate practices that originate in the dominant society? How are the complex historical and cultural processes in such a context of domination related? These questions impel this study as I describe and interpret a culturally organized political and social movement at Lac du Flambeau in the late twentieth century that centered primarily on a dispute within and without the community over spearfishing walleyed pike.

The history and value of the use of off-reservation resources before and since the court decision of 1983, the formation and emergence of a militant faction that aggressively hunted and spearfished, and the events, images, and arguments that were engineered, evoked, and assembled when contesting the agenda of the Lac du Flambeau tribal council, clearly indicate that Lac du Flambeau remains a separate and culturally distinct community. It is in this sense that Lac du Flambeau is an emergent center in "their own system of the world" (Sahlins 1988:4). Though colonized and transformed, this society is largely organized by an order of value that is both continuous with and a transformation of Ojibwe culture in other locations throughout the upper Great Lakes over the course of the last 350 years. Yet Lac du Flambeau undeniably has been integrated into the global economy and culture for 250 years. Indeed, its genesis lay in the interaction of global forces. Nonetheless, it has continued to grow and transform as a social and cultural entity whose members share an image of it as separate.

The revitalization and reimagining of the Waswagoninniwug Anishinaabeg in the late twentieth century did not occur in a cultural or historical vacuum. Anishinaabe people have participated in authoring their own history within the world-system for a long time. After a description of the Lac du Flambeau community, I turn to the seventeenth and eighteenth centuries and examine the relationship between three key features of Objibwe life: the fur trade, the Midewiwin ceremonial complex, and warfare. When discussing these early years and Anishinaabe responses to contact, I present a model for understanding subsequent culture history at Lac du Flambeau that attends to the ways in which culture as a meaningful order is revealed in a community history. Attention is then given to how the subsequent imposed and imported modes of material and symbolic production—lumbering, tourism, Indian guiding, and commercial hunting—simultaneously facilitated the reproduction of what were understood to be traditional Indian signs and practices and transformed the identity, society, and culture of the band's members.

A number of mid-twentieth-century psychological and anthropological accounts of the Lac du Flambeau Ojibwes (Barnouw 1950, 1961; Boggs 1954, 1956, 1958; Caudill 1949; Gillan 1942; Gillan and Raimy 1940; Hay n.d.) and their neighbors at Lac Courte Oreilles (James 1954a, 1954b, 1961, 1970) represent them as acculturating and becoming rural Chippewa Americans. There is much to be gleaned from these studies. However, the local and worldwide reemergence and revaluation of indigenous culture and identity that began in the 1960s and 1970s (Friedman 1994, 1999) challenge the assumptions of such an acculturation paradigm.

Greater scholarly emphasis is now being placed on the ways in which so-called peripheral peoples manage their relationship to the metropolitan core of the world-system (Wolf 1982; Hall 1986; Champagne 1989; Faiman-Silva 1997; Pickering 2000). My study follows on those and is an extended argument for a kind of perspectival relativism: an account of how the Indian people of Lac du Flambeau have reproduced a culturally continuous historical distinctness in spite and because of the nature of their encompassment. It is a cultural account of incorporation, an effort to show how this local cultural world is embedded in a larger impersonal system of political economy, to paraphrase Marcus and Fisher (1986:77).

This alternative cultural history takes "peripheral" peoples seriously as they imagine themselves and act as if they reside not on the peripheral of the modern world-system but at the centers of local systems of the world (for example, Sahlins 1985, 1988, 1993; Friedman 1994).

The people of Lac du Flambeau are inclined toward and capable of improvising relationships based on a hunting and gathering model of relations with sources of wealth and power that are imagined to be beyond the borders of their community. Individual and collective actions are motivated by presumptions of reciprocity. Flambeau people thus do not understand themselves to be dependent, do not act in ways that are epiphenomenal or peripheral, and in this sense are agents of their own history.

Loretta Fowler (1987:242) has shown in her study of Gros Ventre culture and history—the Ojibwes have referred to the Gros Ventre people, originally from the headwaters area of the Mississippi (Warren 1984:178), as *Gi-autch-in-in-e-wug,* "men of the olden time"—that "cultural continuity hinges not on lack of change but on people's interpretations of change." So, for example, Lac du Flambeau gave up intertribal warfare toward the end of the nineteenth century. However, by sending disproportionate numbers of young people into the American armed services, the community could imagine and represent itself as both patriotic and true to an important dimension of its historical self-image as a warrior people. Its long-standing athletic prowess in the region is another aspect of this dimension of community identity. Both practices reproduce the internal social relations that warfare entailed. Historical dispositions or inclinations to improvisationally engage in certain kinds of undertakings—the *habitus,* in Bourdieu's (1977) formulation—can be reproduced in novel or reimagined cultural practices.

Traditional Ojibwe activities such as hunting and fishing endured and were revalued as resistant symbols of ethnicity by virtue of their being contested, if not criminalized, by the dominant society even as engagement with that society deepened. Both hunting and fishing ironically require participation in the region's wage economy in order to procure the necessary tools to conduct them. Lac du Flambeau's Indians depend on automobiles, rifles, ammunition, gasoline engines, aluminum boats, six-volt car batteries, construction helmets, and halogen lamps to hunt and fish.

The core of this book traces the development of off-reservation spearfishing and the nearly seven years of social and political conflict it engendered, beginning with a U.S. Appeals Court decision in January of 1983 and concluding with a referendum vote at Lac du Flambeau in October of 1989. Three underlying cultural processes emerge from the events of this time. The relationship between structure and agency is thrown into relief through the cooperation and conflicts of political actors located within networks of relationships that were organized by two related, sometimes overlapping, yet ultimately distinct cultures. I also assess the connection between the terms of the social conflict and the nature of the symbolism deployed for reconstructing a distinct cultural and social identity. As important are the internal debates within Flambeau society, which reveal some of the contradictions in the lived experience of a dominated people. At the peak of hostilities between the Flambeau band and the state of Wisconsin and local non-Indians, a modern warrior faction openly opposed a civil faction in the tribal council, effectively revitalizing an essential political dynamic of Ojibwe bands in the nineteenth century. Lac du Flambeau's distinctness and traditionalism were debated within the community during a moment of crisis.

As a sign of its distinction, Flambeau is a community that is concerned about the loss of its language, though there are only a handful of people who speak Anishinaabemowin as their first language; to my knowledge there were no households in which children were learning Anishinaabemowin as their first language in the late twentieth century. The language is taught, however, in the public school, with an emphasis on vocabulary as well as the polite greetings one uses to address and question older relatives. It is also used in worship. In fact, one language teacher recommends learning the language by using it to pray as it is thought to be the only language that animal spirits recognize, a testimony to the endurance of a polytheistic (many spirits or gods) cosmology organized by reciprocal relations between spirits and humans. The group that studies the language also markets tapes and manuals that teach the Flambeau dialect. At the same time, the English spoken at Lac du Flambeau by the descendants of Native speakers is distinct from the English spoken by their non-Indian neighbors, themselves largely the descendants of the speakers of Slavic and Germanic languages. Differences in speech sounds, interjections such as "ho-wah!" as well as the tag "enh" or "enah," for "Yes!" or "Right?" at the ends of sentences, suggest that elements of Anishinaabemowin are widely current in spoken English.

There are other signs of cultural continuity and distinctiveness at Flambeau. A number of families continue to make tobacco sacrifices, hold feasts, have their children named ceremonially, call in traditional doctors from distant communities to conduct healings, or build a four-day fire when a household member dies. Extended family contact is close and constant; as a result, the expectations and obligations of kin relationships organize how and what people say to each other in a distinctive way. "Family" remains the salient and essential political and social concept. A close relationship obtains between brothers, a bond apparent in the modern political conflict over off-reservation rights, and the relationship between male patrilateral cousins (sons of fathers' brothers) resembles that of brothers.[1] Most people recognize family relationships as far out as second and third cousins, and are inclined to do so either to brag about them or to justify complaining about their behavior. Teasing between same-sex, and sexual banter between opposite sex distant, and therefore marriageable, kin is still present.

The community, however, is not cut off from its surroundings and has a longtime relationship with the encompassing society, a complex bond also in evidence among the Menominees who live one hundred miles to the south (Spindler and Spindler 1971). As with any enclave, assimilative processes both erase and produce internal distinctions, operating alongside processes that distinguish Waswaaganaan, Lac du Flambeau Ojibwes. Barnouw noted such an "uneven development of acculturation" in the mid-1940s (1950:79). In the early 1990s, there were Flambeau families who claimed they knew nothing of their tribal language, religion, or clan. Members of some of these families avidly hunt, fish, and socialize in ways distinct from those of the surrounding non-Indians, but others do not. There are groups whom the Spindlers would have described as "elite acculturated" who do not speak Anishinaabemowin, do not hunt, have been employed either off the reservation in nearby white towns or by the tribe for generations, and who would represent their Indianness as residing in a style of responsiveness to others. Some attend Christian churches on the reservation.

During the conflict over treaty rights, Flambeau revealed its vitality as a center of cultural improvisation in the flexibility of its political structure and process. Distinct groups within the community were distinguished on the basis of an imagined past and future, but there was little consensus on the constitution of these groups. This fluid perception reflected the presence of both fairly stable kindreds and less stable factions. Different principles of distinction were relevant to different people: whether one's family was originally from Flambeau, spoke the language, worked for the tribe, typically drank alcohol, inclined toward being employed or on relief, or whether one was thought to be a practicing Christian or a "born-again pagan."

When the reservation was under siege each spring during the mid- and late 1980s, such everyday differences were revalued within an increasingly contentious debate over a larger vision.

1

Cultural Topography and Spearfishing

2. Spearfisher standing in the prow of a boat. Photo courtesy of Tom Maulson.

The Highland Lake District of northern Wisconsin is underlain by a formerly mountainous region that has been worn down to a plain and has more lakes per square mile than almost anywhere else in the world. Vilas County, which contains the Lac du Flambeau reservation, has 346 lakes; neighboring Oneida County has 230. One-half the area is either swampy or has poor soil, and in 1910, at its peak of agricultural productivity, farmland composed only 3 percent of Vilas County and 13 percent of Oneida.

The Northern Highland American Legion State Forest, about five times the size of the reservation and a testimony to the failure of a nineteenth-century agricultural vision for Indians and whites alike (Gough 1997), borders the entire northern and most of the eastern side of the reservation. The Chequamegon National Forest, about twice the size of the reservation, makes up half of the western reservation boundary. In three directions, second-growth wooded trust lands imperceptibly become public lands as one moves away from the chain of Flambeau's lakes. Maple, birch, hemlock, white and red pine, and fir grow on the drier lands, and black spruce, tamarack, and cedar grow in the wetter areas.

The Lac du Flambeau Chippewa reservation, "a tract of land laying about Lac De Flambeau . . . equal in extent to three townships," according to the treaty of 1854 and the action of the Bureau of Land Management that created it twelve years later, lies about fifty miles south by southeast of the mouth of the Montreal River, which drains part of the southern Lake Superior basin. The old Flambeau Trail, running along the river to the chain of lakes just beyond the subcontinental divide, is still marked along Highway 2 by the state of Michigan highway department. Flambeau Lake is connected to that chain and lies at the headwaters of the Flambeau River, which empties into the Chippewa River, a major tributary of the upper Mississippi. Very short portages connect Flambeau with the Wisconsin River as well. A crossroads on high land in the Lake District, the area historically has been rich in wild rice, fish, and game. It is near the geographic center of the "wild rice district" designated by Jenks (1900:1106).

RETURNING HOME

It is 1992.

Approaching from the southeast on state highway 47, running parallel to the railroad track, I am welcomed to the 144-square mile reservation by a wooden sign that reads, "Home of the Lac du Flambeau Band of Lake Superior Chippewa Indians." In March of this year 1992, over fourteen hundred band members live on the reservation, 41 percent of them below the poverty line (*Lac du Flambeau News* 1993:12–13). Only about half of the six hundred tribal members over the age of sixteen are employed. As on so many other reservations, the best land, about one-quarter of the total, is in the possession of non-Indians.

Skirting the edge of Fence Lake, on a two-lane blacktop following the railroad tracks, I pass a used auto dealership, then Angler's Bar, across the street from Yukon Tom's bait shop and filling station. Then, at the corner of County H and the state highway, lies the white cinder block ruins of a gas station once owned by Alex Bobidosh, a professional football player for the short-lived NFL Native American Oorangs. He was a successful businessman and tribal chairman in the late 1930s. Farther down the road, past Raven Lake at Thorofare Road, is Tom and Laura Maulson's T&L minimart, which sells groceries, packaged goods, duty-free cigarettes. Their natural gas distributorship and mini-storage facility are on the same few acres, cleared out of the second-growth forest.

Highways D and 47 come together just past the 47 Bar across from the small but stately brick town hall, where the largely non-Indian town council meets and attempts to work out a relationship between the agendas of the non-Indian and Indian parts of the township. The roads run together for about half a mile. The Baptist church sits among a dozen or so of the community's older homes. The road splits again, in a clearing along the arm of one of the two isthmuses over which the town of Lac du Flambeau spreads. It was the logical site for the lumber mill, built in the 1890s, positioned at the approximate geographic center of the largest lakes on a reservation once covered with white pine that could be floated along the chain of dammed lakes. A few houses from that era stand out among newer housing built over the last century, including public housing referred to as "the projects" and carrying many of the same connotations as their urban counterparts.

The community center dominates the northern part of the clearing and houses most tribal administrative functions: a health clinic, chairman's office, council chambers, enrollment department, tribal court, TRAILS (Testing Reality and Individual Life Styles), and youth and Headstart programs. The building dates to the mid-1970s. On any given day, scores of cars are parked in its lot, as it is the biggest employer on the reservation, although this will change when the new casino is built.

Across the two-lane road, in the tribally owned and operated Ojibwa Mall, is a supermarket, two craft stores, a branch of a local bank, and a gas station employing about a dozen tribal members. Beyond the mall stands Simpson Electric, which occupies a former public school built for the children of white sawmill workers in the early part of the century. It employs 180 people, half of them tribal members. It too is a tribal enterprise, purchased in the mid-1980s after a forty-year presence on the reservation in private ownership.

Following County D south from the community center and across an open field behind the Ojibwa Mall is Jerry's Pizza, owned by tribal member Jerry Maulson, Tom's brother. Next door is the office of the Great Lakes Indian Tribal Council, a state and federal service coordinator for Wisconsin's twelve different tribes. Across the street stands a laundromat and the first Lake of the Torches Casino. The abandoned gas station across the intersection provides some parking for the casino. And across from that, Scott Smith runs the Old Trading Post, a printing business that also sells smoked fish and souvenirs. Behind his little one-story shop is the Indian Bowl, built in 1951 on the site of the lumber mill, where weekly powwows are held in the summer for tourists, who are given paper headbands with brightly colored feathers to wear as they watch the show. Twenty or so dancers, mostly Flambeau tribal members, are paid fifty dollars a night for their work (Nesper forthcoming).

On the lake next to the Indian Bowl is Lac du Flambeau's museum, an octagonal log structure organized around a central life-size diorama of the seasonal subsistence practices of harvesting wild rice, spearfishing through the ice, collecting maple syrup, and trapping. In the early 1990s, it features a wall of photos of Flambeau in the early part of the century and display cases full of beaded bags, sashes, pipes, tools, and drums. Beneath the eaves of a life-size trading post diorama, also replete with goods of Indian and white manufacture, life-size dolls of an Indian couple (in historical outfits that evoke contemporary powwow best) sit stiffly on a bench. Played or cued up on a VCR is the *Enduring Ways of the Lac du Flambeau Chippewa* video, made in the 1980s, which emphasizes cultural continuities between a distant past and the present. Though the narration is occasionally stilted by the self-conscious usage of anthropological terms, the residents' love of their land comes through in the representation of contemporary traditional subsistence and expressive practices. Classes in basketry, beading, and other crafts are held at the museum throughout the summer and provide an opportunity for tribal members to teach their skills to a largely non-Indian clientele.

The Ben Guthrie Public Library (which contains a small reference collection, some fiction and nonfiction works, and the minutes of the tribal council) stands across the street from the recently defunct Ace Hardware; this building will soon house the tribal court and police. The library is in the same building as the post office, which is busy in the mornings and especially on the first morning of the month—locally referred to as "Mother's Day"—when the ADC checks arrive.

Kitty-corner from this complex is the Fireside, the descendent of the first such establishment built by the mixed-blood Guthrie family in the last decade of the nineteenth century. A restaurant in the summer months, the Fireside sells souvenirs, candy, soda pop, and light food goods. It also sells liquor. Behind the cash register, fading in the sunshine and tacked up to the wall, is a small animal skin, mistakenly believed by some in the community to be a Mide bag used for magically shooting *megis* shells into the bodies of adepts during Midewiwin initiations. The skin is an icon of a class of exchanges that have been made over the last two centuries here. It was pawned or sold to Ben Guthrie, as were the carved catlinite pipe bowls, covered with a sheet of glass that made up the coffee table in Guthrie's elegant home. This prominent businessman's avocation was to record the history of the society he was instrumental in transforming. His son, a tribal member, expert fishing decoy carver, minister, former councilman and local activist in heritage tourism efforts, founded the museum and cultural center.

At the south end of Peace Pipe Road, next to an auto repair shop owned by a nontribal member, the "part Cherokee" owners of the Totem Trading Post, a craft shop and video arcade, commissioned Wayne

Valliere, a young tribal member, to build a winter lodge in their fenced yard. Covered with birch bark and tied with basswood fiber to an ironwood frame, it is an accurate and excellent example of a wigwam. Across the street stands the Flame, a restaurant and bar, with its locked and painted over "nigger window"—as tribal member Gilbert Chapman refers to it—a walk-up portal through which Indians were sold liquor in days past, lest they walk into the establishment and frighten the more genteel customers.

South of this commercial district is a residential area of a score or so of homes, some the one-bedroom wooden frame houses abandoned when the lumber mill workers left in the first years of the century, and others the brick three-bedroom split-levels built in the 1960s and 1970s. A mile beyond, near the channel that connects Crawling Stone and Fence Lakes, is the Wildcat Circle neighborhood of recently built tribal housing, named after the tribal chairman who was in office during most of the 1970s and 1980s.

Immediately to the north of the community center is the residential neighborhood referred to as Little Pines, a few streets with twoscore HUD housing units, each separated by a swatch of forest about ten yards wide. Jerry Maulson remembers playing on the frame of a Midewiwin lodge that stood on the site of this neighborhood.

Lac du Flambeau's public school stands to the west of the tribal community building on the shore of Pokegama Lake. Built in the 1930s to replace the boarding school, it is old and inadequate and will be replaced in the fall of 1993 by a new seven-million-dollar building. A *weewas jiimaan* (birch bark canoe) hangs above a trophy display case in the school's main entrance. On the walls of the gymnasium, huge thematic murals depict seasonal activities set in the early nineteenth century: spearing, maple sugaring, family life. They were painted by Ernie St. Germaine when he directed cultural education programs in the mid-1970s. In one of the offices, St. Germaine painted a wall-size mural map of the southwestern Chippewa Indian reservations, a projection of a map published in Danziger's *Chippewas of Lake Superior.*

Foot trails crisscross the sprawling athletic field and connect Little Pines with the grocery store and Simpson's, the school with the community building. Children play ball there in the summer months, while others play there in less socially acceptable ways.

West of the school and across the bridge between Long and Pokegama Lakes, the Presbyterian and Catholic churches face each other. Beyond them, the Outpost Cafe is squeezed between the road and the lake. The Outpost is owned and operated by Tom and Laura Maulson. Tom is the most successful businessman and tribal member at Lac du Flambeau. Though his German-American father owned a roofing business when he married a full-blood Ojibwe woman in the 1930s, Tom made most of his money in a variety of undertakings, not the least of which was running a 100-mile trapline in the 1960s when fur prices were good. In 1992, he owns a natural gas distributorship, a storage facility, a gas station–convenience store, a scuba diving business, and the cafe—all on the reservation and all, in his estimation, almost totally supported by residents of the reservation. He and his wife, the daughter of a local non-Indian Minocqua-Woodruff aristocratic family, live in a sprawling ranch-style home on Lake Pokegama, next to his brother Jerry.

The Outpost Cafe is open every day from about 6:00 A.M. to about 1:00 P.M. and is the only restaurant where one can sit down and have breakfast or lunch all year round. The Outpost is a gathering place for Indians and whites who live on the reservation. Both joke about "Indian" and "white" tables within the restaurant, with the "Indian" tables being those furthest away from the door and closest to the kitchen and lake. The joke acknowledges the pervasiveness of cultural distinctions within a shared social institution. Because the faction within the tribe that favored the exercise of off-reservation hunting, fishing, and gathering rights had emerged largely due to Maulson's ability to broker power, the restaurant has become the center of political activity and opinions critical of the more accommodationist tribal council. Amid recollections of hunting and fishing experiences, narratives of the meaning of off-reservation rights are developed and heard at the Outpost Cafe. As I head out of town, the restaurant is the last commercial establishment before I reach the Niijii Center, which occupies what was once the boys' dormitory building of the boarding school.

The Niijii Center is a big, white three-story building that has a wooden sign affixed to the back reading, "Indian Agency." It houses the tribe's Resource and Realty Office, the Forestry Department, and Family Circles. Family Circles is a proactive response to the Indian Child Welfare Act of 1978 in the form of a culture-based Alcohol and Other Drug Abuse (AODA) Prevention Program funded for five years by the Wisconsin Department of Social Services. Adjacent to its parking lot and near the center of the old boarding school campus is a small dance circle and arbor used chiefly for the summer Sobriety

Powwow in early June. Beyond stands the plastics division of Simpson's, employing a few dozen tribal members.

Where the isthmus widens, I pass the fish hatchery that produces thirty million walleye fry a year for the lakes on the reservation. It is a homegrown industry that has guaranteed the seasonal return of fishing tourists ever since they began to ride the train up to Flambeau to vacation in the area shortly after the lumber mill shut down in 1912. The Long's Point residential neighborhood stretches on both sides of a road by the same name and follows another shoreline of Pokegama Lake. The houses here look rather suburban, being HUD-granted three-bedrooms with driveways built in the 1960s. Some of the older people remember how good this land was for hunting birds after the Second World War.

Across 47 on a spit of land between two lakes is the Wa-Swa-Gon marina and campground, also run by the tribe, where fishing tourists park their RVs for the summer, gas up their boats, and buy bait. Still following 47 to the northwest, I skirt the shore of Flambeau Lake, the probable site of Mahliot's Northwest Company fur trading post in the early years of the nineteenth century. At Cemetery Road, two old Indian Civilian Conservation Camp Quonsets are used to store tribal road equipment.

On the lakeside, a state historical marker calls tourists' attention to Flambeau Lake and "Keeshkemun," who brought his band down from Trout Lake to settle here in the middle of the eighteenth century. Keeshkemun's French name—*La Pierre à affiler,* meaning a sharpening stone that was a European trade good—is an icon of historical transformation (it is typically mistranslated as "Sharpened Stone," which connotes precontact and commercially valuable Paleolithic associations). Along the road and beyond the Catholic cemetery to the northeast, a score of identical HUD three-bedroom rental units sit on half-acre lots cut from the forest, each separated from its neighbor by a stretch of forest a few yards wide. Near some houses are loads of cut wood, racks for hanging deer carcasses, or junked cars, the latter sources not only of automobile parts but of materials that can be adapted for other uses: hose clamps for repairing washing machines, wheels for a barbecue grill or a child's swing, hoods for sleds, trunk springs for fishing spearheads, and headlamps and batteries for shining fish and deer at night.

A small, fading wooden sign just beyond the historical marker points toward the "Old Indian Village" a couple of miles around the north end of Flambeau Lake. Once the enclave of a reactionary nativism in the late nineteenth century and destroyed by a tornado in 1912 (Valaskakis 1988:274), it is a quiet neighborhood in the early 1990s. The families who live there are near the Bear River powwow grounds, where a "Traditional Powwow" has been held since 1984, revitalizing the dance circle that had been abandoned with the building of the Indian Bowl.

On a hill next to an ancient cemetery with wooden spirit houses, a roundhouse had been built in the mid-1970s to replace the much larger, original, and disintegrating Drum Dance structure. In the wintertime, families gather here on Thursday nights for potluck feasts and Indian dancing. During the spring and the fall, runners and walkers of all ages start and finish their weekly jogs on the road in front of the roundhouse. Naming ceremonies and the water ceremonies before the spearfishing season are held here.

There is no lock on the door.

The hill overlooks Medicine Rock, an outcrop at the end of a narrow peninsula in Flambeau Lake where tobacco sacrifices have recently resumed. Some say it moves; others have seen fireballs shooting from it. According to legend, it was the site of the last conflict between the indigenous Dakotas and the Ojibwes who would become Waswaaganan. Emblematic of this old settlement's capacity to absorb and deploy the produce of the encompassing industrial society, the carcass of an automobile from the 1910s rusts half buried in the forest floor near the base of the hill.

SPEARFISHING IN MAY

Don Smith, his son Scott, and I stand around with other men at the permit station waiting for it to open at noon. The tribe issues permits to members here for spearing the off-reservation lakes in the spring. In the fall, the garage is used for deer registration. The tribe sets up a table just inside the big opened door of the garage. Business is conducted through a sliding window on the west wall of the building. A clerk sits at the table, the power of the tribe enhanced by virtue of the arrangement. The window mediates between the spearers milling about and those inside, who have the authority to "name" the lakes that will be speared for the day.

Taped to the outside wall are two lists. The one closest to the window is the order of spearing parties that came up in the lottery for that day. Groups of two, three, or four spearers—often fathers and sons, brothers, cousins—write their tribal ID numbers on a card and put it in a hat. Cards are picked from the hat and an order of priority is established. At noon, as the whistle at Simpson's Plastics blows, the window opens and the clerk is ready to issue permits for the lakes on the second list. These lakes have been "named," the term used to designate lakes that a tribal committee has selected for spearing.

The men know each other well and talk easily with each other. They talk about the numbers of fish they took the night before, and whether they were "hard" or "soft," "went" or "gone," or "were done," that is, had spawned or not. Very precise locations on local lakes anchor conversations: "that shoreline by the bar," "the one across from the islands," "to the left of the landing," "all the way across on the other side." The men joke about the poor lottery numbers they have drawn, whether so-and-so has just awakened or was drinking the night before, why they look so bad, and the verbal abuse received from and given to non-Indians.

The sun is shining. It is about seventy degrees, unseasonably warm for May. That's a very good sign; the nearby lakes will warm up and the walleye will spawn in the rocky shallows, plentiful and easy to spear. The weather accounts for some of the good mood that runs through the group—spearers will get their limits tonight for a change. Some men are in shorts, others in blue jeans. Nearly all wear T-shirts and old baseball caps. A man wearing jeans with no shirt displays spider web tattoos on his elbows and an Indian chief on his inside right forearm. Most of the spearers have longish hair and are in their twenties and thirties.

I have walked with Scott Smith and his father from his father's house a hundred yards away on the shore of the lake. I am acknowledged in a superficial and noncommittal way by men with whom I have spoken but who don't know my name—a slight raising of the eyebrows from one man, a nodding of the head from another. Such gestures are far more intimate than last year at the permit station, when I was ignored. Showing up alone, without a tribal member as a host, made me suspect.

I arrive at Gilbert (Gibby) Chapman's house to accompany him and his partners, who will spear a lake off the reservation that night. Chapman and his son are preparing the equipment and boat, a new Alumacraft with a twenty-five horsepower motor on a new trailer. The boat was lent to Chapman by a man from Eau Claire whom he says he hardly knows. Robert Martin, his regular spearing partner, is in the garage sharpening his spear on an electric grinding stone.

There are no introductions. I tell Robert I went to his wedding three years ago, a ceremony within a feast given for non-Indian supporters of Indian treaty rights. He smiles, but doesn't look up from his work.

"You sharpen the tines every time you go out?" I ask.

"Sometimes more. We had to stop last night to sharpen them."

Misses dull the tines. Walleyes spawn in shallow water on the rock bars every spring for a week or two, when the lakes reach forty-two degrees. The spearers miss perhaps a third to half the time.

I watch for a while.

"You ever see or hit any of those concrete walleye Crist and them put in the lakes?" I ask. Some members of the anti-treaty rights groups Protect America's Rights and Resources and Stop Treaty Abuse/Wisconsin have cast fish decoys, painted them, and placed them on the rock bars in the hopes that the spearers will ruin their equipment attempting to spear them. Tribal member Scott Smith has one mounted on the wall of his print shop complete with underwater vegetation, parodying a sportsman's trophy.

"No," Robert replies. I realize that the question is ridiculous because the ploy is transparent to an experienced spearer. I persist.

"Who makes your spears?" I ask, presuming that he doesn't.

"There's a guy on Cemetery Road."

"Ed Chosa?"

"Yeah. There's another guy who makes them up town," Robert answers, distinguishing between the Old Village of Waswaagoning and the town that grew up around the lumber mill at the end of the last century.

"He can make anything you design." Spearfisher's ideas are realized by craftsmen in steel.

Gibby walks through the garage and asks me if I have seen the fish inside the house. He shows me two muskies and a walleye mounted on the wall of his living room, a well-furnished space virtually indistinguishable from non-Indian living rooms in the north woods of Wisconsin. Chapman tells me he told some guys from Wausau delivering a freezer to his house that the muskies came out of Big Eau Pleine, the lake nearest Wausau. The deliverers swore that there were no fish that size in Big Eau Pleine anymore. "It was bullshit," Gibby admits—his tale was intended to provoke them. In fact he speared the fish at Big St. Germaine Lake, fifteen miles east of the reservation.

The three men get into the front seat of Gibby's son's truck, which pulls the boat trailer; I will follow them fifty miles east to Anvil Lake, bringing along four boat cushions. We stop at T&L for gas and Gibby's son buys a case of Old Style beer and stows it in the boat. On the way, the boat trailer begins shimmying and the men pull over once, then again, to look at the right front wheel of the truck. After we arrive at the landing, Chapman's son crawls under the wheelwell with a wrench and concludes that the problem can wait but will need attention soon.

Meanwhile Gibby and Robert have walked down to the landing and returned with Mike, who is married to a Flambeau tribal member. Mike, about a year out of the Marines, is from a reserve in Canada. A young neotraditionalist leader in his mid-twenties, he has emceed powwows and had prayed in Anishinaabemowin at the Family Circles feast on the previous Friday afternoon. Mike acts surprised to see me in the company of these men he admires.

A temporary employee of the Great Lakes Indian Fish and Wildlife Commission (GLIFWC), Mike is the main warden on the landing that night. He jokes about not letting me out in the boat and asks to see my ID. As I reach for my wallet, he assures me that he is just kidding. He fawns a bit by telling the spearers that the lake is open to as many fish as they want to take that night. The quota for the lake is 299 walleye. It is scheduled for twelve permits but no one else is coming to this lake tonight. Chapman's party is twenty-eighth in the lottery and the lake is likely to be at its peak. Instead of writing three permits for twenty-four fish each, as would be the usual practice, Mike writes out three permits for ninety-nine each. He is being a good guy as he creatively responds to the situation. Now we won't have to come in off the lake to pick up extra permits for the balance of the fish.

Another temporary employee of GLIFWC, a tribal member from Flambeau whose mother is Dakota, remains sitting in Mike's truck. Robert comes sauntering down to the landing and asks Mike if that guy sitting in the cab is eating dog soup, a playful, if derogatory, ethnic slur. There is some joking about somebody looking "Winnebago," Wisconsin's indigenous Siouan people with a pre-casino reputation of being poor because they had little land.[1]

We wait as twilight falls. The other temporary employee asks for my ID; he is not kidding and treats the job more seriously than Mike. I show him my driver's license and he tells me that I can't go out in the boat.

I say loudly enough for Gibby to hear that I've been in the boat the last two nights running, that I am a writer, and that both Larry and Frank, Flambeau's GLIFWC game wardens—whom I refer to only by their first names to signal my familiarity—know I've been going out. Gibby adds, "He is writing a book about all of this." The man backs off, deferring to Chapman. I climb into the boat and we motor off into the growing darkness.

By the time we cross to the north shore of Anvil Lake to get out of the wind, it is dark enough to spear. Gibby proudly announces that he has the most modern equipment, pointing out the switch on the battery he uses to power a halogen automobile headlight carefully duct-taped to a construction helmet (Figure 3). The batteries must be covered, according to state law. Most spearers use plastic milk crates and then cover the container with a piece of plywood. Gibby has built a hinged wooden box out of quarter-inch plywood.

Chapman's adult son will run the motor the whole night. Tonight, Robert will stand in the bow of the boat while Gibby will be stationed on the middle seat. The boat idles down the shore in two or three feet of water on the first run of a stretch of about five hundred yards of shoreline.

The spearers scan the water with their lighted hardhats, occasionally illuminating shoreline features, underwater rocks, and stumps for the benefit of the motorman. It is early in the evening for fish—the small males are coming in from deeper water, but the large females will only come in later. "We have two guys spear at once, so that we're not messing around here all night," I am told as it begins to rain lightly. When the wind is at our backs, the smell of gasoline from the idling engine hangs thick in the air. There is very little conversation, contrasting markedly with the bragging before and after spearfishing, when phrases like "killing," "slaying fish," and "hunting muskies" are spoken with relish.

The spearers illuminate and study the water, heads swaying slowly from side to side. A walleye is speared. The spear swings out of the water with the boat's forward movement and the speared fish drops onto the middle seat of the boat. With a quick jerk, the fish is raked off the spear and dropped into a washtub. The gills flare open as wide as they will go. Gibby, standing and spearing in the middle of the boat, knocks the fish he has taken off with his foot. Both spearers begin

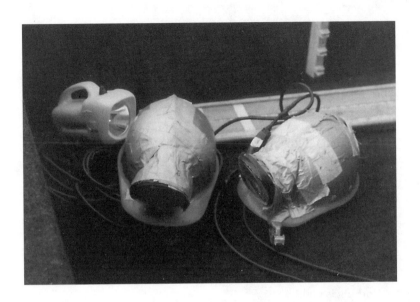

3. Gilbert Chapman and Robert
Martin's modern-day torches:
automobile headlamps duct-taped
to construction helmets. Photo
courtesy of the author.

thrusting, letting the twelve-foot spear shaft slip through their hands and then tightening their grip just after the fish is skewered. They procure fish in flurries, Robert and Gibby taking them as fast as they can; five or six a minute for each spearer, then nothing at all for a few minutes.

They direct the motorman with hand signals, to the right, to the left, turn around and go back. Sometimes one will exclaim "right there," aiming his light on a fish so that the motorman will speed up and pull the boat around to enable a better thrust.

Scores of fish flop in the tub and on the floor of the boat, where a thick pink mixture of lake water, milt, and blood pools. Tonight we can take three hundred, so there is no need to count, at least for a while.

We approach an affluent white home on a bluff, lit with floodlights. A man stands with two women on the pier, their faces in darkness. His arms are crossed across his chest. We pass within fifteen feet of them, so close it is uncomfortable for me not to say anything.

Nothing is said.

We pass them again later; the man is talking on a portable phone. And then again later, he is running a video camera. And no words pass.

The wind begins to pick up as Chapman directs his son to turn the boat around to make another pass along the same shoreline. Gibby asks me for a beer.

His son confides that it used to be "like this"—there were neither protesters nor other boats on the water. He goes on to argue that the harassment began with Dean Crist, who founded the most radical protest organization, Stop Treaty Abuse/Wisconsin. His claim seemingly discounts the three years of protest that occurred before Crist came on the scene or, perhaps, it signals the collapse of a complicated history into the political project of a single, demonized individual. Chapman's son doesn't want to elaborate his point.

We clean ninety-four fish at Scott Smith's father's house, a home on what was once the property of the boarding school on Long Lake. Working in the garage, we listen to a country and western radio station. A tub of fish and a tub for the scraps sit on the floor; a bowl for the fillets is on the makeshift sawhorse and plywood work surface.

We use electric knives. "They cost thirty-five dollars each," Scott complains, "And they are not very good, like a lot of other stuff."

This problem is common at Lac du Flambeau. Many commercially available tools are used more intensively by reservation members than their design can sustain. Electric knives were made to cut roasts on weekends, not to produce twenty or thirty meals every day for a few weeks.

Filleting fish is much easier than scaling them, which was the old way to do it. Don Smith, Scott's father, says that they learned filleting from the Indian guides who did shore lunches thirty or forty years ago for big-city white customers. The guides were paid seven dollars a day by resort owners, who charged white fishermen fifty or sixty dollars. His wife Elane's father, who trapped for years and brought the family up on venison and beaver, won't eat them filleted. Both kinds appear at feasts.

I have difficulty removing all of the meat from the fish. One begins at the head, right behind the gill, holding the knife perpendicular to the length of the fish's body, and cutting down to the spine. Then one rotates the knife ninety degrees and runs it along the side of the spine to within half an inch of the tail. The lower ribs and fatty meat of the belly are cut away, and one cuts the fillet from the skin. The head, spine, and tail are thrown away, dumped in the woods where they will feed porcupines, foxes, and birds. Off Stearns Lake Road, people dump them near a huge white pine that has held an eagle nest for decades. Some dump the remains in the lakes, where they are sometimes mistaken for whole fish by non-Indians opposed to treaty rights, who then accuse Flambeau's Indians of "wasting the resource."

Cleaning walleye is done by feel, not by sight; this is a skill that one doesn't acquire quickly. After the fillets are washed again, we take sharpened hand fillet knives and trim away any gristle, bone, and especially the meat that has been bloodied by the spear's tines. We work for two hours.

Scott Smith will give a thirty-five-inch muskie that his wife, Elane, speared the night before to Johnny Square, a non-Indian who owns a bar and resort on the reservation on Whitefish Lake. Johnny will smoke the muskie after soaking it in brine overnight and offer it to customers at the bar.

Vince St. Germaine stops by to visit. "The bananas in first, then the bigger ones," he reflects, referring to the spawn. He uses the word "herd" and tells of the night a reporter in the boat with them was shocked to see so many fish and to witness thirty being speared in less than ten minutes. St. Germaine says tonight they are going to hunt for muskie because they can catch two each on the lake they are spearing.

"Lot of guys have come in from the city," he says, somewhat cryptically referring to the tribal members returning to the reservation to spear the past weekend.

"Chicago?" I ask, wondering what he means by "the city."

"Yeah. Milwaukee. Minneapolis."

The particular identity of "the city" is incidental. It is not here, Flambeau, and that's what's important. The familiar reference to "guys" is a quiet way of implying that this place is really the center of their lives no matter how far or for how long they have been gone.

Sitting in Scott Smith's print shop, another spearer, Mike Chosa, tells me about Flambeau's history, noting that he shared these stories with anthropologist Nancy Lurie years ago. Chosa flatly declares that the conflict over Indians hunting and fishing off the reservations is about survival. "The kids will become shells without fish, venison, berries. They are used to these foods in all ways. Macaroni will kill them."

A few tribal members who have stopped by the store to visit are half listening to what Mike Chosa is saying to me. Chosa, aware of the audience, pauses and offers his opinion of the social value of the fish.

"We'd have fish fries in Flambeau, a guy would eat forty or fifty fillets, enah?"

They all laugh, deep and long.

2

Anishinaabe Culture

4. A tribal member puts tobacco into the water of the lake as a sacrifice before spearing. Protesters stand behind the spearers and family members on the boat landing. Photo courtesy of Tom Maulson.

The social and political conflict in the 1980s over the meaning of renewed Indian access to the living resources of the lands and lakes between their modern villages was accompanied by a cultural renaissance among western Ojibwe communities. This renewal and the ways in which the conflict were organized and improvised have long and deep historical roots that cannot be understood apart from Anishinaabeg culture. In particular among their traditional beliefs and practices, the special value that the Ojibwes placed on their relationships with nonhuman entities and their attitudes toward warfare helped shape their actions and reactions to events during the "Walleye War."

THE MIDEWIWIN AND THE FUR TRADE

The Algonquian-speaking communities that lived in the upper Great Lakes region traditionally gathered in their largest concentrations at spring and summer fishing sites. As summer wore on, extended family groups fished, picked berries, and gathered wild rice when it ripened; they often returned to the fishing sites for autumn spawning runs. During the winter, people hunted, separating into extended families. In the late winter, a few families came together at the sugar bush to make maple sugar (Cleland 1982; Ritzenthaler 1978:746–747).

None of these Algonquian-speaking communities called themselves "Ojibwes" at the time of white contact in the seventeenth century (Hickerson 1963:70). Only one relatively small group referred to itself by an apparently related and likely parent term. Becoming a single people who would be called and call themselves "Ojibwe" and later "Chippewa" was a process that took place during the seventeenth and early eighteenth centuries. This reimagining of identity occurred in a transformed world produced by contact with fur-trading Europeans, a transformation experienced as an indigenous cultural renaissance and remembered as a migration. The emblem of this change was a ceremonial complex known to us as the Midewiwin.[1]

The Midewiwin was a society of shamans, graded into degrees, who cured and killed using "herbs, missiles, medicine bundles and other objects which had medicinal properties" (Hickerson 1970:52). The ceremonial complex's purpose was to prolong the life of the community by increasing and distributing spiritual power.

Initiation into the society required gifts and fees for the initiators. According to eighteenth- and nineteenth-century accounts, trade goods were required or preferred, an aspect of the Midewiwin that has not been fully appreciated. Trade goods such as European-made beads were easily assimilated into an indigenous system of values in other ways dissimilar to the Europeans' (Hamell 1983). When considered as a series of exchanges, the so-called initiation fees were ultimately procured by hunting and trapping, the most fundamental of relations between indigenous people and the nonhuman world. The bodies of animals were transformed into material wealth that both signaled personal distinction and produced social distinction. The capacity to take animals and accumulate furs itself was a sign of spiritual power; initiation into the Midewiwin thus validated and constituted new social identities. The Midewiwin represented a historically unprecedented realization of *pimadaziwin,* "life in the fullest sense, life in the sense of health, longevity, and well-being, not only for oneself but for one's family." To realize *pimadaziwin* was to be a wealthy person. It was achieved by "individuals who sought and obtained the help of superhuman entities and who conducted themselves in a socially approved manner" (Hallowell 1955:360).

The Midewiwin ceremony flourished in the last quarter of the seventeenth century in an Ojibwe world that was simultaneously being depopulated by disease (Schlesier 1990), reorganizing as multitribal refugee villages in response to Iroquois incursions (White 1992:1–49), and growing more affluent from the fur trade. Non-Indian presence in the Great Lakes and whites' interest in animal skins were made meaningful in the context of the Midewiwin. The influx and ceremonial distribution of wealth entailed by the ceremony reconfigured social relationships and created new social groups. The Midewiwin ceremonies were held at spring fishing sites, where people took consciousness of themselves as a single people; "the *Midewiwin* reinforced social ties among these groups and spread a common body of traditions to people who were usually isolated from each other" (Peers 1994:60).

All of these relations are symbolized in the origin story in which the Anishinaabe migrate from the east to the west, the *megis* shell repeatedly appearing, disappearing, and reappearing on the landscape (Warren 1984:78–82; Hoffman 1891:166; Dewdney 1975:57–80; Benton-Banai 1988:95–103). This sacred history refers to the migration of an ethnogenetic locus, objectified as the "Ojibwe" and realized in the Midewiwin.

The extended family was the elemental social unit during this time. Not only did members of an extended family eat together (Dunning 1959:63–64), they participated in life-crisis ceremonies such as marriage and controlled the means of their own reproduction through hunting territories. An extended family's control of the latter was recognized by others. It has been pointed out (Hallowell 1992:46; Leacock 1954) that such exclusive control over hunting territories was probably a result of the fur trade, with earlier times likely characterized by a more fluid use of the land and its resources.

The process of turning boys into men and girls into women differed, though some symbolic elements were shared. Although it was thought that guardian spirits were valuable to girls and women, the visitations they received were typically spontaneous rather than solicited. Because guardian spirits were considered essential for boys and men, they were sought out more intentionally (Landes 1937:5–8). This difference was realized spatially. As boys expressed increasing interest in hunting and fasting, they moved their sleeping places further away from the women. The movement culminated in the boys being isolated to seek the help of a guardian, presumably beyond where women would gather fuel. This great fast, often lasting ten days, ideally resulted in a spiritual experience that girded their confidence as hunters and warriors. Ojibwe girls became women in isolation within menstrual lodges near their homes. Like first-time warriors, they covered their faces with charcoal and could not touch their bodies with their hands.

The men's productive orientation as hunters took place at some distance from domestic activities. They hunted in the bush, and women retrieved the kill to transform it into food and clothing. These differing roles and tasks were inscribed on their bodies and in characteristic body postures. The nineteenth-century German ethnogeographer Kohl noted that typically Ojibwe men stood around expectantly watching while women worked, and the women were stronger and had rougher hands than men (1985:4). Densmore (1979:30) observed that inside a house, the men would sit cross-legged while women sat on their right foot with their left extended, enabling them to "reach things" better for themselves in their work and for others nearby.

OJIBWE COSMOLOGY

Anishinaabeg personhood is said to have consisted traditionally of three aspects (Jenness 1935). All persons have a body, a soul, and a shadow. Located in the heart, the soul is the seat of will, reason, intelligence, and memory and often travels apart from a person's body. It is reborn after the death of the body. Situated in the brain, the shadow travels out ahead of the body; characteristically enlightening the soul, it is occasionally visible to others as a double of the body. The shadow is also capable of splitting into two conflicting shadows (Jenness 1935:18–20).

All living things are constituted in this way. This includes humans, animals, and spirits like "the culture hero, the thunderbirds both male and female, the master of the fish, the mermaid, some forest spirits and some lakes spirits and the sun, moon, stars, winds, and shells and stones, among others" (Black-Rogers 1977a:143). These "persons" live in social worlds that are structured in the same ways as the human world. "Animals have their families and their homes, like human beings, they meet and act in concert. . . . A cricket that finds food invites all its fellows . . . they have their leading men . . . in each locality . . . [and they] . . . are always larger than the other plants and animals of their kind" (Jenness 1935:22–23).

Unlike other life forms, which have an inherent power to live, human beings need spiritual power gained from relationships with non-human persons in order to realize *pimadaziwin*, life in a complete and full sense. Effective action in the world is a sign of the integrity of these relationships. The nature of this connection between human and non-human persons is revealed in a creation myth performance from Parry Island.

Shauwanagizik, the supernatural being or deity who rules the southern sky, created the animals, birds, and plants at the command of Kitchi Manido, the Great Spirit. After traveling all over the world and summoning different beings to come to him, he returned to the south and sat down on the parry.

The first man who approached him had a long neck and long legs. He said to Shauwanagizik "I have come to visit you." Shauwanigizik answered "I am glad that you have come. You shall be known as crane." Forthwith the man became a crane and flew away.

A big stout man now approached and said "I have come to visit you." Shauwanigizik said "I am glad that you have come. You shall be known as the great horned owl." The man became an owl and flew away. (Jenness 1935:25–26)

Thirty more persons came to visit and were named and transformed into avian and terrestrial animals. Twelve "men" then traveled west. Two were lost, and "because the earth took them to itself, trees and grass were able to grow" (Jenness 1935:26). The rest were transformed into explicitly named varieties of trees. Finally:

Later eight men started from the east and traveled north. First they reached a land of snow. The snow gave place to ice until they came to a huge pillar of ice that stretched up to the sky. Beyond this pillar, in the land of the dead in the west, they saw Nanibush.[2] A woman was planting a garden there; although not dead herself, she had followed her dead child to the west. She told them that they had reached the land of the dead, that after they died they too would join the multitude, that every night Nanibush beat his waterdrum and the people danced in his big wigwam by the light of the fires in the mountains, and that his wigwam had many large pots filled to overflowing with the souls of the food that mankind eats on earth. (Jenness 1935:25–26)

This myth delineates pivotal elements of Ojibwe culture and history. The first person arrives without a name and is transformed into the crane. The Cranes are the first chiefly clan, according to William Whipple Warren, a mid-nineteenth-century mixed-blood ethnohistorian. Cranes are responsible for the most recent phases of the migration of the Ojibwes from the east and for making the Loon clan the first councilors in the lodge (1984:46–53, 86–89). There appears to be some relationship between the historic term "Ojibwe" and a euphemism for the sound of the crane's voice (Hickerson 1970:44). In this myth and the exegesis of other Ojibwe origin myths, Cranes represent the possibility of all subsequent social order. Greenberg and Morrison (1982) as well as Schenk (1997:17–28) argue that the Cranes were the original "Saulteurs" referred to by the Jesuit missionary Dablon in his "Relation" of 1670. Dablon noted that the "Pahouitingouah Irini . . . joined together with three other Nations" (Thwaites 54:133). Greenberg and Morrison consider Dablon's account a version of Warren's later mythopoeic story, in which the Crane calls the Bear, Catfish, Loon, and Moose/Marten groups together (1982:89–91). The latter groups are the named Algonquian communities north of Sault Ste Marie that coalesced into the Ojibwes.

The series of transformations in this myth indicate that all distinctions are the outcome of an unequal relationship between a spirit whose power to transform is based on its superior knowledge of the world and named, gendered persons who are transformed by virtue of their willingness to form exchange relationships. In general, conscious and sentient beings are transformed into nonhuman persons starting with those that mediate elemental realms: birds, squirrels, then amphibious mammals, and finally trees.

A version of this transformation (which highlights a link between violence and proliferation) appears in the story "Clothed-in-Fur," collected by William Jones in the 1920s at Fort William, Ontario. Physical blows delivered to a series of incompetent wives accomplish the creation of the diversity of animals (Overholt and Callicott 1982). A fragment of a version of the myth Jenness published was told to Huron Smith in the 1910s by Jack Doud of Lac du Flambeau. Winnebojo, the culture hero of the Ojibwes, took flesh from his own body, put it in places on the earth, and corn, squash, and bears grew there (Smith 1932:349). The story reinforces the notion of the personhood of all life forms.

In the latter part of the myth collected from Parry Island, Nanibush drums, and the dead feast and dance around the pots overfilled with the souls of animals killed by the living. In the Ojibwe world, the souls of both human and nonhuman persons are reborn, so it is mankind's hunting, fishing, and gathering that is reproductive, nourishing persons in both worlds.

A similarly close relationship between the souls of animals, the living, killing, and eating is further elaborated in a myth where the world is made from the body of a bear. The bear was caused to appear by humans, killed, and then made into the stars.

In the first days two men suddenly appeared sitting opposite each other as if they had just awakened. One was named Bemikkwang, and the other Nigankwam. Each carried a bow and arrow on his right shoulder. Nigankwam rose, went over to a mound, and poked it with the end of his bow. A bear came out, which he shot. Bemikkwang then arose, went over to the mound on the opposite side and poked from it a knife and a large birch-bark pot. The two men skinned the bear, cooked it in the pot, and ate the whole carcass at one meal. Nigankwam then arose, took up the skull of the bear and threw it into the sky, where it became three stars [in the Great Bear]. Bemikkwang arose, took up a vertebrum [*sic*] and threw it into the sky; it also changed into stars. Nigankwam rose again, took up the breastbone and threw it up; it became the Milky Way. Nigankwam and Bemikkwang were the first human beings. Afterward Nigankwam made a woman and had children, who were the ancestors of the present Indians. (Jenness 1935:37)

Bemikkwang is "the thunder that passes without raising a storm"; Nigandwan is "the leader in the clouds, the first thunder to come in the spring of the year" (Jenness 1935:35). Thunder is a *manido*—personified power—and thought to be subordinate only to Gizhe Manido (Kitchi Manido), "not the creator of all things, but the source of all power inherent to a greater or lesser extent in all things that exist" (Jenness 1935:29). The two are prototypical Anishinaabe, since they "suddenly appeared"—Warren notes that the term "is derived from An-ish, aw, meaning without cause, or spontaneous and in-aub-a-we-se, meaning the human body" (Warren 1984:56).

The killing of the bear by First Thunder of the Spring is a paradigmatic sacrificial act. "For 'a bear is just like a human being, and must be honored like a guest from foreign parts'; then the spirit master of the bears will clothe the skeleton of this one with new meat and fur and send it again to the lodge" (Landes 1937:15). The bear is said to be the most nearly human of all animals and the object of the most important eat-all feasts (Thwaites 1897, 6:217–218; Quaife 1921:138–141, 193–195). As Kohl observed: "They regard it almost in the light of a human being. Indeed they will often say that the bear is an 'Anijinabe' (Indian)" (1985:408). The reproductive aspect of the bear's power inheres in the consumption of its flesh. This meal becomes the enabling condition of the cosmos-creating acts that follow, which establish human reproductivity in the form of the first woman.

In his studies of the Cree, Robert Brightman concludes that the eat-all rule for boreal Algonquians was the means by which "the condition of disjunction between human and non-human that existed prior to the kill" is reestablished such that "gifts of animals to hunters —that are initiated by non-human benefactors" become possible (1983:447–448).

Operating within such a "cosmic economy of sharing" (Bird-David 1992:30), an Ojibwe hunter, fisherman, or gatherer perceives and acts within his or her natural environment "as a friend, a relative, a parent who shares resources with them . . . [and] is morally bound to share food and other material resources with them" (1992:31). The world is presumed to be abundant, so "as human agents appropriate their shares they secure further sharing" (1992:32).

WARFARE, SCALPING, AND REGENERATIVE POWER

One of the ways in which life-generating power was acquired in the Ojibwe hunter's traditional cosmos was through skinning. Hunters also took the body parts of enemies killed in low-intensity warfare.[3] Warfare, then, was not just a means of achieving political ends but was another way of acquiring power.

Connections between warfare, skinning, body parts, and power condense and surface in stories about the trickster. Among many other things, the trickster, the eldest of three sons, is the first killer. In the twenty-seven-episode "Wenebojo Myth from Lac du Flambeau" collected by Barnouw in 1944, he transcribes that "Wenebojo, the oldest boy, killed everything he could kill, even the little birds. . . . He even tried to kill both big and little Manidog [spirits] when he saw them" (Barnouw 1970:15). The trickster goes on to kill one brother, "the first time anybody ever died on earth" and then his other brother (Barnouw 1970:19).

The significance of these acts is thrown into relief through the use of skins. One moment in an episode weaves together Wenebojo's reputation, deception, the power of the skinned, and the art of the dispatching act. He comes upon an old toad woman doctor.

She looked at Wenebojo really sharp and said, "You're not Wenebojo are you?"

Wenebojo said, "No I'm not Wenebojo. Would you be alive if I were Wenebojo? If you saw Wenebojo, he'd kill you."

She teaches him how she doctors. As the old toad woman turns to leave, the trickster murders and skins her, attires himself in her skin, and goes off to kill the chiefs of the underworld who had killed his nephew, a wolf (Barnouw 1970: 36, 37). The killings, made possible by the murderous appropriation of the skin, have the same order of consequences as the sacrificial act of eating all of the bear in the story of the first Anishinaabeg discussed earlier: they establish the conditions for the regeneration and transformation of the world. This mythology was realized in history as warfare, motivated by a desire to extract power from other persons and symbolized through the taking of scalps and other body parts.

Discussions of warfare by literate nineteenth-century Ojibwes inevitably generated apologetic historical explanations. The Reverend Peter Jones (Kahkewaquonaby) claimed that the Ojibwes fought with the Nahdoways or the Six Nations Iroquois for vengeance (1861:111). Famed historian George Copway (Kah-ge-ga-gah-bowh) attributed the origins of hostilities between his people and the Sioux to "the question of the right of occupancy of the fisheries at the upper end of Lake Superior and the right to the game of the adjacent woods" (1850:55).

Henry Rowe Schoolcraft, a non-Indian historian, offered a more essentialist interpretation of Ojibwe warfare. He characterized the Chippewas as woodland mystics who "have regarded the use of the bow and arrow, the war club and spear, as the noblest employments of men. . . . [It is] success in war alone that fills the highest aspirations of the Chippewa mind. To hunt well and to fight well, are the first and last themes of their hopes and praises of the living and the dead" (Schoolcraft 1847, 5:150). In his judgment, "the Indian has but one prime honor to grasp; it is the triumph on the war-path; it is rushing upon his enemy, tearing the scalp reeking from his head, and then uttering his terrific su-su-kwon (death whoop). For this craven art he is permitted to mount the honored feather of the war eagle, the king of the carnivorous birds" (Schoolcraft 1847, 2:57).

Committed to assimilating Indians, Schoolcraft of course had his own reasons for graphically describing a rather iconic aspect of indigenous life. His comments make clear, though, that warfare and scalping were valuable means of acquiring spiritual power and prestige, and must therefore have been important and widely shared modes of reproducing society.

In the mid-1760s, the fur trader Alexander Henry was present for the return from a large battle between the Chippewas of Chequamegon and the Nadowessies (Dakotas). The Chippewas lost thirty-five men and told Henry that they were disappointed. "[T]he Nadowessies continued their retreat without doing the honors of war to the slain. To do these honors is to scalp, and to prepare the bodies is to dress and paint the remains of the dead, preparatory to this mark of attention from the enemy: 'The neglect,' said the Chippewa, 'was an affront to us—a disgrace; because we consider it an honor to have the scalps of our countrymen exhibited in the villages of our enemies in testimony to our valor'" (Quaife 1921:196).

The Ojibwes honored Sioux scalps when they took them, and their regenerative power is apparent in the description given by Kohl when he visited the southwestern Ojibwe country in the mid-1850s. He writes of a single scalp, which had been circulating in a village, held by a boy "like little girls do a doll" (Kohl 1985:129). Admired by many, it "was carefully extended on a wooden ring, and so copiously adorned with feathers, gay ribbons, tinkling bells, fox and other tails, that the bloody skin and hair were nearly entirely covered." Kohl also witnessed the emotional effect of taking scalps on a village. "And when they return from the wars their clothes are torn, their moccasins worn out, perhaps their entire flotilla expended. But if they bring scalps with them, the whole camp is drunk with joy, and the women work gladly and patiently for a couple of months to set matters in order again, and repair the deficiencies" (Kohl 1985:67–68).

Densmore was also made aware of the regenerative power of taking scalps. One interlocutor among the Minnesota Ojibwes named Odjib'we had organized a war party against the Dakotas, who had killed his wife's brother. On the way to a certain Dakota village, they came upon an enemy war party; they pursued it and killed one man. Densmore was told that "[t]hey returned home at once and Odjib'we presented the Sioux scalp to his wife De'kum ('Across'), who held it aloft in the victory dance as she sang . . . [a song whose lyrics were] . . . 'Odjib'we, our brother, brings back'" (Densmore 1910:121). Her brother's identity had diffused among the Dakotas and could be reconstituted and returned through the sacrifice of any one of them.

The regenerative reconstituting power of scalps was not limited to restoring relations within families but also revived and reshuffled the relationships between groups. Densmore observed that "gifts were distributed to all the people by members of the warrior's clan; for instance, Odjib'we's dodem (clan animal) was the bear. When he returned bringing a scalp, all the men and women belonging to the Bear Clan danced around him with their arms full of presents, after which they distributed the presents throughout the village" (1910:120).

In 1659, Pierre Radisson had observed a similar practice among the Ottawas living at what is now the village of Reserve at Lac Courte Oreilles (Adams 1961:128–129). Since the dead had returned in the form of scalps, people could now enjoy each other's company. Densmore's comment that "war between Indian tribes was an occupation rather than a calamity" (1910:61) is warranted by evidence from throughout Algonquian country and over the course of a few centuries.

Ojibwe warfare would transform and ramify with political domination and further incorporation into the world-system of societies, but it would also retain traditional ties to the acquisition and regeneration of power. In the twentieth century, when fishing became warfare on the off-reservation lakes, the bodies of fish took on some of the symbolism, deep emotional resonance, and reconstituting social and spiritual power formerly associated with human body parts.

3

Hunting, Fishing, and "Violating"

5. Boy holding a speared walleye.
Photo courtesy of Amoose, GLIFWC
staff and Bad River tribal member.

For the Ojibwe bands of the late eighteenth and early nineteenth centuries, "leadership was based upon skill as a hunter and trapper, on maturity, wisdom, guidance, articulateness, and control of supernatural power" (Smith 1973:13, paraphrasing Rogers 1962:266). Successful men drew others around them. With the treaty period came a concentration of power in the hands of chiefs who mediated the relationships between Ojibwes and non-Indians. Such leadership was typically contested (Kugel 1985), preserving a diffusion of power in the face of external centralizing influences.

The importance of access to forms of wealth and power such as hunting, warfare, and trade was reflected by the political organization of southwestern Ojibwe villages. By the early nineteenth century, six bands were discernible in the Lac du Flambeau area; they became the Lac du Flambeau Chippewas later in the century. They occupied Flambeau Lake, Trout Lake (Ma-tak-e-ge-ihik), Turtle Lake/Portage (Keche-non-ah-ge-vun)—referred to as Mercer by Amikonze of Lac du Flambeau in 1924—Lac Vieux Desert (Kitikitgan), the Wisconsin River (Monse-o-ne), and Pelican Lake (Ke-chi-waub-i-jish) (see Bokern 1987:72). The village at Flambeau Lake was central because the Midewiwin ceremonies were conducted there (Warren 1984:193). Flambeau Lake village had been established by the Crane clan leader, Keeshkemun, identified by Warren as chief of the Lake Superior Ojibwes. When the British sought the aid of Wisconsin Ojibwes against the American revolutionaries, they attempted and failed to enlist Keeshkemun's help (Warren 1984:373). Britain's inability to put down the rebellion led to the domination of the Americans in the Great Lakes region.

The national expansion into the Great Plains in the nineteenth century motivated business interests to seek a means of access to the lumber in northern Wisconsin. Indians who signed a treaty in 1837, therefore, understood it to be a sale of only pine trees (Satz 1991:18). Article

5 of the treaty stipulated hunting, fishing, and gathering rights: "The privilege of hunting, fishing, and gathering the wild rice, upon the lands, the rivers and the lakes included in the territory ceded, is guaranteed to the Indians, during the pleasure of the President of the United States" (Kappler 1904–41:492). Five chiefs from Lac du Flambeau signed that treaty: Pish-ka-ga-ghe (the White Crow), Na-wa-ge-wa (the Knee), O-ge-ma-ga (the Dandy), Pa-se-quam-jis (the Commissioner), and Wa-be-ne-me (the White Thunder) (Satz 1991:156).

A treaty signed five years later ceded rights to contiguous lands bordering on Lake Superior, which were desired by the government for copper mining and to consolidate control of the southern shore of Lake Superior. The treaty of 1842 was also signed by the first chief, White Crow from Flambeau, May-toc-cus-e-quay, and She-maw-gon-e (1991:173). Certain usufructuary rights were guaranteed: "The Indians stipulate for the right of hunting on the ceded territory, with the other usual privileges of occupancy, until required to be removed by the President of the United States" (Kappler 1904–41:542–543). Chiefs from the nearby Wisconsin River and Lac Vieux Desert signed the 1842 treaty as well, which shows a measure of growing local autonomy and geographic dispersal.

Shortly after the treaty of 1842 and throughout the 1840s, the United States government made unsuccessful attempts to relocate the Wisconsin Chippewas to lands west of the Mississippi River (Satz 1991; Clifton 1987). In 1850, the commissioner of Indian Affairs and the secretary of the interior persuaded President Fillmore to issue an executive order revoking the Chippewas' privileges of occupancy and requiring them to remove to their unceded lands in Minnesota. The Indians were incredulous at this shift in policy, since they had never understood themselves to have agreed to such a contingency. Pez-heke, the first chief of the LaPointe band and signatory to the 1837 and 1842 treaties, traveled to Washington DC and convinced the president to rescind the executive order. In exchange for yet another cession of lands in 1854, the Ojibwes negotiated permanent reservations within the ceded territory (Satz 1991:68).

The delegation from Flambeau that signed the 1854 treaty was complex in organization. The two first chiefs, Aw-mo-se and Oscaw-bayis, were apparently followed by two second chiefs—Ke-nish-te-no and Me-gee-see with Aw-mo-se, and Que-we-zance and Ne-gig with Oscawbayis (Satz 1991:185). Three headmen's names were associated with the first group and two with the second. The Flambeau delegation came from two distinct villages: Aw-mo-se was the civil chief of the village at Flambeau Lake (Warren 1984:47, 192, 319) and Oscawbayis led a settlement to the south on the Tomahawk River (Jones et al. 1924:9).

A dual political structure is revealed by the sequence of signatures of the 1854 treaty—first chiefs represented civil authorities, while the headmen spoke for the warriors. This dual structure was an important and common feature of Indian polities in the Woodlands. At the village level, it facilitated the development of opposing factions, often in the form of young men—fledgling and full-fledged warriors—taking issue with the counsel of the civil chiefs (Hickerson 1962:52–53).

Entwined with the dual political structure was a commitment to the idea that every individual had to have a guardian spirit and the belief that sacrificing a variety of "persons" was the condition of society's existence. Guardian spirits were called *pawaganak* (dream visitors) but also *adisokanak* (legendary spirits) and, collectively, *mishomisaanan*, that is, "grandfathers." Living grandfathers were inclined to counsel peace where spiritual grandfathers were often called on for help in war. The wisdom of the old and the energy of the young were equally valued in Ojibwe villages. "[W]isdom was the obligation of the older civil leaders and recklessness the prerogative of the young" (Hickerson 1962:53). Villages were thus typically unstable, with older civil leaders acting conservatively out of accumulated experience and the young men seeking that qualifying experience in warfare.

The value placed on individual autonomy, conjoined with the wealth that came into Ojibwe society through the fur trade, caused leadership roles to proliferate and diffuse across civic, military, and religious domains, all parties variously cooperating and competing —war chiefs, pipe chiefs, clan chiefs, talking chiefs, trading chiefs, and multiple degrees of authority within the Midewiwin (Hickerson 1962:47).

The continuing extension of American hegemony and the decline of the fur trade drew to a close a period of cultural florescence in Wisconsin Ojibwe history and ushered in a time of more profound accommodation of non-Indian interests and presence. During this historical phase, Ojibwe societies were greatly transformed but not absorbed, because both settler colonialism and corporate capitalism came with explicit designs for the place of Indians in the total social order.

In his report to the commissioner of Indian Affairs in 1854, Agent

Gilbert described the Flambeau people as living in a "state of destitution and poverty absolutely shocking." One-fourth of Flambeau's population had succumbed to smallpox but the survivors were unwilling to abandon their homes in favor of La Pointe (RCIA 1854:30). In fact, the Flambeau Ojibwes were anxious to have their reservations surveyed in order to keep the white loggers out (RCIA 1859:73). According to the agent, settled whites in the area were also interested in containing Indians on the reservations to put an end to their habit of roaming about the white settlements on the Chippewa and St. Croix Rivers (RCIA 1861:75).

Lac du Flambeau at this time was quite unlike some of the other Lake Superior Chippewa reservations, which were in closer contact with whites and "making progress in civilized pursuits" by learning to farm, converting to Christianity, and hiding their polytheism more carefully. The state and federal governments facilitated the cutting down of the pine forest, which had been the original objective of the first treaty cession in 1837. The booming lumber industry fostered wage labor opportunities for Ojibwes, but it also created "the cutover," a deforested eighteen-county region covering the northern third of the state (Gough 1997:10). Although this devastation adversely affected the fish populations, after a short while the growth of young forest increased astronomically the number of deer (Habeck and Curtis 1959:49). The state then assumed the role of reshaping a productive ecology by regulating harvests and restructuring game populations.

Despite escalating cultural changes in the Northwoods, traditional subsistence practices and sharing within extended families continued to be practiced at Lac du Flambeau, aided by its relative inaccessibility, poor conditions for agriculture, richness of lakes and forest, the availability of day labor opportunities in the lumber camps, and a lack of U.S. government personnel to implement local programs. The construction of a sawmill three miles from the village of Waswaaganing in 1894, on the heels of the coming of the railroad five years earlier, had some centralizing effects, creating sectors of Flambeau society that were more dependent on outside modes of production.

An equally far-reaching change was the building of a hatchery in 1914, intended to stock the lakes on the reservation with walleyed pike, a species that sportfishing tourists would pay Indians to guide them to. These fish would also become favored by Lac du Flambeau spearfishers, in part because their eyes are big and noticeably reflect the light. Although the collective social life continued to be organized around episodically available resources,[1] the hatchery precipitated a stronger state legal presence on the reservation. This transformation soon fused Indian cultural identity with the practice of "violating."

VIOLATING AS A WAY OF LIFE

As the state came to look upon the natural resources of the northland as a springboard for a tourist industry and as a form of income for itself, it grew less and less tolerant of Indians hunting, fishing, and gathering off of the reservations. The Ojibwes of Flambeau, however, remembered the treaties and so, in varying degrees, continued to seek off-reservation resources throughout the nineteenth and twentieth centuries; firsthand recollection of treaty rights lasted into the twentieth century. In 1897, two elderly Lac du Flambeau men in possession of venison outside the reservation boundaries were arrested by state game wardens and taken to Hurley, forty miles away. The official at the reservation wrote to the agent at Ashland: "I believe in enforcing the game law on white men as well as indians. But to be so harsh on these old men who were told when the treatys were made with them that the game belonged to them and they should have the privilege of hunting any where they pleased the punishment seems to me to be out of proportion to the offence" (Vine 1897).

Over three decades later, treaty rights were still vividly recalled. At a general council of the chiefs of Ojibwe bands from Wisconsin, Michigan, and Minnesota in 1931, attorney Thomas St. Germaine of Lac du Flambeau "gave a lengthy talk on the hunting and fishing part of the treaty" of 1854 (Ojibwe General Council 1931:2). The chiefs concluded that "the hunting and fishing rights were reserved." St. Germaine made the same points in 1934 at the Hayward Congress—a two-day meeting scheduled by John Collier, Commissioner of Indian Affairs in the Roosevelt administrations, to discuss the proposed Indian Reorganization Act with Indian people from the Midwest. He insisted on talking about Indian water rights, hunting, fishing, and gathering rights, and the illegality of the state's assumption of jurisdiction (Satz 1994:210).

However unbroken were the memories of off-reservation rights to the Indians, those rights were forcefully denied by the expanding state of Wisconsin. The consequence of the state's denial and actions to support that denial was and is a culturally distinct form of illegal hunting called "violating" that both distinguished Flambeau's residents from mainstream American society and brought them further in some ways into the local economy. For example, the trade in wild game in the city of Chicago in the 1870s was worth five hundred thousand dollars a year (Oberly 1991:84); there is some evidence that Ojibwes facilitated this thriving trade legally "as hunters, trappers and guides" until the state forbade the export of venison in 1883 and thereafter continued their hunting and trading practices illegally.

The commodification of the state's wildlife had important implications for the Ojibwes. Although the state imposed a season on deer hunting as early as 1851 and proscribed gill netting in 1853, it was not until 1868 that the limited seasons for deer, game birds, and furbearing animals were applied to the "uncivilized Indians." The law reduced drastically the land base of the traditional economy from 16,000,000 acres to 450,000 (Oberly 1991:81) and criminalized a traditional way of life, though it would not be enforced in the ceded territory for another twenty-one years (Silvern 1997:495).

In the commercial realm, the 1870s brought the first publications of guidebooks for fishing in northern Wisconsin. Accommodating and promoting these new uses of land and resources was an emerging economic infrastructure that included guides, cooks, and oarsmen (Les 1988:2), facilitated by a grant to the Wisconsin Central Railroad of a right-of-way forty miles wide between Steven's Point in the middle of the state and Ashland on the southern shore of Lake Superior. In 1878 the state prohibited the use of spears, nets, seines, baskets, grapnels, traps—any method other than hook and line—to take game fish. Both Indian and white settlers in the Lac du Flambeau region had relied on such devices to fish.

In 1879 the Wisconsin Supreme Court, apparently without reference to the treaties, ruled that Indians were subject to state laws on their reservations. The first closed seasons on game fish were established two years later, followed by a series of species-specific bag and size limits in the first years of the twentieth century. In 1883 the state prohibited the export of venison, shortened the hunting season from November 1 to December 15, and criminalized hunting at night with lights (Schorger 1953:213). In 1887, the same year that the General Allotment Act was passed, Wisconsin shortened the deer season to twenty days and began appointing fish and game wardens (Oberly 1991:84). Hunting licenses were required of all deer hunters for the first time in 1897. Two years later, no game at all could be taken without a license (WDNR n.d.:1).

In 1908, in *State v. Morrin,* the Wisconsin Supreme Court found that the off-reservation rights of the Wisconsin Ojibwes had been abrogated by Wisconsin statehood in 1848. The Ojibwes and the Wisconsin Conservation Commission in the 1920s wrangled over trapping fur-bearing animals because wardens had the responsibility to tag fur-bearers both on and off the reservations. In 1933, the same year that Wisconsin's male residents over the age of eighteen were first required to purchase a fishing license, the Wisconsin Supreme Court in *State v. Johnson* allowed the state to regulate fee-owned land within the border of the reservations. At the same time the Wisconsin Conservation Commission asked the attorney general for a formal opinion to support its position that Indians did not have treaty rights on navigable water on their reservations (Oberly 1991:110). These laws were part of the state government's overall effort to redefine the northern third of the state as a recreational playground.

A 1924 Chicago and Northwestern Railroad map, entitled "Summer Outings," lists fourteen resorts on the Lac du Flambeau reservation and a few score more in the region. A goodly number of tourists at this time were paying Indians seven dollars per day for their knowledge of the lakes in the area (though resort owners mediated the relationship between the Indian guides and their clientele). With the closing of the mill at Flambeau in 1912, guiding tourists to fish and game became an important seasonal source of cash. Charging outsiders a small fee to camp on the reservation supported a fish hatchery, which, in turn, stocked the lakes with the species sportfishers liked to catch. To this day, the hatchery stands across the road from the renovated tribal campground at Flambeau. The entrepreneurial activity of guiding became linked with tradition by the very forces that would threaten the integrity of the reservation in other ways.

The influx of tourists and cash also brought the first cars to Lac du Flambeau. In addition to their usual use, automobiles extended the size of Indian hunting territories and created daytime and nighttime road hunting. In this sense, Lac du Flambeau people assimilated the automobile as a terrestrial canoe. It was ideally suited for hunting the old logging roads at night in somewhat the same way that Flambeau parents and grandparents had hunted the lakes at night in canoes.

People born in the 1930s and 1940s recall being taught to hunt from cars at night. It was the Depression, and hunting was one of the few local industries that was booming. A new road between Flambeau and Boulder Junction, built by the Civilian Conservation Corps workers on the reservation, effectively improved a hunting corridor for Indian people with access to automobiles.

A report in the *Wisconsin Conservation Bulletin* of December 1938 recounted the breaking up of a venison bootlegging ring operating out of Lac du Flambeau that had been supplying taverns and roadhouses in Wisconsin and Illinois. The counsel for the defense had "produced ancient treaties and other Indian laws to support contention that the Indians were legally entitled to hunt either on or off the reservation at any time" (1938:9). Widespread violating in the 1930s and 1940s also took place at Lac Courte Oreilles, eighty miles west of Flambeau. One hunter and his friends there were killing one hundred deer a month, collectively worth four hundred dollars, with meat selling for twenty-five to forty cents a pound. There were families at the reservation town of Post who had canned two hundred quarts of venison (James 1954b: 257). In response to meat rationing during World War II, Indian commercial hunters at Lac du Flambeau supplied resorts with venison—which the non-Indian owners passed off to their clientele as beef.

The use of the term "bootlegging" at the time evoked a variety of associations with alcohol. Indeed, the Indian poachers drank. Alcohol had been a part of life at Flambeau since at least the middle of the eighteenth century; it had been intimately connected to hunting and trapping since the French and then the English proffered it as a sign of the friendship that made exchange possible. After the fur trade period, alcohol remained part of the sociality of the hunting mode of life. The high value placed on indigenous knowledge of resources in the growing tourist economy went hand in hand with the guides' access to alcohol, which became one of the means by which they displayed a relative cosmopolitanism.[2]

Eighteen Ojibwe men were arrested and convicted for hunting deer out of season during 1951, commonly being fined and serving jail time. One warden felt that it was very difficult to interrupt "the constant sale of venison to tourists during the summer and deer season" (Oberly 1991:117). A few of the family names on the Wisconsin Conservation Commission arrest lists appeared again thirty-five years later during the spearfishing conflict.

The crackdown on violators accelerated in 1957 with the passage of Public Law 280, which gave the state the right to prosecute criminal cases on most reservations in Wisconsin (Wilkinson 1990:21–23). Deploying current international rhetoric, the Bad River Band declared in 1959 a "state of cold war" between itself and the State Department of Conservation, forbidding wardens from setting foot on tribal land. By the mid-1960s the state's attorney general had taken the position that "Public Law 280 extinguished any federal immunity on the part of Chippewas" (Oberly 1991:122).

The antagonism between the state's game wardens and Indian hunters once again linked Indian economic production with the deadly game of warfare. In the community memory at Flambeau, this tension over subsistence rights evoked times from a couple of centuries before when Ojibwes had been advancing on the Dakotas, looking over their shoulders at every turn. "Meanness," best understood as a capacity and inclination to fight or the appearance of a readiness to fight, became an increasingly important sign of Indian identity, paralleling a similar valuation among the Lumbees of North Carolina (Blu 1980:144–147).[3]

Many people I have spoken with at Flambeau admit to violating at one time or another. All have stories about violating, most very entertaining—recollections of finding deer that were shot, deer shot perfectly, or those not dead when hurriedly brought into the vehicles, eluding the game wardens, and fights with local whites.

Violating is not only economically significant but a very important step for Indian boys becoming men, and to a lesser extent, for girls becoming women. Because the risk of being caught is so great, people learn how to remain cool under somewhat dangerous and quickly changing circumstances, a quality characterized as "equanimity under duress" for the Menominees to the south (Spindler and Spindler 1971:29). Ojibwe men admit to violating with proud defiance, indicating that they perceive the practice as integral to their identity. (It should be noted that many whites in the area violate as well, often for the same reasons: they are poor and need the meat or the cash the meat can bring.)

Hunting at night, or "shining," on the reservation is not against federal or tribal law.[4] It is sometimes undertaken as a family activity with a man's wife, son, or daughter holding the light and shining it out the front passenger seat window. Most of the time, however, there is little game on the reservation.[5] More typically, people go off the reservation to hunt. The men depart in groups of three or more, depending on the time of year, availability of deer, and the anticipated hostility of local whites.

In a typical violating episode, a single deer or a small group of deer is sighted on a hillside or in a field within fifty yards of the pavement, usually at the forest edge. Occupants of the vehicle then scan the highway in both directions for other cars and resume their speed. The location and nearby houses are noted. After driving for about a mile, the hunters return to the place where the deer were sighted. If the deer are still visible and no one else is around, the driver pulls over and one of his companions shoots an animal. The vehicle immediately departs and is driven four or five miles down the road; after allowing time for the deer to die, the hunters return to the kill site. If there are still no other cars in sight, the man who shot the deer, or a designated "dragger," is dropped off to find and gut the deer—ideally out of sight—if it is too heavy to move easily. Pulling away, the driver goes down the road for about ten minutes, turns around, and comes back. When approaching the point where he dropped off his companion—and again, if there is no one else around—he flashes his lights to signal the man waiting with the now-gutted deer. The deer is quickly loaded and the group is on its way.

Through careful and detailed surveys of the deer populations in scores of management units throughout the state, the Wisconsin Department of Natural Resources (DNR) knows where deer are commonly seen and where their trails cross roads and state highways. They know also where to watch for violators.

The zeal with which non-Indian wardens enforce game laws encourages Indian people to believe that *chamukamans* (whites) have little compassion for *shinabs* (Indians) as human beings and value property more than they value human life. One Indian man was arrested and spent six months in jail for hunting without a state license (Satz 1991:88). Many others have had their guns and cars confiscated over the years, often devastating a family's ability to sustain itself. According to tribal member Nick Hockings, in the 1960s and 1970s the fine was about eight hundred dollars, a very large amount of money at the time.

Violators sometimes resist and display their superiority by fooling the wardens. In the early 1990s, Flambeau tribal member Ed Chosa said he took over one hundred deer a year with a small group of hunters, which fed a number of families. He told me that he used to watch the wardens sit in their cars just off the reservation and wave to the non-Indian people leaving the reservation on various errands. He felt that the wardens were more likely to follow the Indian cars, especially if they were transporting a group of people. Ed Chosa remembers that occasionally his non-Indian friends would allow him to lie on the back seat floor of their car so that he wouldn't be followed and could hunt in peace. He hated the DNR wardens, whom, he feels, disdained Indians. The woman he lived with was swamped one April night by a non-Indian driving a motorboat, harassing spearers. Chosa reported that the DNR refused to help, claiming that they had to patrol the spearing and could not assist them.

A prominent tribal member at Lac du Flambeau tells a story of leaving the reservation to spearfish with two other men in two cars. Wardens were watching from across the lake, but the Flambeau men decided not to acknowledge their presence. They quietly slipped the fish into the trunk of one car and then with exaggerated gestures put a bag they had secretly filled with forest litter into the trunk of the other car. The wardens followed the spearfishers and stopped the second car carrying the bag full of brush just before it got to the reservation. The wardens were quite embarrassed when they opened the bag and realized that the fish they knew the men had taken were now safely across the reservation line. In the local idiom, the tribal members had "scored a touchdown"—successfully returning with their quarry through the "goalposts," brown wooden welcome signs on the roads leading into the reservation.

In the same way that "goalposts" and "touchdowns" have different metaphorical extensions, violating means different things for Indians and local whites. For whites—who also tell stories to each other about their violating escapades—violating is a mark of their personal autonomy and cleverness vis-à-vis the state, a measure of their commitment to a traditional individualism. That personal autonomy, however, is not a recognizable sign of membership in a historically distinct group that also has other distinguishing signs and practices. Violating is one of the most important practices in the constitution of Indian manhood, because it is done "to feed our families" and because it is against the white man's law. It is the practice of subsistence under circumstances that resemble warfare, and like warfare, it is a reproductive act.

Violating is undeniably an important dimension of local Indian identity and a sign of personal power. The domination of Indians by way of the enforcement of game laws has provided a key foundation for Flambeau's Indians to construct their own identity in stark oppositional terms, which has contributed to the endurance of their culture. According to Spicer (1971:797), such an "oppositional process is the

essential factor in the formation and development of the persistent
identity systems," accounting for how local Indian cultures like Flambeau manage to survive domination by state organizations.

But such an oppositional mode of generating identity can have far-
reaching unintended consequences. To be an Indian is to commit acts
that non-Indians would classify as illegal.[6] By the same logic, the consequences of economic impoverishment—"its unemployment, its disease and malnutrition, its broken homes, its child abandonment and
neglect, its public welfare dependency, its drunkenness and violence"
(James 1970:438)—run the risk of being seen as signs of ethnic
identity by Indian people. James G. E. Smith addresses this issue: "If
there is a 'culture of poverty' (James 1970) among the Southwestern
Ojibwa, it is not the culture of the poor rural American Whites, which
he characterizes as a poverty of culture. It is, rather, a phase of Ojibwa
culture that is continuously adapting to change while embodying traditional values that are more real than apparent" (Smith 1973:33).
Impoverished conditions are locally understood at Lac du Flambeau
as the outcome of valuing people more than property in a context of
domination.

FISHING AND IDENTITY

When the Ojibwes reconstructed and reimagined their history during
the spearfishing dispute in the late twentieth century, they gave pri-
macy to fishing, emphasizing cultural practices that had previously
been in the background.

A contemporary traditional story of the origin of spearing walleye
at night stresses its importance and close connection to the origin and
identity of the Anishinaabeg who live in the area of Lac du Flambeau.
"How Winaboozhoo Learned to Firehunt" was written by Flambeau
band and Crane clan member Ernie St. Germaine in 1990 and appears in *Winaboozhoo Adisokan,* used as the children's curriculum in
Family Circles. The story is set in the present, at the site of the Old Village where the Bear River flows into Flambeau Lake. A boy asks his
grandfather how the old man learned to spear. Grandfather says his
own grandfather taught him and, perhaps, Winaboozhoo in turn,
taught him. The grandson's question, "Who taught Winaboozhoo?"
sparks the tale.

Winaboozhoo's grandmother notices a fireball, an ominous sign,
dancing along the shore. She fears that the *windigowag*—cannibal

spirits—are angry. But the fireball doesn't show up the second night. Winaboozhoo decides to investigate against his grandmother's will, motivated by her teasing his assumption that the fireball didn't return because of Winaboozhoo's prowess. He arms himself with a "bow, several arrows, a knife, a good sized club, some Ninja stars and handbook on karate" and paddles off toward the fireball. The narration shifts voice here and is told from the grandmother's point of view. She watches the fireball approach her grandson and move on after a long time. He does not return until late the next day, after she has concluded that the fireball was a *windigo* sign. Winaboozhoo tells her about Akiwenzii, an old man whose bad eyes can't bear the sunlight but who likes to eat fish in the spring. Akiwenzii

devised a way that he could even catch them. What he did was make a torch using *wiigwassamakaak*, a birchbark dish, which he filled with *bigiw*, white pine pitch. Then he attached this to poles which he extended out over the front of his *jiimaan* [canoe]. In the evening, he went out on the lake after dark and would put a fire on the *bigiw*. It would burn brightly and even spatter causing little sparks to fly out into the water. *Giigoo* would see this, would get real curious and come to see what this fascinating light was. One of them, *oka*, the walleye, was Akiwenzii's favorite. *Oka*'s eyes would even shine in the light and were easier to see by Akiwenzii. When they came up close to the light, Akiwenzii would spear them. Then he would have a nice feast the next day. . . . Akiwenzii taught Winaboozhoo many tricks. . . . In turn, Winaboozhoo promised to help Akiwenzii however he could. Winaboozhoo promised that as long as he would remember he would never take more *oka* than he could eat by himself, and in that way Akiwenzii would never go hungry. Winaboozhoo later taught the *shinabe* who came to live at Bear River the story of Akiwenzii and in this way, they too learned how to firehunt. This caught on very fast and pretty soon, there were many *jiimanan* out on the water firehunting with their torches. He told them that they should never take more than their families could eat so that the old ones would always have *giigoo* to eat.

Other Anishinaabeg who came to visit here noticed this unusual way of catching fish with torches. So they called these people who lived by Bear River, *Waswaaganan*, or People of the Torches. And this place became known as *Waswaaganing*, or the Place of the Torch People. (St. Germaine 1990:61–62)

This spearfishing story is paradigmatic: *oka* is privileged and singled out from the other fish that spawn in the spring, having been important historically to Indian peoples in the Great Lakes area, the favored object of a practice central to the contemporary identity of the Flambeau Ojibwes. The fire basket itself illustrates a principle in the transformation of tradition: the indigenous prototype is a realization of a historic form in an aboriginal idiom. The torch described in the story is the birch bark version of torches made with iron frames, torches depicted in the Paul Kane painting *Spearing at Torchlight* at the Royal Ontario Museum in Toronto (Satz 1991).

Through Winaboozhoo's use of "Ninja stars and handbook on karate," the storyteller appropriates the present to the past, encompassing the colonizer's temporal linearity in a grand, if also flip, gesture that announces a local center of the world. Lac du Flambeau becomes placed on the same footing as the dominant society through the importation of exotic martial arts that will be put to local ends. It is this sign of cultural autonomy that authorizes the admonition not to take too many fish.

Only on the Great Plains and in the Great Basin culture areas were fish not speared (Rostlund 1952:293). Nocturnal torchlight fishing by Indians is documented throughout the Northwest, from south to central California, and in the entire area between Hudson Bay and the Great Lakes from about the hundredth degree of longitude to the Atlantic seaboard.

The first published description of spearfishing at night is by Le Jeune in the *Relation of 1634*. He describes the practice among Algonquian people in the area of Quebec.

This harpoon fishing is usually done only at night. Two Savages enter a canoe,—one at the stern, who handles the oars, and the other at the bow, who, by the light of a bark torch fastened to the prow of his boat, looks around searchingly for the prey, floating gently along the shores of this great river [the St. Lawrence]. When he sees an Eel, he thrusts his harpoon down, without loosening his hold of it, pierces it . . . , then throws it into his canoe. There are certain ones who will take three hundred in one night, and even more, sometimes very few. It is wonderful how many of these fish are found in this great river, in the months of September and October. (Thwaites 6:311)

David Thompson gives an account of Ojibwe people spearing at Red Lake in Minnesota in mid-April at the turn of the nineteenth century:

The spearing of fish in the night is a favorite mode with them, and gives them a considerable part of their livelihood. The spear handle is a straight pole of ten to twelve feet in length, headed with a barbed iron; A rude narrow basket of iron hoops is fixed to a pole of about six feet in length. A quantity of birch rind is collected and loosely tied in small parcels. When the night comes, the darker the better, two Men and a Boy embark in a Canoe, the one gently and quietly to give motion to the Canoe. The pole and basket is fixed in the Bow under which the Spearman stands, the Birch Rind is set on fire, and burns with a bright light; but only for a short time, the Boy from behind feeds the light, so as to keep a constant blaze. The approach of the flaming light seems to stupefy the fish, as they are all speared in a quiescent state. The Lake or River is thus explored for several hours until the Birch Rind is exhausted, and on a calm night a considerable number is thus caught. Those in my canoe, speared three Sturgeon, each weighing about sixty pounds. (1916:267–268)

Fishing in the early nineteenth century apparently had a deeply embedded, though mundane, value for the Ojibwes. When Flat Mouth, the chief of Leech Lake village, was in Washington discussing treaty payments, he used the expression "his house smelled so fishy" (Hickerson 1962:93) as a euphemism for a man's poverty. Hunting and trapping were signs of distinction, the means of acquiring prestige goods and reflecting engagement with the international economy. Flat Mouth's denigration of fishing suggests that the practice, although a mainstay of the subsistence economy, was not integral to the identity of the Ojibwe bands at the time.

In the 1850s, for the lake tribes, fish, especially whitefish, "was their daily bread" and so the "gagoiked, or fisherman is not celebrated as the hunter is in either poesy or religion" (Kohl 1985:307, 328). Spearfishing was something that men did. Though it could be constructed as a sign of Indian identity, it was one sign among many. It was undertaken by people closely related to each other and taught in a traditional way, with boys rowing the boat or just watching for longer than they really wanted to as their fathers, uncles, older brothers, and cousins speared.

Fishing was interwoven with hunting, since deer frequently stood next to lakes and streams and could often be shot from canoes (Kohl 1985:311–312). The only deer George Copway ever killed with a bow and arrow he shot from a canoe at night. By the light of a candle, "we placed in a three-sided lantern; opening one side, the light was thrown upon the deer only" (Copway 1850:28). There were many deer in the area of Flambeau, evidenced by the fact that François Mah-

liot, a Northwest Company fur factor there, accumulated 528 deer-
skins in a couple of months in 1805 (1910:225). The deer were probably taken using a few deer fences made of downed trees. One of these
fences was fifteen miles long in the area of the Trout Lake village, a few
miles northeast of the present-day reservation (Schorger 1953:203).
Another was nearer to the village of Waswaaganing, after which Fence
Lake on the present reservation was named (Habeck and Curtis
1959:51). Given the history, the names "Lac du Flambeau" and its
Anishinaabemowin equivalent, "Waswaaganing" may be as attributable to the nocturnal hunting of hoofed as finned prey. With the
depletion of wild game for the fur trade, fishing presumably grew in
value over the course of the late eighteenth and early nineteenth centuries.

The cultural importance of *oka,* walleyed pike, before the late twentieth century is equally ambiguous. *Poisson doré* is not specifically indexed in the *Jesuit Relations,* but does appear in lists of species when
fishing is mentioned or described. In the summer of 1849, Captain
John Pope of the U.S. Corps of Engineers made an expedition to the
Red River of the north. On his map, to the south and west of "Waswaaganing or Flambeau L. [Lake]" is marked another body of water,
"Flambeau dore L. [Lake]," near the headwaters of what he refers to
as the Labiche River (Pope 1849). The name marks a remarkable co-
occurrence of both the species of fish and the method by which it was
harvested. The Labiche (hind or doe) River is known today as the
South Fork of the Flambeau River and the lake is Lac Sault Dore. Another lake ten miles due east, near Phillips, preserves the species name
and is called Duroy Lake. Kagagon (okagakan) Slough on the Bad
River Reservation also refers to walleyed pike.

Stizostedion vitreum is singled out in Mahliot's journal (1910:168),
which records two fish being taken in a net on July 11. The technique
of spearing isn't noted, although Mahliot makes seven entries in his
journal during the period that *oka* were likely to have spawned that
year. In his five-page inventory of spearing methods among Wisconsin
Indians, Kuhm refers to sturgeon and whitefish, confirming Densmore's (1979) findings. In Kuhm's glossaries of Indian fish names,
"*oka'o*" occurs third on the list of twenty-one types of fish among the
Menominees, but it is the last fish on the Ojibwe list before four kinds
of crustaceans (1928:108–111). The walleyed pike does not occur at
all on the lists of Winnebago, Sauk, or Potawatomi names of fish. It
could be assumed that walleye was just another fish for the Ojibwes

during the early twentieth century; then again, its appearance so high on the list for the Menominees is interesting, given that they are the indigenous Algonquians in the region.

The fish populations of the inland lakes in the historic period, especially in the eighteenth and early nineteenth centuries, were managed in the sense that they were harvested, but nothing like the way they would come to be managed in the twentieth century. Sediment samples suggest that by the 1850s, changes in fish populations had already taken place due to lumbering and agriculture. Lumbering significantly transformed the fish populations in Michigan, which was cut over by 1900. There is little reason to suspect a qualitatively different impact in Wisconsin, where sixty billion board feet of timber was taken concurrently (Gough 1997:18) in the northern third of the state around Lac du Flambeau. "Lumbermen pushed sawdust and other wastes into lakes and streams, killing fish and ruining spawning grounds along riverbanks; so the sun heated the once shady waters and drove out the cold-water fish. Lumbermen floated logs on spring floods, gouging stream bottoms, channelizing them, and destroying fish habitats" (Doherty 1990:38–39).

These devastated fish populations would both rebound and be intentionally altered to attract fisherman tourists. Sportfishing, according to Betty Les (1988:2), originated on the inland waters of Wisconsin in the 1850s; it "caught hold and emerged into a major pastime" by the 1870s. During this time, the state made its first appropriation of funds to introduce and propagate fish. In 1875 the newly created Fishing Commission established the first fish hatcheries in Madison and Milwaukee. In 1881 the legislature closed the season on walleye and black bass from February 1 to May 1. Two years later the state began its walleye propagation program, producing eight million fingerlings. By 1900 Sears and Montgomery Ward offered a mail-order rod and reel for $1.50, and "using fishing as a drawing card, summer resorts thrived" (Les 1988:3). A hatchery in Woodruff-Minocqua, twelve miles east of the reservation, was built in 1901, two years before publication of the first detailed tourist map of the region.

By 1937 a new hatchery was being built at Lac du Flambeau and was expected to increase the output of (walleyed) pike fry from fifteen million per year to fifty million per year. Forty years later, the Wisconsin Department of Natural Resources distributed annually 59,515,000 walleye fry and 3,261,329 fingerlings, three times more fish than all other managed species combined. As predators of both largemouth and smallmouth bass, walleye had become the most popular sport fish in Wisconsin. Today it is the most extensively propagated fish in the state (Becker 1983:878).

At the beginning of the twenty-first century, the fish hatchery at Lac du Flambeau produces thirty million walleye fry per year and puts most of them in the reservation lakes. These fry are an investment in the local economy because they make the lakes attractive to tourists who consume services on the reservation, including employing guides.

The longtime fishing exploitation of the area by tourists has made guiding them an occupational option for a number of Lac du Flambeau men over the decades. The stereotypical image of the Indian as the one who knew about nature was affirmed by their being hired as guides (James 1961:729). The few surviving men who guided in the period before World War II at Lac du Flambeau recall this work with great affection and nostalgia. At the reservation, guiding was more important to the tribal members than slating the officers for the new government mandated by the Indian Reorganization Act in the mid-1930s. On the day it was decided that Flambeau would elect its leaders, there were not enough people to form a quorum to vote because they were off at the resorts cultivating their customers for the next summer (Huber 1936:26). Apparently, some colonial institutions held more promise to the Flambeau people than others. This choice reflects not only the importance of the role of guide, but also the value placed by both Indians and whites on detailed knowledge of the lakes in the area. Indian professional guiding helped consolidate the meaning of Indianness.

At the same time, the production of tens of millions of walleye fry per year has been going on for more than fifty years at Flambeau. Though this may not have changed the structure of the fish populations in the nine-thousand-acre ten-lake chain of lakes on the reservation that was originally created to float logs to the mill, it does serve to maintain current levels of walleye numbers and index the value of walleye to the reservation. Today, nearly everyone who fishes Flambeau lakes goes to the Flambeau chain, and 90 percent of those fishers are non-Indians. Most Ojibwes, however, have been forced out of the guiding business, since membership in the guiding associations is expensive and use of the most up-to-date equipment is essential.

Spearing before the Treaty Rights Conflict

Questions about first memories of spearing almost invariably elicit recollections of rowing or paddling for an older male relative. A boy works and observes for a period of time before he is permitted to try it. This is traditional pedagogy,[7] a part of initiation into manhood at Flambeau. Being a man very often means being a spearer.

Most tribal members didn't own motors until the 1960s and 1970s. Some speared out of rowboats, standing in the stern with a partner rowing backward. Lacking freezers, the spearfishers took what fish they needed for a day or two and then rowed their tubs back home.

Steve Boggs, who studied child rearing during the winter at Flambeau in 1951–52 (Boggs 1956, 1958), remembers watching people spear from a rowboat on Crawling Stone Lake. He does not recall any Indians owning motors. Don Smith remembered back to his teenage years:

This was in the early '50s. We heard that somebody was spearing with a motor and I couldn't figure out how because I always thought about motorboats going across a lake to beat hell. I didn't know that you could use it to go slow. We would row and you would say, "a little to the right, a little to the left." Now we just use hand signals [demonstrating the technique]. We used to use those six-volt batteries and they wouldn't last very long. Before that you had to hold a flashlight in one [hand] and a spear in the other. It was hard!

Tom Maulson, born in 1941, recalls spearing with the help of the light of a Coleman lantern directed with small sheets of aluminum bent in a semicircle. Another Lac du Flambeau tribal member who lived in Shawano more than one hundred miles south of the reservation spent his boyhood during the 1960s on the reservation and went spearing with his father. He remembers being commanded to pull on the oars of the rowboat one way and then another. "Up to my ankles in walleyes," was his first image in describing what it was like.

In the late 1960s and the early 1970s, when Scott Smith was a boy too young to go out spearing, he took a kitchen fork, flattened it out, and hafted it to a pole to make a spear. Smith and his friends would spear crabs along the lakeshore, which he would take home and present to his mother, who would cook them. According to Ernie St. Germaine, by the 1970s only a few people speared the lakes, perhaps reflecting a decline in the practice.

Standing on the seats of boats rowed backward, spearing fish at night, was a quiet sign of male identity for a long time at Lac du Flambeau. Part of its value is an oppositional contrast with the fishing practice of

Flambeau's white neighbors. Whites hunt and fish during the day after the spawning season for sport, and handicap themselves with minimally adequate mass-produced equipment. Indian people work at fishing at night during the spawn, maximizing their technological assistance using homemade lights and spears.

Whether or not the Anishinaabeg of Waswaaganing were primarily walleye spearfishers in the eighteenth and nineteenth centuries, their responses to a rapidly changing world have included making themselves into nearly exclusively walleye spearfishers in the modern era. It was the state's usurpation of guarantees made in federal treaties and the tacitly legal redefinition of Indian rights beginning in 1868 with the criminalization of subsistence that helped to reconfigure hunting, fishing, and Indian identity. Traditional subsistence activities at Lac du Flambeau now had to be done surreptitiously. As a result they took on the gamelike quality and trappings of warfare, recalling distant memories of conflict over the land with the Dakotas. At the same time, Lac du Flambeau became enveloped by American mainstream society as an effectively proletarianized and underdeveloped enclave. Subsistence hunting, fishing, and gathering had only marginal economic importance for the band as a whole but were critically important to some tribal members. The value of these subsistence practices as signs of Indianness was augmented by the Indian guides, who mediated a relationship between traditional knowledge and contemporary identity. By virtue and in spite of the community's incorporation into the world economic system, by the last quarter of the twentieth century Indian ethnicity at Lac du Flambeau resided in a few signs and practices, oppositionally cast against the world around them.

Contained within the borders of the reservation, the practice of spearfishing was tolerable, even quaint, from the point of view of many non-Indians. For Indians and whites alike, it was a sign of distinction that further authenticated the dances Indians did for the tourists, bolstered the aura of the north as pristine wilderness, and validated Indian images on postcards sold on the main streets of Flambeau, Woodruff, Minocqua, and elsewhere. When the practice took place beyond the borders of the reservation, however, its value and the very meaning of being Indian was profoundly transformed.

4

The War Begins

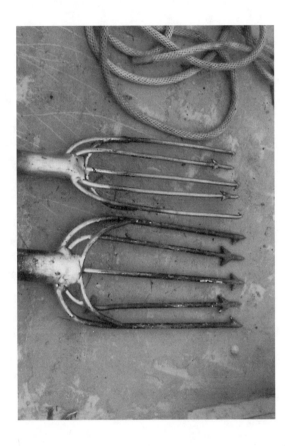

6. The heads of fishing spears belonging to Gilbert Chapman that were made for him by Edward Chosa. Photo courtesy of the author.

Hunting and fishing conditions off the reservations for Indian people had been eroding for nearly a century before litigation in the 1970s altered the relationship between the Wisconsin Chippewa bands and the state. The Great Society programs of the late 1960s, especially Wisconsin Judicare and the Indian Law Center, enabled Wisconsin Indians to litigate their concerns about fishing and hunting more extensively (Wilkinson 1990:23). Access to and deployment of legal resources for tribal ends was an unintended consequence of the post–World War II relocation program that had moved tens of thousands of Indian people to the cities, at least for a time. A supratribal consciousness took root among Indians who moved between urban centers and reservations (Cornell 1988:128–148), resulting in exposure to and sharing of strategies and techniques for transforming the relationship between reservations and the surrounding dominant society.

Ojibwes in Michigan began legally contesting the state's infringement on Indian fishing rights when William Jondreau of L'Anse, Michigan, sued the state in 1965, eventually winning in the state's supreme court in 1971. Citing the right to fish in Lake Superior under the 1854 treaty, the court held that the state could not enforce the licensing or regulating of fishing in Keweenaw Bay on Lake Superior by Chippewas of the L'Anse reservation (Fixico 1987:492). The following year, two Red Cliff tribal members contested the state of Wisconsin's interpretation of the boundaries of their lakeside reservation by gill netting in Lake Superior. As in the Jondreau case, the court upheld the treaty right to fish there. In 1976 Albert "Big Abe" LeBlanc of the Bay Mills band sued under the 1836 treaty and won in the state's supreme court (Doherty 1990). The court remanded the decision to the district courts for clarification, a process that culminated in 1985 but continued in certain aspects until 1990.

In 1978 a number of cases involving the property interests, hunting, and fishing rights of the Ojibwes of northern Wisconsin were argued together in the federal district court in Wisconsin—*U.S. v. Bouchard, U.S. v. Ben Ruby,* and *Lac Courte Oreilles v. Voigt.* One case involved the ownership of the Kakagon Slough on the Bad River Reservation. In another case, the LCO band asserted the right to hunt, fish, and gather off its reservation free of state regulation. This case was initiated when Fred and Mike Tribble of LCO were arrested by Milton Dieckman and Larry Miller of the Wisconsin Department of Natural Resources for spearing through the ice on Chief Lake in February of 1974, just three weeks after Judge Boldt had upheld the right of thirteen Washington bands to half of the salmon on the Columbia River.[1] Don Hanaway, the state's attorney general, later referred to the Tribble incident as "the most important fishing citations ever issued in Wisconsin" (1990:1).

In the first case, Judge Doyle found that the Kakagon Slough was not the exclusive property of the Chippewa Indians. In the second, Judge Doyle determined that the Chippewas did not have the right to hunt, fish, and gather off the reservation free of state regulation. He reasoned that although both the treaties of 1837 and 1842 ceded lands and explicitly reserved the usual rights of occupancy (which the Chippewa Indians understood and intended to mean the right to hunt, fish, and gather throughout the ceded territory), the treaty of 1854, which established the reservations in Wisconsin and ceded lands in Minnesota, did not explicitly reserve these rights for the Wisconsin bands. Doyle concluded that this omission was tantamount to their suspension.

LCO took this decision to the U.S. Court of Appeals. In 1983, in *LCO v. Voigt,* it was reversed and remanded to the district court for clarification of the scope of the rights and the extent of the state's regulatory power. In its reversal, this court distinguished between aboriginal and treaty-recognized use rights, asserting that the Chippewas apparently understood that they would continue to be able to use the land as long as they did not harass the settlers. The major historical source, the annual reports of the agent at LaPointe, failed to show that the Indians had harassed the settlers between the signing of the treaties and the executive order of 1850. This order was found to exceed the powers of the executive because the right to make treaties is reserved to Congress and because the order was formulaic—that is, it did not refer to any alleged depredations committed by the Chippewas.

The appeals court decided that because of the standing of treaty-recognized use rights in law, explicit language in the treaty of 1854 would have been required to suspend the use rights guaranteed in the treaties of 1837 and 1842; insofar as they were not mentioned, they were understood to continue. Furthermore, in his 1978 decision, Judge Doyle had apparently discounted the fact that the usufruct rights of the Minnesota bands that lived within the ceded area specified in the treaty of 1854 were explicitly retained in quite the same way that the rights of the bands within the 1837 and 1842 cessions had also been retained.

FLAMBEAU IN THE WINTER OF 1983

Michael Lutz, staff counsel for the Wisconsin Department of Natural Resources, described the office as "chaotic" on the day in January 1983 when news arrived that the appeals court had reversed and remanded the district court decision.[2] Out of a disinclination to deal with such a large issue through a series of "mini-trials," as Lutz characterized them, the state chose not to enforce the law on Indians hunting off the reservation.

During the winter of 1983 a number of Flambeau tribal members overheard personnel from the Department of Natural Resources discussing the change in policy on their shortwave scanners (such scanners are standard equipment in many reservation homes and vehicles and are used to monitor the wardens). Gilbert Chapman recalls: "That very hour, guys went out to shoot deer, right from the highways." Don Smith remembers hearing the message at about midnight; three men went hunting the next morning. Rueben Zortmann and Ed Chosa took three deer from off the reservation. "In a few days, everybody was out there," Don told me. "They weren't getting too much, but they went out just because they could." Wayne Valliere heard the report the following morning while at breakfast. His father told him that he didn't have to go to high school that morning, gave him his rifle, and sent him off the reservation northeast in search of "Boulder beef." He said that he shot a deer right from the road outside of Boulder Junction, "with white people watching from the cars."

In a special meeting of the tribal council at Lac du Flambeau, the tribe decided to arrange a meeting with the Department of Natural Resources on February 3. The meeting was canceled. The apparent unwillingness of the DNR to meet before a public response suggested to Indian people at Lac du Flambeau that the DNR was interested in whatever political edge might be gained by letting sectors of the white community adjudicate matters, at least until the disposition of the state's request for a rehearing would be made. In the opinion of Jerry Maulson as well as a number of the Flambeau men who led the spearing parties off the reservation in the first two years, "the DNR set us up." They felt that the situation was an outstanding opportunity for the DNR to ally the local community, deflecting long-standing white hostility toward the DNR over the state's management of fish and game. Instead, if the community obliged, the DNR would effectively be orchestrating the outcry.

The first response by the surrounding non-Indian communities to "the *Voigt* decision" was alarmist. The February 3 issue of the local newspaper, the *Lakeland Times,* was headlined, "Ruling Allows Chippewa Indians Off Reservation Hunting Anytime." The paper began its coverage with a polarized apocalyptic vision: "Wholesale slaughter of fish and wild game or a reasonable exercise of treaty rights? Open conflict or meaningful negotiation between Indians, white sportsmen and the DNR? . . . [T]ourism will be devastated if the ruling is not overturned before spring spawning runs of walleyes, musky and other gamefish begins and Indians harvest thousands of vulnerable fish" (*Lakeland Times* 1983a). The article noted that a DNR warden estimated that more than twenty-six deer had been killed the week before north of the reservation in the area of Manitowish Waters.. "You can kiss hunting and fishing and the resort business good-bye if this comes to pass," the warden commented, snidely adding, "Of course, we will always have water-skiing."

Most of the issues and images that would inform the debate between the tribe and the state were incipient in this issue's coverage: "real" Indians existed in the past; contemporary Indians were killers out of control and likely to cause the demise of an economy based more on hunting and fishing tourism than on subsistence hunting and fishing. Fish became the icons of the whites' future, portrayed as "vulnerable" to "wholesale slaughter." Fears about the future of the tourist economy were fanned with the implicit representation of the tribal membership as ungovernable.

The first letter to the editor concerning this issue recommended that the court's decision should be obeyed only if mid-nineteenth-century technology were employed to take deer. Indian practices were considered authentic and respectable only to the extent to which they were anachronistic.

Anti-Indian rhetoric immediately flared, including inflammatory stories in the papers, a call for Indian scalps on a Minocqua radio sta-

tion, and signs appearing in Boulder Junction calling for Indians to
be killed.

A few days later, Bronson LaFollette, the attorney general of Wisconsin, filed for a stay of the appeals court decision pending an appeal to
the supreme court. It was granted, with enforcement to begin on February 19 and to remain in force until an off-reservation deer hunting
season was negotiated the following fall.

On the same day as the attorney general's filing, the Flambeau tribe
released a pointed statement about the issue following a poll vote:

Because of irresponsible and erroneous accounts and editorials regarding
the recent court decision on Indian rights on off-reservation lands and because of the immanent danger which exists to our tribal members who may
exercise their rights the Lac du Flambeau tribal council issues this statement to all media:

We have sent delegates to a meeting of all the Bands at Mt. Telemark.

The Realty/Natural Resources committee met and made recommendations to the tribal council, which are being implemented.

There will be a news conference on February 7 at 10:30 AM at the tribal
Center. (Tribal council minutes, February 10, 1983)

The news conference was convened by Mike Chosa, president of the
Realty/ Natural Resources committee of the council and a descendent
of a "second chief," apparently a headman or leader of warriors from
the Trout Lake area. Chosa's name was derived from the French
"shocher," a kind of wizard. Experienced as an activist, Chosa had
been a student of community organizer Saul Alinsky in Chicago in the
late 1960s and early 1970s and had organized the Chicago Indian Village near Wrigley Field, the first Indian occupation east of Alcatraz.
His father, Ben, a longtime ricer on the reservation, was an educated
man reputed to have subscribed to the *Congressional Record* to monitor legislation on Indians.

Mike Chosa immediately went on the offensive at the news conference by pointing out that "the court has affirmed rights we already
possessed. . . . 150 years ago Indians were more numerous and the resources were more plentiful. Look at it now." He went on to describe
the depletion of fish and game.

Chosa then outlined a series of steps that the tribe was taking to respond to "the challenge of protecting the resources" (*Lakeland Times*
1983b), an expression that attempts to engage the terms of the debate
the newspaper found so congenial. These steps spoke to different au-

diences, carried a complicated semantic load, and served to expand the scope of the controversy.

The first step called on tribal members to voluntarily refrain from taking deer until "the time of the fireflies." Speaking to and about tribal members first was a sign of the extent to which at least some elements within the tribal government understood and realized traditional styles of leadership. An Indian style of leadership that respected the autonomy of individual hunters was distinguished from a non-Indian, coercive authority. The request to wait until "the time of the fireflies" emphasized that a human productive activity was organized around a temporal order reflective of the changes in the natural environment. By not glossing "the time of the fireflies" as "about June," Chosa signaled to both Indian and non-Indian communities that at least some groups on the reservation traded in a language and a system of meaning that could be construed as historical and traditional, a system that presumably antedated the calendrical system the two societies now shared. The first step effectively consolidated and empowered the Indian community.

By calling for "a meeting between the tribe and *responsible DNR officials*" (underlined in the tribal council minutes), the second step criticized the DNR and attempted to exploit hostility in the white community toward the DNR in its regulatory capacity. This step held accountable certain components of the DNR—such as the warden who prophesied the end of tourism and those who authorized him to make such comments—and implicitly acknowledged a long history of harassment and, in some tribal members' views, the DNR's dramatic abdication of its fiduciary responsibility.

The third step called for an informational meeting for tribal members, a sign that the tribe was attempting to assert leadership over an activity that had been conducted autonomously without tribal governmental involvement or interest. As important, this meeting would claim the newly upheld subsistence rights as rights held collectively: rights managed and defined by a representative body, not rights held by individuals by virtue of membership in a tribe.

A fourth item signaled the tribe's sensitivity to its relations with surrounding communities. The governor was called on to address the concerns of non-Indians in the region, a move that preempted the governor's office from taking a hostile stance first. The Realty/Natural Resources Committee was also asked to investigate possibilities for an open forum meeting with Flambeau's neighbors.

The fifth and sixth steps must be understood together. They represent the beginning of a policy, a kind of "Pax Waswaaganing," that reflected Lac du Flambeau's attempt to impose its understanding of the meaning of the *Voigt* decision on the other Wisconsin Chippewa bands. The first of these two steps requested a meeting with the other five bands who had been the plaintiffs in the appeal—Lac Courte Oreilles, Red Cliff, Bad River, Mole Lake, and St. Croix. In fact, the meeting had already been called by Gordon Thayer at Lac Courte Oreilles, who had recognized that the *Voigt* decision affected all the bands and wanted them to gather and discuss it.

The meetings that subsequently took place between the bands gave rise to the Voigt Inter-tribal Task Force. When this body joined the Great Lakes Indian Fisheries Commission, it became the Great Lakes Indian Fish and Wildlife Commission, a federally funded agency that provides assistance to the thirteen member bands in Wisconsin, Michigan, and Minnesota in their conservation and management of fish, wildlife, and traditional pursuits of the Ojibwes. GLIFWC facilitates the development of institutions of tribal self-government to ensure the continued sovereignty of its member bands in the regulation and management of natural resources (GLIFWC 1988:2).

The second of these two steps proposed that the Realty/Natural Resources Committee of Lac du Flambeau implement a conservation code and resource management plan for the ceded territory. This plan attempted to formulate a consensus among the six bands as to the meaning of the *Voigt* decision. These efforts were led by Mike Chosa and Gilbert Chapman, delegated by Flambeau's tribal council to speak with the chairs of the other reservations (tribal council minutes, February 10, 1983).

Like Chosa, Gilbert Chapman had some experience living off the reservation in the city. A relocatee, he had lived and worked in Milwaukee for a number of years. He had also traveled across the American South in the 1950s and 1960s, and he drew upon the racial injustices he witnessed to illuminate his understanding of the relations between Indians and whites in the Northwoods. Chapman often repeated a line he said he had heard from whites in the South: "A nigger will do anything a white man will let him. And it's the same with Indians." He had been a policeman for the town, knew some law, and had written a tribal law enforcement program as a private consultant.

During 1983, Chosa and Chapman represented Flambeau's interests and interpretation of the *Voigt* decision as best they could. They had some difficulty forging a common vision and goals with the other bands. Chapman reported in a letter that the leaders of the Bad River and Red Cliff bands were largely indifferent to the potential change in the status quo that at least certain tribal members at Flambeau saw in the *Voigt* decision. He went so far as to note that:

I told Gurnoe [tribal chairman of the Red Cliff band] that what Red Cliff does on its own reservation is no one else's business but what they did off the reservation in the ceded territory was Lac du Flambeau's business and the business of the other seven Chippewa bands [affected] by the Voigt Decision. After more discussion Mr. Gurnoe and Mr. Ray DePere [tribal chairman of the Bad River band] agreed that *all* the Chippewa Bands have to work very closely together in forming some management plans for the ceded areas or we may have some problems exercising our rights. (Tribal council minutes, April 11, 1983)

The tribal council at St. Croix, according to Chapman, was also less than imaginative about the ramifications of the *Voigt* decision. All they wanted from the state, he recalls, were free fishing licenses for each tribal member. "I called them the Zebco tribe," he told me, impugning their Indianness—Zebco is a brand of sports fishing tackle. Flambeau's perception of St. Croix as timid is shared by Mike Chosa's brother Ed,[3] who said that once when he was visiting in that area, he shocked his hosts by violating, taking fish and deer to feed the gathering of guests at the home at which he was staying. The large numbers of deer and fish at St. Croix prompted Ed Chosa to ask why no one was taking them. When he was told that the game were "out of season," Chosa scoffed and said he would hunt and fish whenever and however he pleased.

The Flambeau delegation also encountered resistance from the Mole Lake band, who did not practice spearfishing as intensely as some of the other tribes. Chapman remembers the threat used to achieve consensus: "Mole Lake was not interested in spearing, but wanted wild rice. They have very few lakes in their area that are good spearing lakes. I told them that they wouldn't take a pound of wild rice off the reservation if they didn't support Flambeau's spearing because the rice was ours too."

The *Voigt* decision spurred the creation of a judiciary at Lac du Flambeau. At a February 21, 1983 meeting, the tribal council passed a resolution retaining the legal services of James Jannetta, who had been introduced to the council the previous week. A non-Indian, Jannetta was the counsel for the group of bands on an appeal of the *Doyle* decision, and had helped the Sault Ste Marie band secure commercial fishing rights in Lake Superior. One of the first projects he undertook was designing and implementing a tribal court. Such a judiciary would allow the tribe maximum jurisdiction over its children under the 1978 Indian Child Welfare Act and preempt state jurisdiction in light of *Lac Courte Oreilles v. Voigt* (tribal council minutes, February 21, 1983; April 11, 1983). One of the first two judges was Tom Maulson.

Tom Maulson was soon appointed to take Mike Chosa's position as a delegate to the other bands. In addition to his own business interests, he had taught, worked as tribal policeman, been chairman of the tribe's housing committee, and served with Chosa on the Realty/Natural Resources Committee at the time of the *Voigt* decision.

Maulson came to play an instrumental role in the ensuing bitter dispute over spearfishing rights. Multiple signs of leadership converge in him. Born on the day the Japanese attacked Pearl Harbor, he is a twin, a traditional sign of power, and large in size, another sign of special status since it expresses the Ojibwe belief that the leader of any group of "persons" is always larger than the others. His many travels and his success as an athlete, soldier, and businessman off the reservation point to a certain amount of spiritual power. Maulson's teaching about Indian identity at the reservation school gave further credibility to his claims to leadership. Some of his young students would be among those in the forefront of the fishing rights struggle in the years to come.

But in the early 1980s Flambeau's Indians were not skilled at off-reservation politics and negotiating, according to Mike Chosa. "They thought that negotiations meant giving things away. They were so happy to be sitting there with white people." This inexperience rapidly changed. Soon the sons and grandsons, daughters and granddaughters, of Ojibwe guides and commercial hunters, grown sophisticated by conflict and experience in larger political spheres, would pursue this cause with a vengeance born of a long-standing hostility toward the state.

THE FIRST OFF-RESERVATION SPEARING SEASON

In October of 1983, the United States Supreme Court refused to hear the state's appeal of the *Voigt* decision. At the same time, Judge Doyle decided not to mediate the irresolvable issues that were surfacing in the negotiations between the Ojibwe bands and the state. The state had to acquiesce to negotiate with the bands. For the first time, the state of Wisconsin had to confront realistically the implications of tribal sovereignty and accept that it did not fully control what went on within its borders.[4] Also for the first time, the members of the Voigt Inter-tribal Task Force came to understand and define the treaty rights as tribal and not individual property, and they asserted the necessity for tribal self-regulation. Both sides agreed to start with deer, and an interim deer hunting agreement was worked out in the fall of 1983, establishing a season from November 13 to December 31.

The Voigt Inter-tribal Task Force and the DNR reached the first spearfishing agreement in 1985. The 1985 season would last seven consecutive days, from dusk until dawn, and take place between "ice-out" and May 3—the first day of the hook and line season and thus effectively the beginning of the new year for non-Indians involved in tourist-related businesses. Each band could spear six lakes; a list of the locations selected was required to be given to the DNR, an action that came to be called "naming a lake." The bands agreed to give the DNR forty-eight hours' notice when they intended to begin to spear. No lake named could be less than five hundred acres or protected as a refuge or for research by the state.

Fish longer than twenty inches were designated off-limits to the Ojibwe spearfishers. Through this regulation, the state sought to protect the lucrative sportsmen's trophy fishery. This age-class of fish was effectively worth hundreds of dollars each in hotel, motel, resort, and restaurant receipts. A subsequent outcry from spearfishers forced some compromise—one fish over twenty inches could be speared per lake each night, two if the lake was bigger than 5,500 acres. The Lac Courte Oreilles and Bad River bands did not accept this compromise and refused to ratify the agreement.

The 1985 agreement also required spearfishers to carry tribal identification cards and cooperate with DNR wardens, who measured each fish upon a boat's return to designated landings. Tribal members were not allowed to sell speared fish or to cross private land to get to designated waters. Tribal, GLIFWC, and DNR wardens were empowered to enforce all regulations and a schedule of fines was established, imposed by tribal courts (if they were in place) or state courts (if they were not).

On paper, the 1985 spearing agreement appeared to be a well-regulated version of the sports fishery, with bag and size limits allocated per person per lake. In actuality, it enabled some tribal members to accrue surpluses and, therefore, power and status, since spearers were permitted to fish on behalf of other tribal members. Flambeau tribal member Don Smith noted that a few spearfishers took many off-reservation walleye that first year.

We pulled into the parking lot there at the landing and there must have been sixty law enforcement and DNR people there and there was only three of us going to spear! There wasn't anybody there on the landings watching us.

. . . The first year, I'm going to just pick a number, say they took 4,000 walleye, me and my two boys took 1,800 of 'em, almost half what all the bands took. I had maps that I got. We used to take a ride around those lakes before we speared them. I have a lot of relatives around this area and they told me where the rock bars were and where to spear.

By the 1992 fishing season, Smith owned four freezers to store all the fish, fowl, and deer that he and his grown sons were taking. His son Scott described the experience of spearing until his arms were so weary that he couldn't lift the spear any longer. He guessed that in one night he took over five hundred walleye.

Scott Smith also spoke of the first night spearing off the reservation as one of the most memorable of his life. He and others went to Tomahawk Lake, a place where non-Indians had been particularly hostile to Indians during his lifetime and the site of a Waswaaganan village well before it. Tomahawk was one of the lakes "named" to be speared by Flambeau on the advice of the interested membership and fish hatchery personnel. Lakes like Tomahawk and Squirrel were relatively close to the reservation and known to be good walleye lakes by the older guides, their children, nephews, and grandchildren.

Tomahawk and Squirrel Lakes had been the sites of permanent villages in living memory, a historical connection not lost on at least some of the spearers. Ed Chosa set loudspeakers on top of his van and blasted powwow music out over the lake while the people speared in celebration of what he described as "a return, a kind of homecoming." They set their boats in the water, started the engines, and went "to beat hell" across the lake, heading for a rock bar where the walleye spawn. This practice came to be known as "a Flambeau trademark," or "the Flambeau method." Other bands, especially the ones who use underwater lights, began spearing right from the landings. During the first years, some of the spearers from the Bad River band were teased by those from Flambeau because they showed up with the short spears used for spearing through the ice in winter. By this point in their history, Flambeau fishermen had been intensively indigenizing modern hunting technology for more than a century.

The distribution and concentration of spearers at the lakes in 1985 had little to do with the fact that each band was permitted to spear six lakes. Theoretically, any fisherman could fish any "named" lake any night, once the tribe had given forty-eight hours' notice on the six lakes that it had selected a few weeks before. Most of the lakes were not being fished in the style that they had been fished on and off the reservation before the turn of the century. The lakes were now the sites of very temporary villages for all practical and cultural reasons, gatherings referred to by Ed as "a real party."

The first group of Flambeau Indians who went off the reservation to spearfish, according to Tom Maulson, were the violators, the people who had always gone off the reservation to hunt and fish. "It's in their blood," Maulson concluded, evoking the romantic image of the subsistence hunter that had evolved over the last century (James 1961:729, 741). "That was our way. We've always hunted and fished off the reservation." Maulson was instrumental in organizing this group.[5]

When visiting people or inviting them to visit his rather plush home behind the fish hatchery, Maulson repeatedly made the argument "Use 'em or lose." This saying was culturally potent and resonated with these hunters' experiences. It expressed the traditional Ojibwe belief, discussed in Chapter 2, that a reciprocal exchange relationship bound human and animal "persons." Through hunting and feasting, humans reproduced animal species. Consuming the corporeal remains of animals honored their spirits and placed them in humanity's debt, thus making hunting and fishing initial generative acts (see Brightman 1976, 1983, 1993). Ignoring resources—be they lakes full of fish or privileges recently reinscribed in federal law—was tantamount to refusing to exchange with the spirits, who would then offer no response of beneficence of any kind at all. The rights and the fish would be lost.

Two important structural features emerged during the first season spearing off the reservation. Many spearfishers went off the reservation, more than were remembered later by the leaders of the first group; the first spearing season was also more anarchic than was later represented by the newspapers and the oral histories of the leaders.

Indians tended to spear in larger groups than when they had previously violated, because of fear for their safety. Tom Maulson remembers that non-Indians "would say to us, 'Wait 'til it gets dark. We're going to kill you fuckers.'" Signs of incoherency and disorganization in the reaction of spearfishers were apparent. Maulson attempted to close Squirrel Lake after the first night, but spearers returned anyway for a number of nights thereafter. A man was arrested for refusing to show his tribal identification at Tomahawk Lake. Nine spearers were cited for taking more than one fish larger than twenty inches. A few citations were handed out for boat light violations, two for spearing in a stream, and two for being over the bag limit of twenty. A prime instigator of spearfishing, Maulson seemed to have little control over how it was carried out.

Many non-Indians at first marveled at the efficiency of spearing as a harvesting technique. Seeing multiple tubs of walleye as well as an occasional large female full of spawn soon turned the curious into critics. ERFE (Equal Rights for Everyone), the first of the anti-treaty protest groups, sprang up during this time.[6] On the last night of the 1985 season, about one hundred people blocked the spearfishers' access to one lake and fired five gunshots at Big Twin Lake. Some non-Indians questioned the appropriateness and even the cultural authenticity of "fish frys and tribal music on boomboxes" (*Lakeland Times* 1986a).

The *Lakeland Times* newspaper amplified the anti-treaty and anti-Indian sentiment growing in the Lakeland communities in the guise of representing itself as forum for dialogue between treaty opponents and treaty supporters. It inflamed local anxieties by headlining the numbers of fish and their gross weight in issue after issue during the spearing season. The paper also printed letters critical of spearing written by people from Illinois, lending support to the fear that spearing was endangering tourism. Separate articles were run on the content of letters to the editor written by the protest leaders. When James Schlender of GLIFWC wrote a letter responding to the paper's coverage of a forum at the Minocqua Community Building, where his tires had been slashed, he was upbraided in print by the editor, who addressed him as "Jim" and suggested that the charges of vandalism might better be laid at the feet of Indians critical of the off-reservation spearing (*Lakeland Times* 1986a).

Perhaps most importantly, the Wisconsin Department of Natural Resources soon dropped all pretense of being an unbiased fiduciary by taking the position that tourism and spearfishing could not coexist in the Northwoods. At what was understood by Indian people to be a joint news conference, the DNR surprised the bands by raising concerns about the biological and social dangers of spearfishing. The DNR recommended "that this practice should not continue in the future" and that the state should "engage in negotiations with the Chippewa bands to compensate the bands for their non-exercise of open water spearing in 1986" (Meyer 1985:4–5).

Very different parties reacted quite negatively to this proposal. The state attorney general chastised the secretary of the DNR for making such a premature suggestion, since the entire scope of the treaty rights was still being litigated in federal court and the state and the bands were operating under interim agreements.

Placing an exchange value on spearfishing offended the bands since there has always been a strong sense among tribal members that greed, symbolized by money, is in many ways at the heart of ethnic whiteness and opposed to things Indian. When I hear tribal members use the word "Indian" as an adjective for an object, such as a car or road, they mean that it was imaginatively improvised, produced by hand, or jerry-rigged using available materials.[7] An "Indian" project, whatever it might be, is undertaken for its distinctive social or use value; money is a sign of the opposite—exchangeability and alienation.

Finally, there was also a negative public response to the DNR's proposal since state taxes would pay for such a forbearance agreement. Popular concern was raised about the equity of the state subsidizing the present consequences of past federal actions: why should state taxes be allocated to the bands to pay for an agreement made when Wisconsin was still a territory and not yet a state? This criticism would be heard repeatedly in the years ahead.

THE STAR LAKE CONTROVERSY

The interim agreement for the 1986 season between the state and the bands allowed for a nine-day season, to end on May 2 when the hook and line season began, and a twenty-five fish bag limit per tribal member each night. Spearfishers could fish until 1:00 A.M. on weekdays and 2:00 A.M. on weekends. The Ojibwe bands would be permitted to take 10 percent of the "total allowable catch" (TAC) per lake. The (TAC) was the number of members of a species that could be sustainably taken from a body of water each year, a figure set at 35 percent of the total estimated population. Because non-Indian communities had been upset about the numbers of fish taken from Squirrel and Toma-hawk Lakes the previous season, the harvest was distributed across a greater number of lakes. Three lakes per night could be designated, but no lake could be speared on two consecutive nights. Unlike the year before, in 1986 the DNR would not announce which lakes were be-ing speared in an effort to forestall violent scenes on the landings.

A week before Flambeau spearfishers "put their spears in the water" (a favorite expression) in 1986, the *Lakeland Times* gave notice of a rally in Minocqua on Saturday, April 26, sponsored by a new regional anti-Indian organization, Protect American Rights and Resources (PARR). The editors encouraged people to attend the rally to "get your message across" (1986d). Twelve hundred people attended the rally, including Vera Lawrence, a Sault Ste Marie Chippewa band member who called for abrogation of Indian treaties on the grounds that the treaties were made with full-bloods, who now numbered very few at Flambeau.[8]

The PARR rally witnessed one of the first public displays of modern cultural revitalization at Lac du Flambeau. For some time, a spiritual leader from Grand Portage in Minnesota, having dreamed that the unfolding conflict over fishing rights would become important, had been instructing the people of Flambeau in cultural practices that had been forgotten. A number of people were taught how to construct spirit poles, which are placed in front of one's home. These are cedar poles about twenty feet long that are stripped of their bark and branches up to the last few feet; here medicines in the form of tobacco offerings, strips of colored cloth, and eagle feathers are often tied. A rock is often put at the base of the pole and tobacco offerings are placed upon it. Wayne Valliere remembered that this spiritual leader also taught the Flambeau singers four songs that they were to sing when they went to the PARR rally.

Tom Maulson and a group of nearly one hundred people from Lac du Flambeau attended the rally in Minocqua. They brought a drum and an innovative ritual they later referred to as a friendship cere-mony. The presence of the drum was significant to the tribal mem-bers; its use is a mode of establishing a relationship with the non-human persons who empower human beings. The drum that was brought to the rally was a descendent of the Drum Dance drum given to the people of Lac du Flambeau by the Bad River band who, in turn, received it from groups further to the west, who ultimately got it from their old rivals, the Dakotas. The Dakotas received it when a woman who was hiding in a lake from the U.S. Army was taken up into the spirit world and given instructions about the making and decorating of the drum and the songs and offices that went with it. Once the drum was made and its offices of belt carrier and pipe carrier filled, the soldiers came to dance. The drum thus represents an imaginative encompassment of one's enemies, largely on one's own terms (Vennum 1982; Barret 1911; Densmore 1910; Slotkin 1957).

What transpired that day was understood by the Flambeau people to have been influenced and guided by the spirits. As Wayne Valliere, a young man at the time, began to sing the first song, he noticed that all of the scowling protesters, adorned in blaze orange jackets (a symbol of anti-treaty sentiment), hats, and anti-Indian buttons, turned to look at him. Amid catcalls and hooting, he kept singing. Then the crowd stared up at the sky. "I saw them look up and I looked up and I saw an eagle making twenty-foot circles over the drum. He did that through the whole song, four times through. We sang three more songs and by the end those people were quiet. Then we walked through that whole town carrying that drum."

For the singer, the eagle represented a validation of what he calls the ways of the 'gete Anishinaabe'—"the ancient Indians" (Baraga 1992:128). Even the newspaper noted that an eagle circled the park during the rally, "a sign of strength to the Chippewa" (*Lakeland Times* 1986e).

The appearance of the eagle and the lack of violent confrontation helped consolidate the moral superiority of the Indian people who brought the drum to the rally; they attributed the peaceful outcome of the event to the power of the drum. This would not be the last time that a drum played a significant role in the spearfishing conflict. Such a turn of events also worked to further bolster the validity of their revitalized traditions and the credibility of the spiritual leader from Grand Portage.

One telling flash point of controversy did erupt during the Minocqua rally. When the crowd, dressed in the blaze orange of hunters, faced the American flag for the pledge of allegiance, Tom Maulson and his twin brother Jerry turned their backs. The brothers claimed later they were turning away from the protesters, not the flag. The media and growing anti-spearing protest movement, however, seized on this act, and it was referred to time and again in the pages of the *Lakeland Times*. For anti-treaty whites, the gesture symbolized the antithesis between an emerging Indian sovereignty and loyalty to the United

States. Most Indian people, on the other hand, understood the Maulsons' gesture and saw the criticism as yet another attempt by outsiders to define their identity, this time by impugning Indian patriotism.

Spearfishers from Lac du Flambeau fished twelve lakes in 1986 and took 5,743 walleye. This total represents 79 percent of the fish taken by the four bands that speared, a near tripling of the number of lakes and fish over the previous year and a marked increase in spearers who went off the reservation (Kmiecik 1987).

The season began for Lac du Flambeau with twenty-three spearers taking 273 walleye at Big Arbor Vitae Lake less than twenty miles east of the reservation on the night of April 18. The most productive night was April 24 on the Turtle-Flambeau Flowage, where fifty-four spearers took 1,192 walleye in seventy boat-hours at the average rate of 17 fish per boat-hour. The quantities suggest that the spearing was treated as a hunting expedition rather than acquiring fish for a feast. Maulson recalls that the spearfishers were not sure that the Turtle-Flambeau Flowage could be harvested because flowing water offers less visibility and increases the difficulty of spotting walleye. Flambeau leaders like Maulson had encouraged spearers to go to Turtle-Flambeau because it was not attracting as many non-Indian protesters as those lakes closer to Minocqua-Woodruff.

The most memorable night of the 1986 season was its last, when forty-eight spearfishers took 792 walleye from Star Lake. Tribal members could not be refused access to a lake no matter how many speared; there was no provision for regulating the number of spearers on any particular body of water because it had never been a problem. More than seventy spearfishers went to Star Lake that night, far more than anticipated. Three factors contributed to this turn of events. It was the last night of the season; the spearers had been rained out the previous Friday night; all the other walleye lakes had already been speared.

At one point during the evening, George Meyer, the chief enforcement officer of the DNR, and Tom Maulson got into a very heated argument about the numbers of spearers arriving on the asphalt boat landing ramp that led into the water. According to Maulson, Meyer wanted him to stop the spearers, something that Maulson had no authority to do. Maulson instead asked Meyer for permission to fish North Twin Lake, where they had been the night before and had taken only about one-fifth of the fish they had speared in 1985. Meyer refused, citing the agreement that a lake would not be speared two nights in a row. Maulson, however, reminded him that he had permitted the spearing of the Flambeau Flowage on two consecutive nights earlier in the week. Both Don Smith and Gilbert Chapman remembered that this argument ended when Maulson and Meyer were forced to move off the ramp to avoid a boat trailer backing into the water.

This moment, this night, galvanized the conflict. The forty-eight persons who speared Star Lake took almost eight hundred walleye, averaging sixteen fish each. The DNR and local non-Indian media blamed Tom Maulson for what they described as an "overharvest" of Star Lake; protesters called it a "rape" (*Lakeland Times* 1986f). Maulson responded to reporters' questions about the violation of the agreement to take 10 percent of the TAC by raising general concerns about how whites use resources and abuse Indians. He observed that reservation lakes are disproportionately fished by non-Indians, that the spearers are subject to gunshots on the lakes, and, most recently, that they had witnessed hundreds of people calling for the abrogation of treaties and termination in the town of Minocqua (*Lakeland Times* 1986e). The media condensed and simplified these complaints and concluded that the Indian "overharvest" of Star Lake was a retaliation for the PARR rally in Minocqua.

The incident at Star Lake drew the attention of the regional metropolitan newspapers, which ran front-page articles and editorials. For the first time, the spearfishing conflict was more than a local issue. Some of these papers criticized the non-Indians for holding a PARR rally so close to the reservation and echoed Maulson by pointing out that Indians were sometimes shot at while fishing, blocked from getting to landings, verbally abused, and run off the road (*Milwaukee Journal* 1986b). Such articles drew the ire of the local non-Indian community around Lac du Flambeau whose hostility for the cities of Madison, Milwaukee, and especially Chicago was always just beneath the surface.[9]

The secretary of the DNR registered written protests with Maulson, the tribe, and GLIFWC, calling into question the bands' ability to regulate themselves and the future of the state's negotiations with them. He claimed: "The Lac du Flambeau tribe placed forty-eight spearers on Star Lake," as if it had all been directed (*Milwaukee Journal* 1986b). Given the nature of Ojibwe leadership, it could not have been so orchestrated.

The 1986 season, and the night at Star Lake in particular, witnessed the emergence of Tom Maulson as the recognizable leader of the spearers in separate but interlinked systems of leadership and responsibility (Figure 7). Since the *Voigt* decision, in addition to being appointed as a tribal judge and the Flambeau representative to the Voigt Task Force, Maulson also chaired the tribal council's Water and Sewer Committee and the Housing Authority. As such, he was a visible and responsible member of a bureaucracy to Indians and non-Indians alike.

Maulson was increasingly treated as a leader by the press and by the negotiators for the state; at the same time, according to Ojibwe conceptions of authority, he could only entreat and encourage spearers, not command them.

Maulson's relative affluence permitted him to act as a more traditional leader. He would be the first to say that he wasn't "a traditional" in the sense of linguistic competence, a personal history of contact with Ojibwe religious practices, and a pervasive disposition, attitude, or gaze that the Spindlers labeled "latescence" (1984: 24–31). He was leading people in what was understood to be a traditional manner in the modern era. Spearfishers would gather at Maulson's house and he feasted them. He had acquired his wealth by hard work and good fortune and deployed it in a traditional way by sharing it, accruing prestige and a loose following of sorts. Aside from giving away or sharing money, food, spears, car batteries, spare parts for twenty-five horsepower gasoline engines, and his boat, he also imparted his knowledge of the lakes, understanding of white political mores and, perhaps most importantly, his vision of a future for Indian families and "our people."

As in earlier times, Tom Maulson led a group of Ojibwes by example, by suggestion, and by persuasive argument. "Nor does the chief dare to give commands to his soldier—he will mildly entreat. . . . If the chiefs possess some influence over them, it is only through liberal presents and the feasts," commented Nicholas Perrot, who lived with Ojibwes in the seventeenth century (Perrot 1911:145). In the nineteenth century, John Tanner, who also lived among Ojibwe people, similarly observed: "An Indian chief when he leads out his war party, has no other means of control over the individuals composing it, than his personal influence gives him" (1830: 35).

Maulson was thus acting as a traditional Ojibwe leader when he admitted, "I had no power to tell the other spearers what to do. I could not stop them from going on the water" (*Milwaukee Journal* 1986a). When the press and the state tried to hold him accountable for the action of the Flambeau collective, he could credibly claim in front of

7. These men were referred to as "the first group of spearers"; the photo was taken at the Wa-Swa-Gon Campground in the late 1980s and became an icon of the movement. From left to right: Robin Cobe, Wally Christensen, Gilbert Chapman, Jerry Maulson, Edward Chosa, John Christensen, Tom Maulson, Nick Chapman, Jerome Cross, Billy Martin, Duane Poupart, Gilbert Chapman Jr., Brooks Big John, Freddy Maulson, Leonard Stone, Scott Vallier, Charlie Chapman, Joey Wildcat, Tom Maulson Jr. At the drum from left to right: Larry Williams, Wally LaBarge, Tommy Williams, Billy Mitchell. Photo courtesy of Tom Maulson.

Indian people that he was not responsible for what "our Indian fishermen do"—such a presumption of authority would have insulted the spearers. By denouncing his leadership role to non-Indians who imagined he directed things, he honored and elevated those who acted in concert with him, affirming long-standing egalitarian political dispositions in Ojibwe society. As spearfishing became increasingly militant and interwoven with cultural revitalization, Maulson's leadership took on the trappings of a modern war chief, who had to be consulted on matters of resource use.

It was a synergistic conjuncture. The more the DNR, the media, and later his own tribal council attempted to hold Maulson accountable for conflicts created by the exercise of off-reservation rights, the more he validated his own leadership position in the eyes of the spearers by disavowing that responsibility. By virtue of a working misunderstanding of Ojibwe conceptions of leadership, Tom Maulson's power grew.

The tribal council meeting that followed the last night at Star Lake drew 101 tribal members, far more than typically attend. The incident was thoroughly discussed, with accommodationists and treaty rights activists arguing about the impact of the event on the tribe's relationship with the "surrounding communities." The senior member of the tribal council, who had served since 1952, worried about the impact of Star Lake on tribal businesses and expressed concern over internal fighting on the reservation. He also spoke of the importance of the treaties, about which he had learned when he was very young (tribal council minutes, May 6, 1986).

Neil Kmiecik, a fisheries biologist at GLIFWC, presented statistical data contrasting the numbers of fish taken in the sport and spear fisheries. Tribal attorney James Jannetta responded to comments about the meaning of this disparity by referring to litigation that was currently underway: "our position is that we can take the whole of the thirty-five percent that is harvestable. But until a judge either accepts or rejects that, we have to make a series of agreements with the state" (tribal council minutes, May 6, 1986).

The nature of Tom Maulson's leadership was raised. "How can someone be a Voigt Representative, tribal judge, and tribal official during the day and just another spearer at night?" a man asked. Jerry Maulson, the vice president of the tribal council, responded: "We are council members when we sit here, not every moment of our lives. People in the community turn the hats on us, sometimes seeing us as chairmen or vice-chairmen"—a bureaucratic structure sometimes contradicted the relations lived in the tribal idiom of kinship. He added, "Lac du Flambeau is named after spearing. If we give that up we might as well change the name of the town, too."

In reflecting on this meeting, Jerry Maulson told me that the tribal council tacitly agreed that Tom would continue serving in his various official positions. The diffusion of authority, long noted by observers of Ojibwes (Hickerson 1962:47), is reflected by Maulson's status and the outcome of the tribal council meeting. Maulson had not been appointed, elected, or drafted to the role he was playing; he also would not be actively opposed. The source of his authority to act in a public way with consequences for the band was not located within the band but in a separate realm. Appropriating an idiom from the dominant culture, it was said of Tom that everything he touched turned to gold.

The Star Lake incident continued to reverberate across the state. PARR attempted to pressure the state government in Madison to act, announcing that its members would boycott fishing and hunting licenses until the treaty rights issue was addressed. The decision not to publicize the location of lakes to be speared was criticized on First Amendment grounds. The DNR was condemned by the bands for not assuming some of the responsibility for exceeding the quota, since it shared in designing the regulatory procedures. In a letter to the chairman of Lac du Flambeau's tribal council, the congressman from the Flambeau region, David Obey, denounced spearfishing and withdrew his support for federal funds for the fish hatchery at Lac du Flambeau (*Lakeland Times* 1986g). He subsequently sent copies of this announcement to the chairs of the other tribal councils with notes congratulating them for the ways in which they had conducted their tribe's harvests. Such an attempt to isolate Flambeau from the other bands did not succeed; Lac du Flambeau's actions were defended in the pages of *Masinaigan*, GLIFWC's quarterly publication, which represents all of the bands. The Flambeau tribal council, in a press conference on May 6, voiced its support for Tom Maulson as their negotiator, called for the resignation of the DNR's chief negotiator, took collective responsibility for exceeding the quota, and announced that it was preparing a united response to Congressmen Obey's threat (*Lakeland Times* 1986g). By the end of May 1986, Tom Maulson succeeded James Schlender of Lac Courte Oreilles as the elected chairman of the Voigt Inter-tribal Task Force. He also convinced Lac du Flambeau that the job was worth a salary of twelve thousand dollars per year.

The locus of both the conflict and negotiation had clearly shifted from Lac Courte Oreilles, where it had started, eighty miles east to Lac du Flambeau.

ESCALATION IN 1987

Continuing negotiations between the bands and the DNR yielded another interim spearfishing agreement for the 1987 season. Each tribe could designate a fifteen-day season and inform the DNR forty-eight hours before it was to commence. For 142 lakes covering at least five hundred acres, the total allowable catch doubled to 20 percent. A permit system was implemented in response to problems encountered the previous year, with the number of permits determined by dividing the remaining tribal quota for a lake by the nightly bag limits. Permits were available at tribal offices and at the "named" lakes. Retained from the previous year's agreement was the twenty-inch maximum length on speared walleyes (with two exceptions: one between twenty and twenty-four inches in length, and a second one of any size).

In early 1987, the Flambeau tribal council passed a motion banning the *Lakeland Times* from tribal council meetings, owing to its "derogatory items concerning the tribe" (tribal council minutes, January 13, 1987). In February, Judge Doyle handed down the first of the remanded federal court decisions. He found that Indians were not confined to the hunting and fishing methods their ancestors relied upon in the mid–nineteenth century when the treaties were signed; they could take advantage of modern improvements in hunting and fishing techniques (*LCO et al. v. State of Wisconsin* 1987a). Rather than dampen public criticism of the "traditionality" of contemporary Ojibwa fishing practices, this ruling amplified feelings of powerlessness and frustration among local whites and made apparent that they were not likely to receive relief from the federal judiciary. Judge Doyle further found that since Indians had engaged in commerce during the treaty times, they could trade and sell their produce to non-Indians today. Usufruct rights were not in effect on land held privately as of March 8, 1983, the day the court denied the state's motion for a rehearing of the original case. No allocation of the resource, however, was warranted insofar as the bands had the right to make "a modest living" from hunting and fishing (*LCO et al. v. State of Wisconsin* 1987a).

Opposition to spearfishing continued to swell. The *Lakeland Times,* whose ex-editor, Larry Greschner, had just become the executive director of PARR, proclaimed that this recent decision "gives the Chippewa Indians almost unlimited hunting and fishing rights in northern Wisconsin" and it reproduced the entire forty-three-page text of the ruling (*Lakeland Times* 1987a). Apocalyptic visions of the death of the regional economy again abounded in its op-ed pages; letters proliferated, calling the treaties anachronistic and attempting to minimize the cultural differences between Indians and non-Indians by evoking the issue of blood quantum and the 1924 act of Congress that made Indians citizens (*Lakeland Times* 1987a).

Tommy Thompson, the new Republican governor of the state— who had campaigned the year before telling audiences in the north country that spearing was wrong and that he opposed treaty rights— met with fifty PARR members in Wausau, seventy miles south of Lac du Flambeau. The governor vowed to seek appeal of Judge Doyle's decision, voiced his support for PARR's goals, but also conveyed the disinclination of the state legislature to act in the protest organization's favor (*Lakeland Times* 1987b). PARR's conference in Wausau was attended by 475 people in late March, when the organization pledged itself to "overturn treaties." Attendees included Vera Lawrence and James Clifton of the anthropology department at the University of Wisconsin at Green Bay. Clifton provided succor to the PARR leaders by challenging the cultural bases of Indian political aspirations. The conference received a great deal of media attention—six daily papers, four weeklies, four TV stations, and several radio stations (*Lakeland Times* 1987c).

Lac du Flambeau spearfishers harvested 15,378 walleye in 1987, representing 72 percent of the walleye taken by the five bands that speared (Kmiecik and Shively 1988). A total of 206 fishermen were issued 695 permits, and they took an average of 75 walleye each at the rate of 12 fish per hour. The number of spearers almost doubled from 1986, with the total quantity of fish exceeding the previous year by two and one-half times.

More Indians were eating more fish from off-reservation lakes than they had in more than a century, revitalizing a version of the mid-nineteenth-century early spring subsistence economy. Of Flambeau spearers, 43 percent went out for one night in fifteen; 59 percent for one or two nights; and nine Flambeau spearers went out on ten of the fifteen nights in the season. Of the entire population of the reservation, 15 percent, all men, was represented on the lakes in the spring of 1987. All the other bands taken together had only one spearer go out for ten or more nights.

On April 15, the first day of their season, the Flambeau spearers fished six different lakes in groups ranging from five to twenty spearers, taking a total of 1,729 walleye. The new pattern of fishing four to six lakes a night continued for the duration of the season. This different fishing strategy can be attributed to three factors: the newly charged atmosphere of the landings, which were attracting more protesters; increasing numbers of spearers; and growing competition between spearers to get to the good walleye lakes within the constraints of the permit system. Landings were no longer nightly fishing camps and the sites of feasts—spearfishers went on to lakes to get fish and immediately left. Three-quarters of the lakes were speared only one night, and most of the tribal quota was taken in that night. The social activities that had expanded off the reservation in the first year of spearing contracted now to the reservation.

Spearfishing was becoming more like the tense, nineteenth-century hunting forays into "the debatable zone" along the present Wisconsin-Minnesota border, an area also hunted and claimed by the Dakotas (Hickerson 1970:143–146). Ojibwe spearfishing in the late 1980s began taking on the quality of warfare. Prophesy reemerged and played a key role in this unfolding drama.

On Sunday night, April 26, twelve Flambeau spearers fished Butternut Lake, located about thirty miles west of the reservation. They speared 40 percent of the allotted walleye. The events of that night made Butternut Lake one of the most important symbols in the Walleye War and escalated the militarization of spearfishing.

Butternut Lake lies close to Park Falls, which was the home base of PARR. It was known at Flambeau that protesters were gathering there after Maulson named the lake; the spearers found it amusing that the protesters were disappointed when the Flambeau spearfishers didn't materialize for a few nights. The protesters' growing frustration was fueled on April 26 by two further factors: it was the first anniversary of the incident at Star Lake, and it was the day following a huge PARR rally of two thousand in Minocqua.

In the early part of the evening, before it was dark, Indians, non-Indians, police, and wardens mingled on the landings. Some commented on the appearance of Larry Petersen, president of PARR—his presence marked the seriousness of the moral objection of some whites to spearing. There were verbal taunts and scattered rock throw-ing, but the spearfishers had encountered this level of opposition before.

As darkness fell, more and more protesters arrived, many appar-ently recruited from local bars. By 11:00 P.M., the crowd was variously estimated at between 250 and 500 people, a far bigger group than the eleven law enforcement personnel present could manage. The pro-testers grew angrier and bolder; the size of the rocks thrown became dangerously large. The ugliness of the taunts escalated, racial slurs were yelled, and the groups on the landing began to segregate. Ac-cording to Neil Kmiecik, "instead of being on the boat landing we were gradually moving out onto the peninsula. The force of the non-Indians' anger caused people to move away from them." Tom Maul-son and Ed Chosa recalled that the Flambeau spearers who could get out of their boats could not leave the landing since they were trapped on a thin peninsula stretching out into the lake, separated from the protesters by a line of DNR officials who could do no more than keep the two groups apart.

The growing terror and rage of that night stand out vividly in the memory of the Flambeau spearers. Neil Kmiecik remembers: "I was bending over to count fish and a rock came over my head and hit the boat that was next to me."

Ed Chosa admits: "I was afraid for the first time at Butternut. The police were egging the crowd on. I said to George Meyer that some-body was going to get killed any moment. . . . It was bad until the boats came in, and then it was worse."

"We were backed up against the water," Tom Maulson recalls. "That cop from town was saying to the protesters that it was an illegal gather-ing, an unlawful gathering, and those guys were telling him to get fucked and that they were going to kill us."

In telling the story to me, Maulson growls at this point, imitating the protesters: head down, slouched in his chair, eyes staring at an imag-ined, hated enemy. "All we had was rocks that we picked up. The rocks they had were flying over our heads. I figured that we were going to be killed. I was just looking at those guys wondering which one I was gonna take with me." Maulson then heard his grandmother, who had "walked on" a number of years earlier, say, "It's going to be alright, Sonny."

Law enforcement from four counties and police officers with dogs from the city of Superior finally arrived and cleared the landing by about 2:00 A.M.

The tribal council at Flambeau reacted with anger the next day. The events at Butternut Lake were "fanning the flames of racial hatred. . . . It was racism in its rawest, ugliest form. . . . It was especially sad to see how many in the mob had brought their children to the scene, as if it were a sporting event. In this way, racial hatred is transmitted to a new generation. . . . At another time they wore brown shirts and swastikas or hid behind white sheets and burnt crosses. . . . We will return to Butternut" (*Lakeland Times* 1987d).

The perception that opposition to spearfishing was racist marks the incident at Butternut Lake as a moral turning point in the conflict. Very few at Flambeau had described the opposition to spearing in racial terms before April 26; after that night, nearly everyone did.

Lac du Flambeau ended its spearing season four nights later by returning to Butternut Lake, where 150 police allowed only people with tribal identification access to the landing. In part due to the efforts of Tom Maulson, over 200 Indian people from three states made a ceremonial return to the lake. The Flambeau, Lac Courte Oreilles, and Mole Lake bands sent drum groups. *Masinaigan,* which heavily covered the spearfishing season, reported that two eagles flew over the landing (1987). An elder conducted a pipe ceremony, tobacco was placed in the water, four boats were sent out, and each came back with one fish.

The speeches given during this last day of the 1987 season echoed the persistent themes of the growing conflict, underlined with heightened defiance. Tom Maulson sounded notes of unity and identity at the ceremony: "We are strong as a nation. . . . We were on this landing right here. They wanted to kill us. There's no way they are going to do that. We're back." Mike Allen, Flambeau's tribal chairman and a growing rival of Maulson, endorsed his sentiments and raised the specter of historical legacy: "We can't allow ourselves to be robbed of our heritage and future by vigilantes. We must return to the scene of such things to show unity" (*Masinaigan* 1987). Ben Chosa, a great-grandson of a Trout Lake village war chief, explicitly linked their contemporary subsistence rights with the distinct history and identity of the Ojibwe bands: "Our chiefs reserved that right for us. These are all their descendants. Spearing itself is traditional. It's over thousands of years old. Just like the whites when they harvest their wheat. We did it all over, not just on reservation lakes" (*Lakeland Times* 1987e).

The second of the remanded court decisions was made after the spearfishing season, in August 1987. Barbara Crabb, a new federal judge, found that the state's regulatory power over the exercise of the off-reservation rights extended to the conservation of particular species or resources in a particular area and to public health and safety, but to "no other purpose." She found that "the plaintiffs' rights were paramount but not exclusive," but that "the state could not regulate to assure tribal compliance with moderate living standards . . . unless allocation of particular resources became necessary" (*LCO v. Wisconsin* 1987b). Crabb's decision motivated the state of Wisconsin to seek a settlement with the bands reservation by reservation.

The ruling threw into relief internal differences at the Lac du Flambeau reservation, a modern schism that continued to widen and deepen along traditional lines in the years that followed. More accommodationist members of the Flambeau tribal council, chaired by Mike Allen, worked to democratize the value of the treaty rights. Only a small fraction of the tribal membership was exercising the off-reservation subsistence rights. Treaty rights thus had little practical value for most tribal members. Allen and the majority of Lac du Flambeau's tribal council hoped to consolidate, transform, and distribute to their constituents the increasing value of the treaty rights in the form of per capita payments, jobs, and social services the state was willing to exchange for forbearance. Furthermore, they sought to win a peace dividend in the region, whose lakes and forests would then return to their previous status as resources to be marketed at a higher price to urban tourists. Indians would presumably benefit from such growth in the tourist economy.

The value of the treaty rights was increasing with the conflict, and the Flambeau tribal council sought to manage it for the good of the tribe. Flambeau's attorney, James Jannetta, had earlier taken the position that the entire total allowable catch of the lakes in the ceded territory was so great that the bands could, if they fully exercised their rights, preempt the sports fishery. Given the ambivalence of Flambeau's members about the value of the sports fishery to the economy of the reservation and the band's logistical incapability of harvesting all that it could claim, the tribal leadership was reluctant and unable to rally around a denunciation of tourism. The council responded positively to the state of Wisconsin's interest in seeking a settlement out of court. In the summer of 1987, the Lac du Flambeau band began negotiating with the state for a cash settlement.

In conjunction with this move, in an attempt to consolidate and enhance the power of his office, tribal chairman Mike Allen successfully persuaded the Constitution and By-laws Committee to make the chairmanship a full-time position extendable to more than two terms. Chairman Allen was a quiet and honorable man, trying to be a *min ogima*, a good chief, as he understood the responsibility. In the opinion of some, he had been elected due to his big family, his prowess as an athlete and fighter, and because he did not see himself as better than the average person on the reservation—an important quality of leadership in a community that values egalitarian relations. Allen's strength was further consolidated by winning the rescindment of a council resolution that forbade poll votes. Tribal business could now be conducted outside of the confines of scheduled meetings, facilitating quick and confidential responses to the negotiation process with the state (tribal council minutes, November 2, 1987).

By the fall of 1987, most of the negotiations between the bands and the state were taking place in closed-door sessions. A number of spearers became increasingly suspicious of the nature and extent of those discussions, believing that such tactics of confidentiality and secrecy had no legitimate place in traditional Ojibwe political culture. The civic component of Flambeau politics came increasingly under fire by its ascending warrior component, the activist, neotraditional spearfishers whose informal leader was Tom Maulson. The civic and warrior functions of Flambeau's government, previously complementary, had now begun to compete for legitimacy in representing the will of the entire community.

TREATY BEER AND WALLEYE WARRIORS IN 1988

There were no significant changes in the interim spearfishing agreement between the state and the bands for the 1988 season. The DNR did interdict drinking on the landings, largely in response to what had happened the year before at Butternut Lake. Extensive adjustments were made in law enforcement.

Canine units were used on boat landings and a National Guard helicopter manned by law enforcement personnel kept watch over the lakes. In addition, detachments of officers from counties throughout the state were housed at centrally located National Guard armories ready to respond to a boat landing at a moment's notice.

Other logistical planning also helped to send the message that law enforcement officials were prepared to deal with disturbances at boat landings. High power lights were used to illuminate the landings; police lines were established to separate protesters from tribal fisherman; and officers exhibited riot gear as part of their equipment at the boat landings. (Schlender 1991:11)

The outside response to the crisis became more complicated in 1988. Citizens for Treaty Rights, the first non-Indian treaty support organization, was founded, originating in the Eagle River area forty miles to the east of Lac du Flambeau. The group organized a ceremonial planting of a "Tree of Peace" on the Flambeau reservation by Mohawk Chief Jake Swamp. The *Lakeland Times* (1988b) reported on the group's activities: "Citizens For Treaty Rights plans to plant a 'peace tree' on Lac du Flambeau, throw a dinner there, but then will come back to Minocqua boat landings for its candle light vigil accompanied by tom-tom music."

Opposition to spearfishing continued to intensify, mostly through the efforts of Stop Treaty Abuse/Wisconsin (STA/W), a radical protest organization led by Dean Crist, a local businessman. Identifying itself with the 1960s civil rights movement, STA/W urged people to come to the landings, organized protests, and paid the legal fees of those arrested (*Lakeland Times* 1988g). PARR had no official presence at the boat landings, preferring to concentrate on lobbying efforts in Madison and Washington DC, but STA/W took the protests right into the lakes to disrupt spearfishing. A caustic writer to the *Lakeland Times* urged citizens to take to the water to oppose spearing: "Stop sucking your thumbs and act. . . . Go to the landings and scream. . . . If you manage to get your boats in the water, run it at half throttle and stay a few hundred feet away from the native Americans exercising their rights. They will welcome your presence because it creates more of a challenge when the water is high" (*Lakeland Times* 1988a). Indians and whites now clashed on the water as well as on the landings. "Protest boats dragged anchors across walleye spawning beds. . . . Chippewa boats were rammed, two Chippewa boats were swamped" (Schlender 1991:12).

In order to pay for anti-spearing television and radio ads in the region, Dean Crist completed a deal to brew and market an alcoholic beverage called Treaty Beer. Billed as "the true brew of the working man," Treaty Beer attempted to weave together anti-treaty and antigovernment sentiment, the economic interests of resort owners, and the values of the working class. A typical half-page advertisement in the *Lakeland Times* ran:

Attention Resort Owners: When you order your summer beer inventory
Please remember this:
—Treaty Beer gives all its profits to fight the economic blackmail that is currently threatening your industry.
—The new Treaty Beer is one of the best quality beers in the US
To all those resort owners who have told us that they will only stock Treaty Beer, God Bless You. (*Lakeland Times* 1988c)

The iconography of the Treaty Beer cans (Figure 8) expresses relationships between a number of powerful symbols and fundamental cultural categories. Of particular interest here is the can's juxtaposition of special rights and equal rights. The ideology represented by the phrase "equal rights" underlies American individualism and implies that society is legitimately the outcome of the interaction between individuals who undertake their projects on an equal footing. "Treaty rights" is a diametrically opposed concept because it implies that society is structured before, and privileged above, the fact of individual existence. Acceptance of such special rights legitimizes the notion that equality between individuals is in fact a mystification of the power relations that organize the daily experience of working people.

Two hundred different people from Lac du Flambeau used spearing permits in 1988, harvesting nearly seventeen thousand walleye from fifty-five lakes. The spearfishers took fish at almost identical rates as the year before and followed the same dispersed fishing strategy, naming up to ten lakes per night. On April 18, the opening night of Flambeau's season, most spearers traveled to the Turtle-Flambeau Flowage, a lake with by far the highest quota of fish and the fewest protesters. Six thousand walleye were eventually taken there. A group of fourteen returned to Butternut Lake, accompanied by some sixty supporters and confronted by about seventy-five protesters.

In the first of a series of arrests that propelled him to the forefront of the anti-treaty rights movement, Dean Crist of STA/W broke a side-view mirror off a vehicle owned by a tribal member at Butternut Lake and was arrested for disorderly conduct, hit and run property damage, and reckless driving.

The conflict escalated, though the level of protest varied considerably from lake to lake. At the Turtle-Flambeau Flowage, the spearers

8. This business in the town of
Minocqua advertised Treaty Beer.
The iconography on the posters is
duplicated on each can. Photo
courtesy of Tom Maulson.

remained relatively undisturbed, while on some lakes five or more boats carrying protesters would converge on a single spearing craft. A non-Indian man was arrested on federal charges for the possession of seven pipe bombs.

Competition for fishing locations and varied relations with outsiders heightened tensions among some of the Ojibwe bands. Every night, fishermen from the Lac Court Oreilles band speared the Chippewa Flowage—created in 1921 against their wishes (see Rasmussen 1998)—taking a total of 513 walleye of the 12,000 quota. The Lac Courte Oreilles band had informally asked Flambeau not to spear the Chippewa Flowage. Nevertheless, thirty-six Flambeau members speared there on the night of April 29 and took 829 walleye, returning the next night to spear an additional 294 fish. As Gilbert Chapman remembers it, their actions upset some Lac Courte Oreilles tribal members because they feared their good relations with the local tourist and resort interests would be undermined. The zeal of some Flambeau spearers and a strain of intertribal competition are evident in Chapman's recollections of the 1988 season: "We speared in the four directions. No one went as far south as we did. No one went as far in any direction as we did. We speared over at Kentuck Lake. We went over to the Flowage and took 2,000 in one night! They [Lac Courte Oreilles] took 225 after the fish were through spawning!"

On the last night of the season, as tribal chairman Mike Allen had promised, the Flambeau spearers again returned to Butternut Lake. Seventeen spearers harvested 89 walleyes, a take whose value was primarily symbolic.

The label "Walleye warriors" appeared for the first time in 1988 as a mocking reference to a baseball-style cap worn by Tom Maulson and his adherents. Maulson's wife Laura had noticed the hat in a sporting goods store window in Minneapolis and bought it for him while he was attending a conference for tribal judges. Maulson had the hat redesigned and reproduced, adding to it an image of a walleye and the words "Lac du Flambeau Wisconsin." The hats were given as gifts to spearers at T&L, Maulson's gas station and convenience store, further strengthening his position as a modern traditional leader. Some wearers added a spear to the decoration.

The redesigned baseball cap effectively became the headdress of a contemporary Ojibwe warrior society, weaving together several strands of Flambeau's culture and history. As sporting goods apparel and modern headdress, the hat fused the identity of the warrior with the violating hunter/fisherman who provides for his family. The baseball cap form itself had multiple subtle resonances—it evoked Flambeau's historic athletic prowess, transformed white sports regalia into warrior society regalia as an appropriative act paradigmatic of hunters, ironically linked a mainstream American sport with the Indians' cat-and-mouse game of violating, and subversively commented on non-Indians' definitions of what constitutes Indian tradition and what does not.

IDENTIFICATION AND CONFLICT

A ubiquitous slogan, "Save a Walleye . . . Spear an Indian,"[10] became an icon of the depth of the conflict and provided a glimpse of the great emotional and cultural value placed on walleye by both sides (Figure 9). The equation of human and nonhuman life implicit in the exhortation represents a necessary condition for a conflict between Indians and non-Indians. Some whites equated an Indian life to the life of a fish. At the height of the conflict the *Wausau Daily Herald* went so far as to publish a drawing by a North Lakeland elementary school student of a fish spearing an Indian (1989b).

The spearfishers in turn cemented the equation in their own way by risking their lives to harvest those fish. Some fought or were willing to die for the right to spear walleye because the fish had become essential symbols of contemporary Indian identity. Such a determination to spearfish and a readiness to die, combined with spearfishing's intimate connection to Ojibwe identity and values, inform Wayne Valliere's account of an emotionally tense confrontation and cultural clash at a landing.

I would find the loudest one [protester] and walk right up to him and let him know that I wasn't afraid of him. They would think, "This guy is crazy," and they would quiet down. You can't be afraid of them. My wife was spit on. I took out my handkerchief and wiped it off her face. I wanted to gut that guy just like a deer. I usually carried my hunting knife with me and it's razor sharp. I could gut him pretty quick.

I walked up to him and I said that life here is short and that someday we were going to die and the spirits, they remember everything, they were going to ask him why it was that he did that to that Anishinaabe woman that time. Maybe they won't let him in right there over that and maybe that they would send him right to hell for doing that. Many times my mother and my

9. Protester holding a "Save a
Walleye . . . Spear an Indian" sign.
Photo courtesy of the GLIFWC.

wife pleaded with me, pleaded with me, not to go out for fear that some-thing was going to happen. But I didn't want my children to have to take over this fight. If you are going to die, that's it. I believe in destiny. That's how the traditional Ojibwe believe. It's all determined how you are going to die.

A sacrificial attitude cast as traditional value pervades the young man's view of spearfishing. The moderate response of the narrator to the as-sault on his wife expresses a longstanding cultural ideal of emotional restraint (see Spindler 1978:718), traditionally realized in the warrior who insults his captor by showing indifference to pain. His choice not to retaliate seems to be motivated by an indigenized polytheistic Chris-tianity that preserves the fatalism of the historical Ojibwe worldview.

The equation of humans and fish embedded in "Save a Walleye . . . Spear an Indian" also resonates with traditional Ojibwe cosmology. As discussed earlier, Flambeau Indians and *oka,* walleyed pike, are closely and reciprocally connected because walleye are "persons" in a tradi-tional Ojibwe view of life (Hallowell 1992). Such transformed proto-human persons, the focus of modern conflict, can be potentially em-powering and medicinal for those associated with them. Ernie St. Germaine explained to me: "Those deer, those fish that are out there are making medicine right now. If you come to me and ask me to heal you, I can do that. But you will have to understand a number of things first. There is a lot that goes into it. Right now, out there, there is a fish or a deer or some animal that is eating something. They are making medicine for you. That's their purpose in life and their only purpose. I find that animal for you and that will cure you. It will heal you."

Unlike Indian people, whites in the Walleye War did not give the im-pression that they were willing to die for the fish, despite occasional dramatic displays.[11] Many non-Indians, however, paralleled the spear-fishers in the importance they placed on walleye for the cultural vital-ity and future of the Northwoods. The pervasive hostility toward In-dian spearing and anxiety about the numbers of fish being taken encouraged some to believe that lakes without walleye or with lower walleye bag limits would translate into resorts without vacationers.[12] A depressed tourist economy would be detrimental to their quality of life and force resident whites back to the cities from which they or their ancestors had fled.

The identification of non-Indians with walleye did give rise to a powerful and pervasive metaphor: spearfishing as rape. This analogy, in which walleye are effectively cast as victimized persons, surfaced repeatedly throughout the conflict. Indians spear the walleye when they are spawning in the spring, a time, according to protesters, when the fish are particularly vulnerable, responding blindly and altruistically to the drive to reproduce. Fishing with rod and reel is a sporting contest; spearing fish in the shallows while they spawn is violent and unjust.

A letter to the editor of the *Lakeland Times,* published toward the end of the 1988 season, rehearses an anthropomorphic image of walleye victimized while altruistically spawning:

Swiftly Red thrust the spear. There's a moment of pain as the steel skewers her flesh, the terror. She tries to run but cannot, her tail whips the weeds into shreds. A storm of bottom muck and vegetation swirls about spear and fish. In a frenzy, she summons all her power and manages to squirm ahead a few feet, but the boat and spearman move with her. The human muscles are more than a match for her mightiest efforts and soon it is all over. Her strength ebbs and Red lifts her into the boat. . . .

On the canoe bottom she lives out the last moments of her life. Death had always been close, and now that it has struck, it did little more than chill her.

Short hours before she had done her part in helping to stem the tide that was running even faster against her kind. Now only death and defeat are reflected in her gaunt features and staring eyes.

Adapted from David Reddick's *The Mighty Muskellunge.* (*Lakeland Times* 1988d)

In speeches made by protest leaders and in my conversations with protesters on the boat landings, spearfishing was described a number of times as "raping the resources" (*Lakeland Times* 1988e, 1988f); this phrase initially appeared in the protests in Michigan against the Ojibwe tribes' treaty rights to fish commercially in Lake Michigan (Doherty 1990:69). The rape metaphor also molds the iconography of the Treaty Beer can, where a vulnerable walleye is depicted as being speared from below where it cannot see.

For the most part, men articulated this analogy, essentially signaling that the conflict was over the control of living, reproducing property, or gendered capital. Such rhetoric drew its power from a reactionary conception of womanhood in human society, since it is clearly predicated on the assumption that the walleye are vulnerable, altruistic, and female. More than once in letters to the editor, the national debate between pro-life and pro-choice was drawn on as a way to understand what was going on between Indians, whites, and the walleyes of the northern lakes (*Lakeland Times* 1988e, 1988f).

Because walleye are speared during the spawning season, many whites assume that most of the fish taken are female. In fact, most are male, partially due to the size restrictions placed on those speared. In 1990, for example, 84.6 percent of the walleye taken were males (Kmiecik and Shively 1990:2). Interestingly, the local newspapers frequently published photos of anglers holding large fish, the largest very likely female; no separate mention is made of the fishes' sex, implicitly suggesting that it is the same as the angler. The message is effectively repeated: big fish taken in a proper sporting manner with rod and reel are likely male; the fish speared by Indians are probably female.

The rape metaphor is also cast more broadly against the Indians' use of the lakes themselves. The lakes "open," in current terminology, shortly after the ice melts; the walleye spawn when the water reaches forty-two degrees Fahrenheit, usually a week to ten days later. Winter is widely imagined to be a time of rest and regeneration. The lakes have been covered with ice and then with a blanket of snow. There is a freshness and newness to the lakes that are imagined to be violated by the harvest activity of spearing.

By the late 1980s, the battle over spearfishing was conducted in metaphors as much as at the landings. Both sides of the conflict over walleye identified with the fish, seeing them as persons in evocative, culturally resonant, yet very different ways.

The struggle that had begun at Lac Courte Oreilles and Bad River in the mid-1970s had come to be dominated by Lac du Flambeau in the late 1980s. When Lac du Flambeau had "receded into the 1970s behind boarded windows of empty shops" (Valaskakis 1988:281), their relatives at Lac Courte Oreilles had nourished the seeds of a native nationalism. In 1985, however, some members of the Lac du Flambeau band took to spearfishing off their reservation with enthusiasm and in a spirit of celebration. Local protest movements soon emerged to shape reactions of confusion and then anger as connections were feared and drawn between the drama of the Indian harvest and the fragility of the tourist economy. The emerging, ramifying, and conflicting ideologies of treaty rights and equal rights polarized Indian and many non-Indians.

As the hostility and numbers of whites on the boat landings increased between 1985 and 1988, the spearing parties correspondingly grew in size. What had been versions of the spring spearing camps of previous centuries—small extended family groups that included old people and children—now took on the appearance of war parties, as the spearing groups became more homogeneous in age and gender. As this subsistence practice became increasingly contested, it evoked and condensed generations of experience of gamelike and warlike conflict with outsiders. An important component of Lac du Flambeau's modern cultural identity became revitalized and essentialized around spearing.

For most of the twentieth century, the differences between Indians and whites in the Lac du Flambeau region had been eroding or growing more subtle and private, though an inchoate sense of distinction remained. With the reinstatement of treaty rights and the accompanying contentious process of their definition and exercise, the differences between local whites and Indians proliferated. These clashes of identities and worlds, fought with rocks and metaphors, would soon come to a dramatic climax.

5

The War Within

10. Lac du Flambeau tribal member Gilbert (Gibby) Chapman wearing his trademark "Chippewa and Proud" shirt. Photo courtesy of the author.

The year 1989 proved to be a watershed in the Walleye War. The conflict continued to intensify and broaden, as recounted in Chapter 6. As important, the spearfishing controversy drove further wedges into the social and political fissures already forming at Lac du Flambeau, among the bands, and even in the non-Indian communities. Such internal conflicts would do much to impel and shape the organization of particular spearfishing expeditions and, more widely, the direction and character of the overall struggle in the months and years to come. The style in which various Ojibwe leaders, organizations, and members attempted to manage the conflict came to combine revitalized warrior practices, some of the elements of violating, and long-standing diplomatic orientations. The improvisational political actions taken by the leaders at Lac du Flambeau were informed by the reinvention of Ojibwe distinctness.

The traditional egalitarianism and autonomy of the Ojibwe bands and the relative importance of their local identities threatened to undermine the Pax Waswaagoning and the bands' solidarity in dealing with the state. The Red Cliff and Bad River bands had concluded their own agreements with the state in the early 1970s over the netting of whitefish in Lake Superior. The small and relatively poor Mole Lake and St. Croix bands were more interested in rice than walleye; spearfishing forays to distant lakes held little appeal. The Lac Courte Oreilles band preferred hunting deer to fishing, and they had sufficient deer in their area to satisfy demand. There were many at the Lac du Flambeau reservation, however, who had become violators and walleye spearfishers over the course of the twentieth century. Some of these spearers were aggressive and ambitious individuals whose personal agendas would be well served by a regional conflict over subsistence practices and the reorganization of local Indian identity.

Tensions among bands were mounting in August 1988, when the

tribal chairman of Lac Courte Oreilles invited Flambeau to a meeting at a halfway point between the two reservations to discuss Flambeau's controversial spearing of the Chippewa Flowage that spring. The halfway point suggestion intentionally imitated the diplomatic style used by rival "families" in gangster movies, the evocation of mafiosi acknowledging the strained relations between the bands and resonating with a sense of an embattled sovereignty. The meeting never took place, and a compromise was worked out between the chairmen of the two tribes. Most members of the Flambeau tribal council resisted a meeting between the two tribal councils without the presence of the other four bands, so Lac du Flambeau hosted a meeting of all six Wisconsin bands in early 1989, allocating four hundred dollars to prepare a feast for their representatives (tribal council minutes, January 2, 1989).

Conjoining feast and intertribal business was a significant step toward a collective revitalization along historically cultural lines, and it would not be the last time that feasting played a key role in the conflict. The Ojibwe cosmological roots of feasting lay in the relations of reciprocity between humans and nonhumans, wherein the spirits of the animals are placed in humans' debt by virtue of the sacrificial consumption of their bodies (Brightman 1976, 1983, 1993). The feast also showed that Flambeau's relative success in bargaining out of strength with the other tribes in years past had opened the possibility of a more gentle incorporation of their resources and interests into Flambeau's project.

Although the bands agreed not to spear the Chippewa Flowage in 1989, Lac du Flambeau chose to reiterate its more autonomous position on off-reservation spearing at a special meeting of the tribal council: "Each tribe has a right that's unlimited in the ceded territory. There are no bodies of water that belong to a specific tribe" (tribal council minutes, January 30, 1989). The position is grounded in a history of local political autonomy.

The tradition of band autonomy worked against the efficacy of their collective relationship with the state of Wisconsin and other authorities. According to Don Hanaway (1990:11), the state of Wisconsin's attorney general at the time, the Ojibwe bands declared that they wanted to negotiate separately in the summer of 1988. The Lac Courte Oreilles band, however, announced that it would not negotiate with the state at all over its off-reservation rights. Months later, pressure from outside authorities grew considerably. In mid-April 1989, the six tribal chairmen of the Lake Superior Chippewa bands received a letter from the eleven members of the Wisconsin congressional delegation written on Representative Dave Obey's letterhead calling on them to "be sensitive enough to exercise restraint" in spearfishing. The letter went on:

Obviously if the tribes choose they can legally exercise these rights without exhibiting due sensitivities to the needs of other groups. But the tribes will then have to appreciate that if they do engage in tribal activities that needlessly inflame the situation and needlessly abuse the rights of other groups to share the resource, then members of the congressional delegation will certainly have to take in account the tribes' lack of cooperation and their lack of sensitivity in assessing tribal requests for federal grants and projects. (Obey 1989)

Given the amount of federal money funneled into Lac du Flambeau and other bands, this threat from the congressional delegation clearly signaled that support of the exercise of treaty rights was likely to be a costly decision. That same afternoon, Governor Thompson privileged the relations of some bands to the state—effectively highlighting their differences—by thanking three of them for reducing their proposed spearing harvests. Flambeau was not among them (tribal council minutes, April 17, 1989).

But cooperation between a tribal council and the state did not guarantee success. The tribal council of the Mole Lake band reached an agreement with the state leasing their collectively held rights for some 10 million dollars (2.56 million for health and welfare and 7.78 million for economic development) over ten years. Tribal members would be permitted to spear one hundred fish per year off the reservation, but not sell them; they would not be able to net or snag fish, road hunt, or shine deer; the members of Mole Lake would also forego all timber interests in the ceded territory and the right to seek recompense for past damages. The tribal council at Mole Lake miscalculated the value of these contested rights, even though the membership could hardly afford to exercise them. The Mole Lake band went against their tribal council and voted overwhelmingly (131–24) against forbearance of their rights (*Lakeland Times* 1989a). Such internal resistance to a tribal government's authority and negotiations with the state foreshadowed a struggle that was building at Lac du Flambeau.

THE WA-SWA-GON TREATY ASSOCIATION

In the spring of 1989 the Flambeau tribal council continued to explore the benefits of exchanging off-reservation rights (exercised by a minority of tribal members) for funds and programs that would ostensibly benefit the entire reservation and further consolidate the council's power. On March 13, the council received a petition signed by 350 Lac du Flambeau members "requesting that the Council cease all negotiations to sell, lease or rent the treaty rights" (tribal council minutes, March 13, 1989). Attending the meeting were fifty tribal members, most spearers or the female relatives of "spearing families." They expressed concern about the council's negotiations with the state, asserting that the tribal members "should have been consulted first to see how they felt." They demanded "that a public meeting for the members be called before negotiations," and reminded the council that "Minnesota tribes are in a predicament because of this" (tribal council minutes, March 13, 1989). Sensitive to the charge that they were poor leaders, and wary of 350 signatures that could constitute a majority voting block in a tribal election, the council did not ignore the petition. Negotiations with the state stalled for three months until they were resumed in the middle of June.

The petition was the first clearly successful act of what came to be known as the Wa-Swa-Gon Treaty Association (WTA), a community organization that was the brainchild of former *Voigt* negotiator Gilbert Chapman and spearfishing leader Tom Maulson. The Wa-Swa-Gon Treaty Association opposed accommodating the state's interests through leasing off-reservation subsistence rights and worked instead to reorient tribal members toward more traditional cultural values and goals. The roots of the association can be traced to a long-standing tension within Ojibwe society between a decentralizing "consensual democracy and egalitarianism" (Smith 1973:13) and more codified, hierarchical differentiation and centralization arising out of the reservation's colonial condition.

The Ojibwe hunting bands, historically prone to fission, had begun to consolidate and concentrate on the reservations in the last quarter of the nineteenth century. The creation of more centralized tribal councils in the first half of the twentieth century did not fully displace ideas and practices originating in the autonomy of extended families in winter, when they traditionally broke into smaller groups to hunt. In the nineteenth century, when the fur trade created conditions for the concentration of bands at Chequamegon and the villages in the wild rice lake district, Ojibwe communities split over the extent to which to accommodate outside interests (Kugel 1985; Hickerson 1970). The Walleye War produced a similar dispute over the legitimacy of republican tribal government, when that government again pursued a course of action perceived to adversely affect a group within the Ojibwe community—the power of the "spearing families" was threatened by the actions and policy of the tribal government.

Such a long-standing tradition of egalitarianism and distrust of centralized government gird tribal member Dorothy Thoms's explanation to me of the origin of the Wa-Swa-Gon Treaty Association. "It was laying too quiet at the council. They were all under the chairman's thumb. We were concerned about their negotiating with the state behind our backs so we got together. First a few of us, then a dozen or so, now there are forty or fifty of us."

The identity and objectives of the new association rapidly crystallized. At the next regular meeting of the Flambeau tribal council two weeks later, a letter from the WTA was read. Its statement was intended to "clarify any misunderstanding that may have developed in the recent weeks regarding what our group is all about." The letter bore a logo two and one-half inches in diameter of a flaming birch bark torch circled by the group's name. A gloss on the logo offered: "A group of concerned tribal members of the Lac du Flambeau Band of Lake Superior Chippewa Indians." The use of the old name and the appropriation of the visual symbol of the torch were intended to revive the traditional cultural identity of the reservation and recall the practice of hunting and fishing at night. It sought to remind people, especially the members of the council, that, in the words of Tom Maulson's twin brother Jerry, "Lac du Flambeau is named after spearing" (tribal council minutes, May 6, 1986). At the time, the only other institution on the reservation that bore the name Wa-Swa-Gon was the tribal campground, managed by Tom Maulson.

The goals and objectives of the Wa-Swa-Gon Treaty Association were itemized in the letter:

1. Preserve Treaties
2. Safe off reservation harvests.
3. Need for more communication between council and tribal members.

4. Provide for elderly, children and shut-ins.
5. Protect and preserve resources in ceded territory.
6. Educate public and tribal members about treaties.
7. Preserve our native heritage.

The letter added that the association would be engaging in fund raising, contacting other organizations for support, and promoting a
peace rally to be held in Torpy Park. It concluded: "This letter is out
of courtesy and for your information only" (tribal council minutes,
March 13, 1989).

The letter has an officious quality that appears to imitate a common
style of tribal communications. The objectives of the association emphasized heavily two tradition-related themes—the significance of the
treaty rights and the need to promote Flambeau's distinct cultural heritage. The objectives also pointed outward to the need for public education and outreach, and the forging of alliances beyond the borders
of the reservation.

The strategic decision by the association to enumerate and pursue
a variety of issues is traceable in some senses to the Red Power movement of the more activist 1970s. Mike Chosa, one of the leaders
of the association, was a student, it will be recalled, of Saul Alinsky's Industrial Areas Foundation. Chosa had helped organize a sit-in at a Chicago Bureau of Indian Affairs office and the "Chicago American Indian Village" occupation at the corner of Waveland and Seminary
Avenues near Wrigley Field.[1] One of the elements of Alinsky's strategy
for community organizing is to form coalitions on multiple issues
(Alinsky 1971:76–78) in an attempt to embrace and empower as many
people as possible in a radically democratic political project. Chosa's
association with Alinsky and his rich activist experience allowed him
to counsel influential spearers like Gilbert Chapman and affect to
some degree the strategies and objectives of the Wa-Swa-Gon Treaty
Association.

TWO ORGANIZATIONS

There were a number of important differences between the Flambeau
tribal council and the Wa-Swa-Gon Treaty Association, attributable in
part to the structural tensions between exclusionary and egalitarian
impulses in modern Ojibwe society.

The Flambeau tribe is federally recognized as a semisovereign organization, incorporated in 1937 under the Indian Reorganization Act. The tribal council has taken over many of the functions of the Bureau of Indian Affairs since the passage of the 1975 Indian Self-determination and Educational Assistance Act. It is both a government and an employment and social service agency. For most of the time since the late 1930s, the majority of the tribe's operating funds have been largely fixed and supplied by the federal government. This centralized economic power made it difficult for some tribal members to actively oppose the tribal council or overtly support the Wa-Swa-Gon Treaty Association. "People were afraid of what the tribe would do to them," Nick Hockings recalled. "We were told we couldn't meet on tribal land. There wasn't a casino at the time, so jobs were hard to get and easy to lose. There were people who were sympathetic to what we were about, but they thought that if they were seen coming to our homes they might lose their jobs."

The tribal government's "enrollment department" is prominent and manages the criteria by which membership is determined; it holds the power to recommend to the tribal council upgrading quanta of "Lac du Flambeau Chippewa Indian blood" for purposes of selectively expanding the population to whom tribal benefits apply. Membership criteria are specified in the second article of the tribal constitution. At the time of the Walleye War, tribal members were required to possess at least one-quarter Lac du Flambeau blood. The children of members with less than half Flambeau blood who married either non-Indians or non-Flambeau members could not be Flambeau tribal members. Many publicly advertised meetings on the reservation are for "Members Only," and the tribal council is inclined to close its meetings to nontribal members when discussing what it considers to be sensitive matters.

In stark contrast, the Wa-Swa-Gon Treaty Association recruited people on the reservation who were excluded from or at the margins of the tribe. Included were the non-Indian spouses of at least two early members—both active in the formulation of the group's identity—as well as non-Ojibwes from other reservations. One non-Indian member was married to a woman (whose mother was a tribal member) who considered herself to be an Indian but had less than the one-quarter quantum of Lac du Flambeau Chippewa Indian blood required to be on the rolls. The group's organizers had been improvising their material livings for their entire lives; most were private businessmen of one sort or another. Though they had held positions within the tribal organization from time to time, they were neither long tenured nor were they secure by virtue of familial connections. Wa-Swa-Gon's resources, unlike the tribal government's, were the sum of its changing membership and relationships with others beyond Flambeau. Specifying borders would not be in the interest of those who used the image and name of the association for their political projects. Meetings were open to whoever desired to come. The association was ostensibly recruiting and initiating a program of action not on ethnic or racial bases but built around a shared interest in contesting the exercise of power by the tribal council and reimagining a more autonomous future—politically and culturally—for the reservation.

The Wa-Swa-Gon Treaty Association also drew upon historical modes of recruitment by attempting to win the support of elders through feasts and gifts of fish and game. In so doing, the group grounded its politics in the authority of tradition by displaying its respect for community elders, who are still valued on the reservation.[2]

BEYOND THE BORDERS

A key step in building alliances between the Wa-Swa-Gon Treaty Association and non-Indians was a conference held on April 7 and 8, 1989, at the Northland College campus in nearby Woodruff. Entitled "Weaving the Web" (from a line in an invented but nonetheless famous Chief Seattle speech), the conference was organized and hosted by Nick Van Der Puy. At the time, Van Der Puy was a professional fishing and hunting guide and an activist in the Eagle River–based Citizens for Treaty Rights, a non-Indian treaty support organization that had been founded the previous year. The lectures, reminiscences, and testimonies over the course of the conference helped cement relationships between the Indian leadership of the local struggle and non-Indian and Indian members of other institutions.

The event was encouraged by the leadership of the Wa-Swa-Gon Treaty Association as well as by Walter Bresette of the Red Cliff band. A participant at Mike Chosa's Indian Village in Chicago, the spokesman for GLIFWC, and the founder of the Lake Superior Green Party, Bresette was emerging as the preeminent public intellectual commenting on the larger significance of treaty rights.[3]

The Weaving the Web conference featured lectures, poetry, oral history, musical performances, a sunrise pipe ceremony, and a feast. By facilitating an exchange of perspectives from different institutions around the state, it simultaneously globalized local concerns and localized global ones, placing a new order of resources at the disposal of the leaders of the off-reservation treaty rights movement. The conference also began the process of promoting the Ojibwe spearfishing struggle as the most important peace and justice issue in Wisconsin.

In attendance were the leading members of the Wa-Swa-Gon Treaty Association, DNR and GLIFWC biologists, spiritual and traditional leaders from the Lac Courte Oreilles reservation, and members of the regional academic community. No one from Woodruff or Minocqua, the two biggest non-Indian towns closest to the Flambeau reservation, attended. Most of those present were non-Indian supporters from Madison, Milwaukee, and Chicago as members of the Indian Treaty Rights Committee; from HONOR (Honor Our Neighbors' Origins and Rights), a coalition of progressive and religious Indian and non-Indian organizations; and members of the Witness for Non-Violence, who would soon play an important role at the landings.

Witness for Non-Violence is a nonviolent activist association that began in 1987, modeled on the Big Mountain Witness (itself taking after the organization Witness for Peace, which brought people to Latin America to see a version of political conflict not reported by the federal government or the mainstream media). Witness was formed in response to Walter Bresette's call to activists in Milwaukee and Madison to come to northern Wisconsin instead of going all the way to Nicaragua if they were interested in documenting injustices (Whaley and Bresette 1994:50–51). According its recruitment brochure, the Witness seeks to "diffuse violent situations and protect the rights and dignity of people under attack. Witnessing in northern Wisconsin is a peaceful, non-confrontational observation of the situation. Our presence is meant to convey calm in the midst of tension. By shining a witnessing light on the situation, we hope to lessen the chance of harassment and violence, and to document and testify to any and all violations of the law that we see."

Witness for Non-Violence decided not to engage the protesters on the landings in conversations about the treaty issue, a change in policy that reflected a belief by the leaders that their reports would have greater credibility for state agencies if they submerged their support for the movement in favor of documenting what happened routinely on the landings. Prospective participants agreed to be trained in "witnessing" before going to a landing, a prerequisite insisted upon by the Witness leadership. Training sessions took place in a few of the region's larger cities. At those sessions, participants were initiated into the group through rehearsals of typically hostile encounters on the boat landings. Clearly, this "Witness training" was a rite of passage that purported to create identification with the Indian spearfishers.

Witnesses were simultaneously active and passive on the landings, fulfilling their purpose to "shine a witnessing light," a phrase I often heard repeated on the landings in 1989. On the one hand, the Witness leaders told recruits not to "wear buttons, political shirts or even vaguely different clothing," not to "identify your vehicle by leaving stickers or literature visible or standing around it near a landing," or "needlessly identify yourself or others as treaty supporters." On the other hand, they were instructed to "stand with the Chippewa and their families as a supportive presence," "stand between people in a potentially confrontational circumstance," and "not use the 'silent treatment' on protesters talking rationally to you." In their literature and training sessions, prospective Witnesses were admonished to be sensitive to "Chippewa" or "Native American" culture, not to engage or antagonize the protesters, and to "take detailed notes continually, even if you are also recording or photographing."

Indian treaty rights advocates largely supported the Witness for Non-Violence organization. Maggie Johnson, her sister Dorothy Thoms, and her daughter Anita, all members of the Wa-Swa-Gon Treaty Association and longtime activists, met with the leaders of Witness for Non-Violence on Saturday evening during the Weaving the Web conference to help plan the nature of the group's presence on the boat landings in the fishing season to come. The Indian women became the liaison between Witness for Non-Violence and the Wa-Swa-Gon Treaty Association. They fed and housed the Witnesses who came up from the cities on weekends to attend the boat landings. Nick Hockings generously included the Witnesses in his vision of a future where racial distinctions would be preserved—if demoted in importance. He, too, offered his home to these supporters, who could be seen in the mornings in the front yard cleaning the dozens of fish he had speared the night before while they had stood on the landings witnessing.

Wa-Swa-Gon Treaty Association members used the Witnesses' interest in the conflict and their willingness to be "supporters" to embarrass and chide the tribal council as well as fellow tribal members who were afraid to go out and spear. Tom Maulson and Scott Smith in particular appreciated the outsiders' involvement in the struggle, because it helped to deracialize the conflict and confuse the protesters. If the protesting whites could see other whites supporting Indians, their model of the conflict as understandable in racial terms would be challenged. Other spearers, however, felt that the presence of supportive non-Indians from downstate further and unnecessarily antagonized the local whites. In fact, though, few spearfishers already committed to the off-reservation spearing had much contact with the Witnesses. Many Witnesses were ignored on the landings and in most contexts on the reservation.

The keynote address at the Weaving the Web conference was given by Edward Benton-Banai. A member of the Lac Courte Oreilles band and one of the earliest members of the American Indian Movement in Minneapolis, Benton-Banai had led the takeover of Winter Dam on the Lac Courte Oreilles reservation in 1971, on the occasion of the proposed renewal of its fifty-year lease (Avruch 1972). He had been a leader in the movement to revitalize Anishinaabe culture and identity for nearly twenty years, and had written *The Mishomis Book: The Voice of the Ojibway*, an influential account, widely read in the region, of Anishinaabe culture, history, and prophecy. His remarks at the conference centered on the responsibilities of the present generation of Anishinaabe people to preserve the environment for the "Seventh Generation," as the people seven generations ago, in his understanding, were looking to the future when they signed the treaties. His keynote address conveyed a traditionalist understanding of the current conflict by setting it within an Ojibwe historical context.

Gene Begay, also from Lac Courte Oreilles, conducted a sunrise ceremony on Saturday morning in Torpy Park, the site of PARR rallies.[4] Begay (Niigaaniigaabow, "Leading Man") prayed in Anishinaabemowin, a sign of genuine traditionality among non-Indians and the few tribal members present. He then said his prayer in English, repeating single words and phrases, leaving some untranslated, retaining the tonal aspect of oratory in Anishinaabemowin:

> What I want to say to you is that this wind that we feel this morning
>   has meaning to it.
> It brings to us a message for the Anishinaabeg people.
> This wind here that's coming,
> this is where one of the Ojibway spirits resides.[5]

This *noodin* [wind] that we see coming here,
It brings to us a message of this day,
that what we are going to be doing here is good,
that we should no longer be ascared [*sic*],
the Anishinaabeg people.
We have the power of the Great Spirit in us.
What we're doing here is right.
(Fotsch 1989)

I also told the spirits that we want to have a good feeling with the
    white people around here
who have their laws that they write on paper,
and the tribe will abide by that . . .
And they [treaty opponents] do not understand the Anishinaabe
    way,
in which this has been given down to us,
the right to hunt and fish.
And that we don't mean to harm them,
that we are exercising our rights as Anishinaabe people.
(*Wausau Sunday Herald* 1989)

Begay opened the prayer by noting and therefore establishing a relationship between the conference and the weather, or, more deeply, a connection between the exercise of off-reservation rights and the spirit that is the wind. By so doing, he included those gathered into an enchanted world that is, perhaps, most saliently characterized by the absence of coincidence and the connectivity of all natural and social phenomena.

His use of the term "Anishinaabe" was ambiguous; it is an indigenous word, unlike "Indian," "Chippewa," or "Ojibwe." Its use marks the speaker's intent to locate himself at a definitional center of sorts, marking inclusion and exclusion on the basis of a spiritual if not cultural disposition. The act of giving the speech grounded the authority to make distinctions within a group that has been delineated and objectified by others. It was apparent to anyone present that the group gathered for the ceremony was not entirely made up of tribal members of Lake Superior Chippewa bands; Begay's employment of the term "Anishinaabe" demoted the importance of tribal membership and reconstituted the assemblage as a people who stood in opposition to those "who do not understand the Anishinaabe way." The culminating sunrise ceremony was a mechanism intended to create a certain type of person, one who would become instrumental to the Wa-Swa-Gon Treaty Association.

THE PROPER COURSE OF ACTION

PARR held a rally in Minocqua on April 15, 1989, the weekend after the Weaving the Web conference. Many of the two thousand protesters again wore blaze orange as a sign of opposition to treaty rights. Vera Lawrence returned to denounce the legitimacy of treaty rights if exercised by less than full-blood Indians. Tom Maulson opposed this idea, criticizing a pervasive non-Indian inclination to define Indian identity in racial terms and to mistake the Indian blood metaphors for references to actual physical substance. Nonviolence guided the actions of some of the approximately fifty Indian people from Lac du Flambeau who attended the rally. Echoing nonviolent civil rights tactics, the Valliere brothers brought the drum; Migizikwe, holding her pipe, told the protesters, "God bless you" as they left the park to march through the streets of Minocqua-Woodruff.

The PARR rally though threw into relief some key internal differences among the spearfishers and their supporters. For some time, those who exercised the off-reservation rights had disagreed about how to react to protesters. Should they respond with violence to verbal harassment, damage to their boats, trailers, and vehicles, and gunshots?

Like the Flambeau tribal council, modern war chief Tom Maulson advocated a nonviolent stance. Nothing about his actions on the landings suggested any fear of physical confrontation—he frequently verbally sparred with protesters addressing him in less than respectful ways. As indicated earlier, Maulson's memory of the confrontation at Butternut Lake in 1987, where he believed his death was imminent, included a wish to take others with him.[6] At over six feet tall and 250 pounds, Maulson always had the option to resort to physical force—which, no doubt, gave him confidence to try other means first.

In Maulson's judgment, though, the process of forging a coalition between Indians and non-Indians required a nonviolent ideology. Such a pacifist set of beliefs could be found in local interpretations of a widely circulating Osh-ki-bi-ma-di-zeeg prophecy set forth by Lac Courte Oreilles tribal member Edward Benton-Banai.

In *The Mishomis Book,* Edward Benton-Banai had revealed a millenarian prophecy that seemed to have implications for the current struggle between Indians and non-Indians:

The seventh prophet that came to the people long ago was said to be different from the other prophets. He was young and had a strange light in his eyes. He said, In the time of the Seventh Fire an *Osh-ki-bi-ma-di-zeeg* (New People) will emerge. They will retrace their steps to find what was left by the trail. Their steps will take them to the elders who they will ask to guide them on their journey. But many of the elders will have fallen asleep. They will awaken to this new time with nothing to offer. Some of the elders will be silent out of fear. Some of the elders will be silent because no one will ask anything of them. The New People will have to be careful in how they approach the elders. The task of the New People will not be easy.

If the New People will remain strong in their quest, the Waterdrum of the Midewiwin Lodge will again sound its voice. There will be a rebirth of the Anishinaabe Nation and rekindling of old flames. The Sacred Fire will again be lit.

It is at this time that the Light-skinned Race will be given a choice between two roads. If they choose the right road, the Seventh Fire will light the Eighth and Final Fire—an eternal Fire of peace, love, brotherhood and sisterhood. If the Light-skinned Race makes the wrong choice of roads, then the destruction they brought with them in coming to this country will come back to them and cause much suffering and death to all the Earth's people.[7] (1988:92–93)

The Osh-ki-bi-ma-di-zeeg prophecy, like Begay's prayer at the conference, is inclusive and nonviolent. The text clearly indicates that the "New People" are the descendants of Indians; the future, however, is in the hands of the whites, in the form of "a choice between two roads." If the whites make the desirable choice, a permanent egalitarian community characterized by "peace, love, brotherhood and sisterhood" will come to pass. According to Nick Hockings, a neotraditional spearfisher from Lac du Flambeau who had became a Baha'i, the emergence of the Seventh and Eighth Fire elided the original opposition between Native and nonnative so that everyone who was interested in and committed to treaty rights became Osh-ki-bi-ma-di-zeeg. In his understanding, people of all colors were returning to "Turtle Island"—that is, North America, indigenously conceived—having fulfilled the responsibilities that the Creator had given their ancestors according to their race.

In practical terms, however, Maulson could not easily exclude from the treaty rights movement tribal members who were not fully committed to nonviolence. Among the first group of men who went off the reservation in 1985 and 1986 were a number of very tough individuals who were longtime violators and marginally employed in the cash economy. They were "hard partyers" in the judgment of some and "outlaws" according to others. Because these spearers were willing to fish under fire, they were critical to the continuation and defense of spearfishing. The off-reservation treaty rights movement not only could accommodate militancy but required it.

One of the more influential and militant spearers was Gilbert Chapman. On the Saturday afternoon of the PARR rally, while some Indians marched peacefully, Chapman parked his van in Torpy Park, displaying a cased .357 magnum revolver plainly (and legally) on the dashboard and large posters in the windows that read:

Chippewa and Proud

Fearless	Peaceful
Unified	American
Courageous	Righteous
Kind	Respected

Wearing a T-shirt that bore the same message (see p. 107), Chapman walked through the crowd, starting in the front and weaving his way to the back. No one said anything to him. Onlookers would read his T-shirt message, look at him, and, in his recollection, look away.

Chapman believed that many whites were not willing to go so far as to fight to protect the walleye, and that provocation and aggression would drive away those protesters not fully committed, leaving the hardened core to be dealt with by Indians or state law enforcement. He felt that the spearfishers had made a mistake at Big Twin Lake the last night of the first off-reservation spearing season when they didn't fight the protesters.[8] Though the spearers had been outnumbered, Chapman believed that had "we put a bunch of them in the hospital that night," it would have sent a forceful and decisive message to antagonistic whites.

Gibby Chapman provoked in many ways, including tacking up Lac du Flambeau casino posters over PARR rally advertisements and wearing his Chippewa and Proud T-shirt in non-Indian bars and restaurants. On the landings, he enjoyed the confrontations (as did a number of others), taking pleasure in threatening people whom he sensed did not fully appreciate the lengths to which some Indians were willing to go to spear fish. When law enforcement threatened to withdraw police protection for the spearers, he packed four guns in his truck and carried at least one in his boat. "I'll shoot my way in there and I'll shoot my way out. . . . We're Lac du Flambeau. That means hunting at night.

We've been shooting at night for a long time. Those white people know that." On the water, when once approached by a boat containing protesters, Chapman invited them to come closer and then threatened them with his fishing spear. "If you think this hurts on the way in, wait till I pull it out." Alarmed, the protesters called over to a DNR police boat that a spearer had threatened them. "You bet you're being threatened," Chapman replied.

Two non-Indian brothers who lived at Mercer had worked once with Chapman. Spotting the brothers at the Flambeau Flowage among the protesters, he told them to leave everybody else alone. "My boat is white," he announced. "It's easy to see on the water. You wanna fuck with somebody, you leave my people alone, fuck with me."

They never showed up.

Chapman's verbal parries mark an important aesthetic of Ojibwe warfare: a kind of artful, if in this case crude, provocation that extends and transforms the everyday teasing between friends, male cross-cousins, and brothers-in-law (Dunning 1959:124–128). This attitude and rhetorical strategy were very much evident two years later, when a proposed Native American curriculum for public schools was attacked in the local newspaper by PARR leaders as biased in favor of Indians— chiefly because no mention was made of the fact that some scholars gloss Ojibwe as "Roasters," a reference to torture if not cannibalism (*Lakeland Times* 1991). Chapman's response was to draft a letter to the editor of his own. He gave a preview of it as he sat with half a dozen men in their forties and fifties in the Outpost Cafe. Using my presence and interest as an opportunity to talk to the group, he yelled to me that he was up until midnight last night, and he pantomimed writing. "I wrote that stuff about roasting. You white people roasted six million Jews, then on August 6 you roasted eighty thousand Japs. Then because you liked the smell, you roasted another hundred thousand three days later and you have the audacity to come down on us for putting a roasted white man on a birch bark sandwich now and then." His comment received a big and long laugh from everyone who was sitting together.

Many Anishinaabes still think of themselves as hunters, people who must kill in order to live. Violence is the very condition of life. The absence of an explicit and stable consensus on the place of violence in the treaty rights movement was a measure of the movement's deep resonance with traditional dispositions. But in the end, the nonviolent political realists, who pointed out that the spearfishers were far outnumbered, were able to rein in those urging confrontation by promoting an ideology built around *ogitchida.*

The terms *ogitchida* and *ogitchidakwe,* meaning "head warrior" and "female warrior" and contrasting with *zhimaagaanish,* "soldier" (Baraga 1992:237), began gaining currency at Lac du Flambeau in 1989, when they were reintroduced by Edward Benton-Banai. *Ogitchida* is used and described in the missionary Boutwell's journal in the 1830s (Hickerson 1962:56). It had been revitalized earlier at the turn of the twentieth century in reference to the officers of the Big Drum (Rynkiewich 1980:92; Vennum 1982:76). *Ogitchida* became equated with individual Indian people who fought for the preservation of Ojibwe distinctness and rights to self-determination. After the 1989 season, spearfishers were said to be *ogitchida;* their mothers, wives, and sisters who waited on the landings for them to return were called *ogitchidakwe,* as were Yolanda St. Germaine, Victoria Chosa, Goldie Larsen, and other Flambeau women tribal members who spearfished. Even some non-Ojibwes were considered to be *ogitchida.* The terms connoted a disposition and an attitude that signaled motivation more than engaging in a particular practice.

The reintroduced *ogitchida* was not without controversy at Flambeau. It was viewed by some as depreciating the value of veterans. According to Ernie St. Germaine, some older members of the community felt that "it was absurd for anyone to say that spearers were veterans because they 'faced the enemy'—a bunch of rabble-rousers who tossed insults and rocks at them. It's a disgrace and insult to those who died, bloody and torn in the mud on foreign soil so that these spearers could one day understand the freedom and right to spear and hunt."

By the spring of 1989, Lac du Flambeau's internal conflict had widened and deepened. As the spearfishing dispute flared dramatically beyond its borders, the struggle also intensified between Flambeau's modern civic and warrior factions—the tribal council and the Wa-Swa-Gon Treaty Association.

6

Spearing in the Four Directions

11. Tribal members Tom Maulson
and his son put in a boat at a
landing among sheriff's police and
protesters. Photo courtesy of Tom
Maulson.

The 1989 spearing season unfolded accompanied by a complicated interplay between the leaders of two factions on the reservation at Lac du Flambeau, five other bands of Wisconsin Ojibwes who were also spearing, non-Indian citizen treaty protesters and supporters, the governor, state and federal congressional representatives, the American Indian Movement, and a federal district judge.

As in previous years, the St. Croix band inaugurated the season, spearing 150 miles west of Lac du Flambeau where the lakes tend to open up earlier than in the north central part of Wisconsin. Within days, seventeen Flambeau spearfishers drove for three hours to the southern limit of the ceded territory in Marathon County and took 604 walleye from the Big Eau Pleine Reservoir, which had never been speared before and had not existed in the nineteenth century when the treaties were signed. Another nine spearers went to Lake Nokomis, an hour south of the reservation, and took 248 fish; five others speared the Willow Reservoir, taking 94 walleye.

The first night's catch was given to the elders on the reservation, according to Tom Maulson, who continued to be sought out by the media and was willing to interpret the significance of spearfishing. His claim was taken up by the media and used by some protesters over the course of the season to negatively shape outsiders' perceptions of spearing and the escalating conflict. Maulson's knowledge of how the fish were being used implied that the spearfishing movement had an organizational coherence, contesting the usual media representation of the conflict as between individual, named, and identified non-Indians and a group of unidentified and undifferentiated Indians. The spearers were clearly led by a recognizable leader, albeit in a fashion largely unfamiliar to non-Indians. The practice of giving fish to the elders implied the existence of a coherent community as well as the presence of a distinct, traditional moral order at Flambeau.

OPPOSITION

The print media's coverage of the 1989 season, featuring front-page stories and headlines beginning more than a week before the first spears went into the water, encouraged attendance at the landings. Each issue of the *Wausau Daily Herald,* for example, displayed a map above the nameplate on the front page with a tally by band and county of the number of spearfishers and total walleye taken at each lake.[1] Northern Wisconsin's counties appeared in two colors on the map; counties with lakes speared that day were labeled and colored yellow, while all others remained unlabeled and shown in green. Recalling the image on the Treaty Beer can and posters, superimposed diagonally across the entire map was a fishing spear with a fish impaled through the belly on the five-tined head—a physical impossibility, since fish don't swim upside down.

Rendering the spearfishing information as a banner above the newspaper's nameplate effectively represented spearing and the attendant protesting as an athletic event (Schlender 1991:13). Like the daily box scores and weather reports—more the signs of seasons and permanent institutional contexts than events—spearing was now being depicted as a perennial spectacle, a representation that spurred both observers and protesters to flock to the landings.

The numbers of protesters at the named lakes in 1989 did increase significantly over the previous year, although little attempt was made to distinguish "spectators" or "observers" from protesters. Building on established homeowners' associations in the neighborhoods of the lakes, "lake watch groups" instituted by STA/W were able to disseminate information about spearfishing activity with great efficiency. Every night of the eleven-day season, at least 250 people attended at least one landing each night. Other protesters launched boats to make what were euphemistically called "observation runs," harassing spearfishers by intentionally creating wakes that made spearing difficult and dangerous. In some cases a dozen protest boats converged on a single spearing boat. Indian spearing boats were swamped or rammed; DNR patrol boats were far outnumbered and had difficulty keeping up with the conflict on water (Whaley and Bresette 1994: 107).

Although protesters did not attend the lakes speared by Lac Courte Oreilles, they met St. Croix spearers at Half Moon and Balsam Lakes (Schlender 1991:13). Flambeau spearfishers encountered opposition at the Big Eau Pleine Reservoir and Lake Nokomis.

On Wednesday night, the second night of the season, Flambeau speared seven different lakes in Oneida County. Eighteen spearers accompanied Tom Maulson to the Rainbow Flowage, east of Minocqua-Woodruff and west of Eagle River, where they took 375 walleye.[2] A caravan of twelve cars, three pulling small boats—each with a tub, a couple of spears, helmets with headlamps affixed and DC batteries —left T&L on the reservation as the sun drew close to the horizon through the trees.

With a National Guard helicopter hovering overhead, they pulled into the landing at Rainbow Flowage. Most parked among the trees. Flambeau tribal member Tinker Schuman (Migizikwe) conducted a pipe ceremony on the landing, attended by spearers and family members. Non-Indians and women were directed to only touch the pipe, indicating that the Witnesses, who imagined themselves to be on an equal footing in an alliance with Indian spearfishers (Whaley and Bresette 1994), were being assimilated as wives and sisters. Six squad cars of sheriff's police arrived and began stringing plastic tape around an area of the landing that would be restricted to all but spearing tribal members. Sarah Baccus of Witness for Non-Violence was interviewed by a local television station. Most of the spearers worked on equipment and waited for the evening to grow dark.

Thirty-five protesters crossed the sheriff's line that night in a prearranged act of civil disobedience and were arrested for disorderly conduct or obstruction. Their arrest bolstered STA/W's continuing attempts to represent the relationship between non-Indians and treaty fishermen as analogous to the relationship between blacks and whites in the South during the civil rights movement. The division between Indian fishermen, who could move wherever they wanted to, and non-Indians, who were restricted, facilitated this model of the conflict.[3] The Rhinelander paper went so far as to add a side bar entitled, "Who Was Arrested?" listing all of the names (*Rhinelander Daily News* 1989a).

The conflict escalated further the next day when the state's Natural Resource Board announced the long-anticipated bag limit reductions for walleye on all lakes in the ceded territory named by the bands (*Milwaukee Journal* 1989a). In March, Judge Barbara Crabb had ruled on the state's right to regulate the off-reservation walleye and muskellunge fisheries. She had determined that the tribes could regulate themselves if they implemented a number of conservation-based measures and procedures that the DNR was proposing for the management of the treaty harvest of these species. The greatest contestable issue had been the method of determining the quantities of fish that could be harvested from a given lake. The DNR called for no more than 35 percent of the total allowable catch to be taken by spearfishers and anglers combined. Over the course of the fourteen-day trial, the judge was convinced by DNR biologists' skillful and controversial (Kmiecik and Shively 1990:2) use of data gathered over the last few spearing seasons. Though the DNR would be able to determine the numerical value of the safe harvest, the tribes were permitted to take up to 100 percent of that figure.

The public and media's emphasis on the resulting lower daily bag limits for fishing (*Milwaukee Journal* 1989a) shifted the political cost of this conservation measure by the DNR to the Indian spearers. The DNR had been releasing information about this change in policy for some time. Non-Indian resort owners and others dependent on the tourist economy knew that bag limits would become less than the long-standing ratio of five walleye per angler per lake per day, with the exact number determined by the total walleye speared and the state's confidence in the accuracy of its fish population estimate. Most local resorts in fact had fewer bookings than the previous year (*Lakeland Times* 1989c). The effect of this uncertainty, the possible positive benefits of preventing Indians from spearing or taking their quota, and the April 30 release of the revised bag limits on the 254 lakes named by the bands (*Milwaukee Journal* 1989c) provoked many to go to the landings.

The Walleye War showed no signs of abating. Between six hundred and one thousand protesters gathered at North Twin Lake on Saturday night, April 29. They hurled rocks at the Flambeau spearfishers, hitting Nick Hockings and Ray Cadotte; shots were even fired at some spearers.

On the following night, Flambeau speared nine lakes, most of them close to the reservation in Oneida County, taking almost nine hundred walleye, the third biggest night of the season. Gilbert Chapman was said to have vigorously and provocatively spearfished along the shorelines of Minocqua. When he took a muskie in full view of the diners at Bosacki's Restaurant—then thought of by Indian people as a safe place to express anti-Indian sentiment openly—"enough people got up from their tables and rushed over to the windows to nearly tip the whole building into the lake!" Never one to miss an opportunity to

antagonize, Chapman told a Milwaukee reporter that he feeds muskies to his dogs.

On Monday and Tuesday nights, May 1 and 2, Flambeau spearfishers were stoned and their vehicles damaged as they left Bearskin and
Plum Lakes in Oneida and Vilas Counties. News sources estimated the
protesters at eight hundred at Plum Lake, marking an increase from
the previous week. The first felony arrests were made in separate inci-
dents at two other landings, where protesters attacked police (*Wausau
Daily Herald* 1989c). The Maki brothers of Lac du Flambeau speared
the nearby Willow Reservoir. As they pulled away from the landing, a
protester yelled that the only good Indian is a dead Indian. Telling the
reporter the story the following day, the brothers signaled a note of
warfare by emphasizing the value of recognition in the face of the
threat of personal extinction: "It makes you want to go out and get
more fish by spearing" (*Wausau Daily Herald* 1989e).

DRUM AND FLAG

This season the chairman of the St. Croix band had invited the American Indian Movement (AIM) to the landings. Such outreach and mobi-
lization beyond reservation borders supported the objectives of the
Wa-Swa-Gon Treaty Association but ran counter to the wishes of the
Executive Committee of Flambeau's tribal council, which had decided
to discourage anyone other than spearfishers from going to the
landings.

On Saturday night, April 29, members of AIM from Minneapolis appeared at the landing at North Twin Lake. They brought two key cultural items that spoke to entwined and deepening dimensions of the
spearfishing conflict—a drum and what was at the time called "the
AIM flag." Though a descendent of the Dream Dance drum had been
used for a number of years at rallies, there were elders at Lac du Flambeau and elsewhere who criticized the Flambeau spearers for involving in a hostile situation a drum associated with peace. Urban Indians,
for whom the drum was a sign of a more general identity and an instru-
ment of indigenous spiritual power, were responsible for actually
bringing a drum to a boat landing. According to Jerry Maulson, when
the drum was brought out for the first time at North Twin Lake, "It
calmed people down, Indian people, and it frightened the ones who
didn't understand it, mostly non-Indians." The decision to use a drum

helped shape events in 1989 and became the focal point of the season's memorable last night at Butternut Lake.

The drum appeared with the AIM flag, an American flag with an image of a Plains warrior holding a pipe superimposed on the stripes. First produced in Turkey and marketed in Europe in the mid-1980s, the AIM flag provoked the oppositional display of more conventional American flags by protesters at the landings. What had been an argument about the legitimacy of collectively held usufruct rights now also became a contest of representing the relationship between cultures and nation.

The AIM flag is a political community's representation of itself that posits a symbiotic relationship between two irreducible identities and formally equates them. The superimposition of a stereotypical Indian person on an American flag carried by Indian people suggests an unbreakable bond between the government of the United States and Indian people, a connection that entails a deep and long-standing moral obligation to each other. The AIM flag is simultaneously patriotic and, from a non-Indian anti-treaty perspective, a desecration. It is an image of both a necessary relationship and an unavoidable opposition.

Tom Maulson spoke publicly on a similar theme of opposition and interdependence between Indian peoples and the United States at the same time that the flag appeared in the spearfishing conflict. When Maulson was interviewed on April 28, he commented about threatening phone calls by noting: "We always get those crank calls. If we take them seriously, we'd be like groundhogs under the ground. People should not have to live under these conditions. There is supposed to be God Bless America" (*Wausau Daily Herald* 1989b). Maulson also stressed how treaty rights bound the United States and the bands together, as a claim on the United States that was also integral to modern Native culture: "The Tribe was only exercising *an historical right*. In fact, he said, it's more than just a right, it's a tradition, a part of Chippewa culture. 'You just don't give it away. It has lifted me up. The treaty is a very vital part of my life now. It's part of history. It's something that nobody can take away from me now'" (*Milwaukee Journal* 1989b).

THE INNER STRUGGLE CONTINUES

The contest for legitimacy and representation at Lac du Flambeau grew increasingly complicated. Gilbert Chapman informed the media of the existence of the Wa-Swa-Gon Treaty Association and announced that the group opposed negotiating with the state over the exercise of the off-reservation rights. They took the position that all necessary negotiations had taken place in 1837 and 1842, when the original treaties were signed. Chapman told reporters that the WTA had sixty members. Goldie Larson, Nick Hockings, and Tom Maulson publicly echoed his words and sentiment (*Wausau Daily Herald* 1989a).

Tribal Council Chairman Mike Allen, however, also continued to speak officially and publicly about the tribe's interest in negotiating with the state (*Wausau Daily Herald* 1989a). Asserting his traditional, if not constitutional, responsibility to protect his people, Allen threatened to take 100 percent of safe harvest unless the state's law enforcement established a safe area for spearers, their families, and their vehicles; cleared the landings of protesters after the first rock was thrown; and provided a police escort for tribal vehicles leaving the landings (*Wausau Daily Herald* 1989a).[4] The governor immediately responded, asking the tribes to quit spearing before the sports angling season began at midnight on that coming Friday, May 5 (*Wausau Daily Herald* 1989d).

The timing of Allen's threat may have been motivated by an attempt to outflank the leaders of AIM, who had announced a rally at Flambeau and a march in either Minocqua or Park Falls on May 5. Allen shortly afterward made a more earnest attempt to encompass AIM's and WTA's project by calling the upcoming events a "rally and feast to welcome non-Indian anglers to Wisconsin for the opening of the fishing season." AIM's initiative was recast to explicitly include non-Indians, to throw into relief traditional Ojibwe generosity, and to once again recognize and capitalize on the long-standing cultural power of the feast. Allen proclaimed that the rally and feast "will provide an opportunity for people of goodwill, Indian and non-Indian alike, to gather in solidarity against the outpouring of racial hatred that has been directed against us. We will control access to the reservation to ensure that only people of goodwill will attend. We will not greet anglers with rocks and insults. We will instead welcome them to our land and hope that they can learn to share as we have" (*Wausau Daily Herald* 1989e).

The idea that moderately affluent downstate and big-city sportfishers would attend a rally in support of Ojibwe spearing represents a barely credible, disingenuous misunderstanding of those outsiders. Allen's rhetoric recalls the type of symbolic competition identified by Schwimmer (1972)—in this case, Indians, the subordinate group, represent themselves as morally superior to more powerful, nonreservation groups by offering and sharing food in exchange for the goodwill that visiting traditionally represents for the band. In contrast, the local non-Indians return rocks and insults for Indian goodwill when Flambeau tribal members visit lakes off the reservation. Chairman Allen's addition of a feast to the forthcoming rally continued the traditional practice that had been brought into play the previous summer during the spearfishing disagreement with the Lac Courte Oreilles band.

The same day that Allen was attempting to shape AIM and WTA's efforts, Dean Crist, the spokesman for STA/W, told 150 supporters that he wanted to close down one weekend of spearing in one county, even if it meant more arrests (*Wausau Daily Herald* 1989d). Repeated in the local papers and electronic media, Crist's announcement raised expectations that the forthcoming weekend would bring a dramatic event.

On Wednesday, May 3, the governor reacted further to Allen's threat by instructing the state attorney general to file two motions in the federal district court—the first to stop the band from taking 100 percent of safe harvest; the second to prevent the band from spearing after midnight on Friday, just prior to the opening of the sports angling season on that Saturday, May 6. Judge Barbara Crabb was to hear the governor's request. Though both motions were originally said to be intended to restore public safety, the following day the assistant attorney general said that the motion to stop Lac du Flambeau from taking 100 percent of safe harvest was "to protect fish resources" (*Rhinelander Daily News* 1989b), an explicit critique of Judge Crabb's previous assessment of the biological impact of spearfishing.

In his five-page opinion of Friday, May 5, Judge Crabb denied the governor's motions, likening the situation to the civil rights battle of the 1960s. In this case, it was Indian people whose rights to fish were being infringed upon by lawless protest. She concluded her opinion:

If this court holds that violent and lawless protests can determine the rights of the residents of this state, what message will that send? Will that not encourage others to seek to resolve disputes by physical intimidation? And will that not make the next peacekeeping effort even more difficult than this one has been?

It is the state's burden to show that it is entitled to a preliminary injunction. To do that, it must show that it has a factual and legal basis for its position, that it has not adequate remedy at law, that the public interest would not be disserved by the issuance of an injunction. The state has not met that burden. (*News from Indian Country* 1989a:4)

On the previous Wednesday evening, the leaders of Flambeau's civic and war factions addressed the reservation's spearfishers in an extraordinary meeting in the parking lot of the T&L complex.[5] The local press was not permitted to attend. Tribal Council Chairman Mike Allen and Tom Maulson stood on opposite ends of a porch eight feet wide of a building that Maulson was leasing to the tribe and that housed both the tribal attorney's office and a GLIFWC office where wardens provided spearing permits to tribal members.

Both leaders took turns speaking to the group, never referring to each other's words. Allen repeated the phrase, "cool heads will prevail," and encouraged the spearers to continue to endure abuse without retaliation. Maulson also encouraged restraint and complimented the men on their ability to put up with a difficult situation. Allen went further and asked the spearfishers if they would consider "giving them a day of grace." The tribal council chairman and Maulson had already agreed to seek a night off because they knew that they would both be downstate in court with the tribe's lawyers, listening to the governor ask the federal judge to issue an injunction to stop the spearing.

"Then let's go to Butternut tomorrow night," someone said.

"Tomorrow night?" asked Maulson, looking over the group, seeking a consensus.

"Let's go there Saturday night, after the rally, when we have a lot of support," someone else offered. Men began to quietly converse with each other, and no consensus was apparent.

VIOLENCE AND MYTHOPOEIA AT TROUT LAKE

Despite discussion about "a day of grace" at the Wednesday meeting at Flambeau, the reservation named nine lakes on Friday, May 5, and fished three—Long, Forest, and Trout—in Vilas County. In the recollection of Tom Maulson, "Gibby and them" wanted to go out and get fish. With the regulatory process unfolding within an Ojibwe order of value, there was no reservation mechanism in place to prevent Gilbert Chapman and other spearers from ignoring the request of the tribal leadership.

Trout is a big lake just a few miles northeast of the reservation. It was the site of Lac du Flambeau's parent village under the leadership of Keeshkemun's father, Shadawish, in the middle of the eighteenth century (Warren 1984:192) and remained occupied well into the nineteenth by about fifteen families (Winn 1923:44). It was cold and windy that Friday night, with the windchill nearly five degrees below zero. A few years later, Nick Hockings said that they would not have speared on such a night on the reservation, but went out with whitecaps on the lakes and snow in the air as a response to the challenge from STA/W to close down spearfishing for a weekend.

An estimated 1,500 people, mostly protesters, came to Trout Lake that night (*Wausau Daily Herald* 1989i). Over the course of the evening, the police force was increased from 90 to between 250 and 350. About 500 people had earlier attended a STA/W rally in the nearby town of Arbor Vitae, where a strategy was devised to close down the spearing by crossing police lines and occupying the landing.

Tom Maulson recalls that Trout Lake was the most dangerous night in all of the years of spearing. Rocks were thrown and racial epithets yelled by an angry crowd barely contained by snow fences, screaming usually from the dark of trees enclosing the strips of concrete that stretched into the shallow water of Trout Lake.[6] Hundreds of increasingly agitated protesters chanted "bullshit" louder and louder, and the police grew more vigilant and visibly nervous as boat lights approached the landing out of an undifferentiated darkness. The night oscillated wildly between the boredom of standing around without focus for long periods of time in the early spring cold and the sudden fear of not knowing what would happen when a half a dozen police would suddenly erupt from around the snow fences and forcibly arrest a protester. Emotional states were fragile and shifting. Some in the crowd laughed and were enjoying themselves; others watched calmly yet attentively. Some were violently angry; others visibly drunk; and many appeared to be afraid. What would happen next?

Advancing and surging across the police lines again and again, some in the crowd scuffled and threatened the spearfishers. One protester, claiming that an AIM member had hit him, was trying to attack a drummer when Tom Maulson grabbed him by the shoulders of his coat. "He was a skinny tall kid and he was a jumpin' all around like a rabbit. But I had him good and I wasn't going to let him go unless one of his people took him. They had us surrounded. I knew what Custer felt like then. They could have killed us all, and they was saying that that is what they wanted to do."

Maulson had brought his army-issue M-1 with a hundred rounds, but had left it in his truck. "We left the guns in the van locked up but took the clips with us," Gilbert Chapman remembers. "We thought they were going to kill us." He was searched that night.

"I was apprehensive when they broke through the police line at Trout Lake," Chapman said gravely. "We grabbed things to protect ourselves and walked up toward them with the lake to our backs and they stopped."

A Flambeau man twenty years younger than Chapman stayed in his pickup truck, with a loaded rifle behind the seat. Believing they were going to be killed, he vowed that if the crowd came any closer he would grab the gun and start shooting. He never reached for his weapon. A wind suddenly came off the lake and the protesters "went down, they didn't sit down, but they went down. It was a spirit came through there."

That Friday night, 109 protesters were arrested, most for planned acts of civil disobedience. By repeatedly prodding the advancing line of protesters with their nightsticks, the sheriff's police forced the crowd back and down before they could succeed in taking the space. The landing remained open.

Despite poor weather and imminent violence, fourteen Flambeau spearers took 175 walleyes and 27 muskies from Trout Lake, 42 percent of the tribal quota (Kmiecik and Shively 1990).

THE FLAMBEAU RALLY

By Friday, May 5, the spearfishers from Lac du Flambeau had taken 6,553 walleye and 46 muskies. Many hundreds of these fish—and a few deer—were cooked for a feast on Saturday that more than adequately fed about fifteen hundred people gathered for a rally in support of Flambeau spearfishing.

Agreeing with local Indian leaders not to march in Minocqua or Park Falls, leaders of the American Indian Movement predicted that over a thousand people would come to the rally at Lac du Flambeau on Saturday. According to AIM, the groups pledged to be involved included the National Congress of American Indians, the National Council of Churches, the National Rainbow Coalition, the National Organization of Women, Women against Racism, and the Coalition on Racism. William Means (Lakota), brother of Russell Means, called it "the greatest effort behind an American Indian cause since Wounded Knee" (*Wausau Daily Herald* 1989h).

A whirlwind of activity preceded the rally.[7] As promised by Chairman Allen, the Flambeau tribal police stopped cars (apparently looking for weapons) as they approached the parking lot in front of the tribal community center. The lot nearly filled, with many cars displaying strips of red cloth on their antennas that signaled support for the American Indian Movement. A television satellite truck was parked on the street. Hundreds of mostly Indian people poured into the gymnasium where two television cameras focused on singers and the AIM drum at center court. A young man nearby held a staff adorned with dozens of eagle feathers. The AIM flag was tacked to one of the walls beneath a large mural of a spearfishing scene that had been painted by Nick Hockings fifteen years earlier. An independent film crew from the Twin Cities used the flag as background for a documentary they were making.

Shortly after noon, Edward Benton-Banai—by this time the spiritual, if not political, advisor for a number of the treaty activists in the Wa-Swa-Gon Treaty Association—directed the crowd in the gymnasium to gather around what he referred to as an "altar" on the east side of the basketball court beneath the basket. A brass pail full of water sat in the "key"; a star quilt centered in the three-second area provided the obligatory mediation between the sacred ceremonial objects resting on it and secular ground. Stretching from west to east on the blanket were a small bowl of tobacco; a shallow, rectangular birch bark basket about twelve by twenty-four inches in the rice-winnowing style, overflowing with hundreds of cigarettes; and a kettle with a smoldering fire burning within. Some dozen packages of unopened cigarettes lay to the north of the basket and beyond them three packages of Styrofoam drinking cups. A red stone pipe bowl and carved wooden stem—unconnected to each other—rested on a bed of sage to the south of the brass pail. Near the pipe lay an abalone shell containing burning sage and surrounded by a ring of braided sweetgrass. The small brown suitcase in which these items are kept when not being used lay just east of the pipe and stem.

A large drum in the Dream Dance style hung suspended from four carved and curved staffs at the top of the key, each pointed to a cardinal direction.[8] Expressing Nick Hockings's understanding of Benton-Banai's Osh-ki-bi-ma-di-zeeg prophecy concerning a rebirth of the Anishinaabe nation, the drumhead displayed four painted spirit birds, representing the four races of humankind: the red bird to the east was new life, the yellow one to the south stood for thanksgiving, the black spirit bird to the west was death, and the white to the north signaled the direction that reminds people that life is painful, an ordeal.

Drawing attention to his Indian features, Benton-Banai began by introducing himself as Burt Reynolds, to the mild amusement of those gathered. He asked the elders of the community to come closer and sit nearby on chairs being set in an arc around the altar. Pipe carriers were then invited to stand behind the elders. Treating the elders with honor and recognizing their knowledge and experience signaled Benton-Banai's cultural credibility to the audience. He next requested that any FBI agents present step forward so that their tape recorders would pick up everything, a gesture that acknowledged that "the doings," as Ojibwes often refer to ceremonies, were also political.[9]

Six pipe carriers then came out of the growing crowd that now stood on the bleachers on both sides and covered most of the floor. They held their pipes, with stems and bowls now connected—symbolizing the power of uniting complementary principles, since the bowl and stem are gendered male and female. Benton-Banai took a pinch of tobacco from the bowl on the blanket. Holding it in his left hand, he invited anyone to do the same if they wanted to pray in that manner. The audience was asked to come up and put their own tobacco into the common bowl. Taking the basket that was full of cigarettes, one of the pipe carriers offered the cigarettes to the seated elders, who each took one.

A casual, unhurried tone informed the ceremony at this juncture. Those close to the altar tended to watch in silence; others quietly conversed. People who stood in line to take up or deposit tobacco in the common bowl greeted each other and also quietly conversed.

William Means, James Schlender, and Flambeau tribal members Nick Hockings, Joe Stone, Tinker Schuman, and two others filled their pipes. This group, led by Benton-Banai, faced the east, holding their pipes by the bowls with both hands while the stems were pointed at a right angle. Benton-Banai prayed in Anishinaabemowin. They then turned to the south, and he addressed that direction and prayed again. The sound of the Anishinaabemowin language (which very few present could understand), intoned on one pitch, rhythmically dropping an octave or more for a few beats and returning to a sustained monotone, transformed the spectators into participants in a liturgy. By the time Benton-Banai's group turned to the west, most of the people in the gymnasium were also facing that direction. The pipes were offered to the sky above, and then the bowls were touched to the ground. Two pipes—one for men and one for women—were taken around to the seated elders; men tended to take a few whiffs while most women merely touched the stem.

The events at Lac du Flambeau on this day were unfolding and being improvised according to a deep and pervasive cultural logic that engaged some axiomatic relations in Ojibwe life. Cosmologically, "smoking represented man's relationships to his maker, to the world, to the plants, to the animals and to his fellow men; in another sense it was a petition and a thanksgiving" (Johnston 1976:135). Historically and theologically, offerings of tobacco always alter the balance that the spirits redress with their beneficence. In the Ojibwe cosmos, humans are not sinners who sacrifice to produce harmony; instead, the gods are ambivalent but responsive to gifts made by needy, "pitiful" human beings. The practice turns on the relations of reciprocity assumed to exist between classes of living beings. This was just the first sacrificial gift made to the spirits over the course of the Flambeau rally.

Tinker Schuman, a tribal member, poet and pipe-carrier, was then asked to hold a copper pail of water with both hands. She prayed with head bowed and then offered the water to the elders seated in the semicircle around the altar. After the elders were honored with a sip of the blessed water, all those gathered were invited to partake of a cup of water and thus were strengthened, fortified, and incorporated.

An unanticipated event then occurred, which pointed to the deepening ruptures and fissures within the Flambeau community. Don Carufel, a tribal member in his late twenties, unexpectedly rose and asked Benton-Banai if he could speak. Carufel was the son of Dave Carufel, a respected traditional man and devout Catholic who lived in the Old Indian Village. Active in the Native American Church and a tutor of Ojibwe language and culture for one of the most active spearers, Don Carufel was known also as a pacifist voice of conscience.

"Thus far I haven't been willing to express myself concerning the controversy," he began. "I've been trying to ignore it but it won't go away. I feel I must clear my conscience and let people know what is on my mind before it is too late and I find myself wishing I had said something." No explicit mention had been made of the purpose of the gathering to this point. Carufel reminded people of their traditions, that hunting and fishing were sacred activities and had to be carried out in a spirit of thanksgiving. He criticized Indians for being careless about their hunting and gathering traditions, exhorting them not to ignore the variety of foods the earth gives and to take them in a respectful and grateful manner. He asked whether the fish were worth the risk of human life and concluded by claiming that true traditionality was the cultivation of inner peace of mind.[10]

Carufel's pacifist message was at odds with the political purpose of the ceremony. He represented, however, an important segment of a community that was both coming together and being torn apart as it had not been in living memory. His gentle and implicit critique of the rally's objective was not lost on Benton-Banai. Apparently less than fully pleased with Carufel's cautious message, the leader of the pipe ceremony began to tidy up the altar before he finished speaking.

Benton-Banai next invited the audience to come to the altar to pray individually and to take a cigarette or tobacco at any time that day. The attendees were then directed to the bingo hall next door where there would be a rally and a feast.

After the prayer ceremony, hundreds of people, mostly Indian, crowded into Lac du Flambeau's bingo hall. Nearly a dozen leaders sat on a raised platform on folding chairs under the glare of television camera lights, speaking by turns into a bank of microphones. Present as guests of the Lac du Flambeau band were the elected tribal chairmen and councilmen from different reservations as well as James Schlender of GLIFWC, James Yellowbank of the Indian Treaty Rights Committee in Chicago, Sharon Metz of the support coalition, HONOR, Hilary Waukau of the Menominee Sierra Powers of Witness for Non Violence, and William Means of AIM. In a clear separation between the civil and spiritual domains of contemporary Ojibwe culture, no one who had officiated at the earlier pipe ceremony was sitting on the dais.

Chairman Allen read from the decision that Judge Crabb rendered the day before, adding that Lac du Flambeau couldn't back down now since the law was on its side. "We have to continue right now, we have to keep going," he said, indicating that to stop at this point would give victory to the forces of lawlessness. Allen reminded those gathered: "This is a peaceful rally and we are a peaceful people." Without encouraging supporters to join those going out spearing that night, he urged everyone to be peaceful. The chairman ended by repeating what he had told the spearfishers on Wednesday: "cool heads will prevail."

The facts that Flambeau chairman Mike Allen spoke first and that the rally and feast were held in the tribal bingo hall marked the extent to which the tribal council controlled the unfolding of events that day. But the selection of Jerry Maulson as emcee was a compromise, since he was Tom Maulson's twin brother and a strong supporter of the Wa-Swa-Gon Treaty Association. Jerry Maulson first introduced James Schlender of GLIFWC, who criticized the state's management of the spearfishing crisis and reminded the audience of *Worcester v. Georgia,* the 1832 Supreme Court decision finding that the laws of the state of Georgia had no force in the Cherokee Nation, and about which Andrew Jackson is purported to have said, "John Marshall has made his decision, now let him enforce it." Schlender likened the sheriffs to Jackson because at one time they had threatened to refuse to protect the spearfishers from protesters. Exhorting those gathered "to protect our rights and our people by remembering our history, remembering our traditions, and remembering that the drum and the pipe are central," he concluded by thanking AIM for bringing the pipe and the drum to the landings to strengthen the spearers.

Tom Maulson was then introduced in his capacity as tribal judge and chairman of the Voigt Inter-tribal Task Force. Before getting out a full sentence, Maulson began to choke up with emotion. He delivered a string of freely associated remarks that thanked a variety of people, acknowledged the difficulties of spearing, and recognized the need to build bridges between Indian and non-Indian communities.

"This hasn't happened in 147 years," Maulson declared, referring to the treaty of 1842 that ceded the land in the area of Lac du Flambeau. In his inimitable way of speaking, in terms vague enough to incorporate the imaginations and sentiments of his listeners, "this" apparently referenced Flambeau acting in a sovereign manner on the basis of its nation-to-nation relationship with the federal government. Maulson thanked the tribal council and alluded to "our differences. We talked *at* them." Though he did not mention the Wa-Swa-Gon Treaty Association by name—no speaker that day did—his use of the first-person plural implicitly called attention to the association. Thanking James Jannetta, the tribe's attorney, Maulson ended by announcing: "The fish ain't the issue. The treaty is the issue. The treaty is right, *miigwetch* [thank you]."

The complexity of Maulson's position as war leader at the vortex of the forces brought together that day was revealed in the structure of his speech. He was nearly incoherent at first, emotionally over-whelmed by the event. When he could speak, he mixed gratitude with an ad hoc analysis of the day's significance. His oratorical shortcom-ings were his strength, however, as he drew his diverse listeners into sympathetic mutual constructions of his messages.

James Yellowbank (Ho-Chunk) of the Indian Treaty Rights Com-mittee in Chicago next spoke. Yellowbank had become the liaison be-tween Lac du Flambeau and human rights organizations and other In-dian groups during the 1989 spearfishing season. He was skilled in media relations, in organizing a press conference, and in taking a pro-active stance in managing the meaning of the conflict in a larger do-main. Yellowbank had brought his skills as an orator and spin doctor to Flambeau, setting up a telecommunications office in the tribal cen-ter. In an attempt to reveal the spearfishers as morally superior to the whites, he said pointedly at the rally, "They don't strike back. This is something that the world should see." The theme of nonviolence sur-faced repeatedly during the event, portrayed as a conscious decision by Ojibwes and thus a cultural sign of moral superiority.

Apesanahkwat, the Menominee chairman, was more forceful and angry, drawing the most applause so far. Calling the racism the most rancid he had ever witnessed, Apesanahkwat proclaimed, "This land was our land. It was the Chippewa's land. We reserved rights and the whites who were alive at the time agreed to that. Now radicals don't re-spect Indians or their own ancestors." He acknowledged the anger of Indians by first saying that he wasn't sure whether he could tolerate the ridicule the spearers were suffering at the landings. Apesanahkwat then stoked emotional fires by reciting to the crowd the time-honored quote (attributed to the Mexican revolutionary Emiliano Zapata), "it may soon come a time when it is better to die on our feet than live on our knees."

Apesanahkwat concluded by answering Don Carufel's earlier ques-tion concerning the value of the conflict and its relationship to the practice of tradition.

I want to respectfully comment on my brother Donny's comments this morning. Some of us have lost sight of what the clans' responsibilities are. There are warriors. There are spiritual people. There are hunters. Some of them don't share the same ideology in terms of the protecting of the rights and we have to respect that. We have to respect one another. There are civil

leaders who have a responsibility to look at all of these things. So I do respect Donny's comments. And I think that those fish are worth our lives.
Those deer are worth our lives because that's what God gave us.

Apesanahkwat made a strong case for tribalism, reminding the audience about the relationships between traditional social organization,
the symbolic division of labor, and personal autonomy. His conclusion
that their means of sustenance was a gift from "God" implied an understanding of the tribal social order as a sacred order.

The escalating conflict outside the reservation's borders suddenly
intruded into the rally. Emanuel "Doc" Poler, the chairman of the
Mole Lake band of Chippewa Indians, next stood in front of the microphones. "I've got my tobacco in my hand. I'm squeezing it as hard
as I can. I just received an urgent call to return home." About two
dozen Indian students had left Crandon High School the day before
in response to seven white students wearing T-shirts proclaiming anti-
spearfishing messages. Poler told the listeners that he had heard that
people were marching from Crandon to Mole Lake to take over their
bingo hall.

In an oratorical monotone, Lewis Taylor, the chairman of the St.
Croix band, first took credit for asking AIM to help because his band
had not been confident that the state would protect them. He said that
when asked by Congressman Obey what he thought of a bill to guarantee the Chippewas' 10 percent of safe harvest, he told the congressman that he was crazy. Taylor encouraged everyone in the room to go
to the lakes that were going to be speared that night.

Then gaiashkibos,[11] a councilman from Lac Courte Oreilles and the
first vice president of the National Congress of American Indians,
brought a more generous and reflective tone to the dais. He began by
acknowledging the chairmen, friends, non-Indian friends, and the
delegation from Lac Courte Oreilles. After complimenting Judge
Crabb on her "intestinal fortitude" and calling upon the governor of
"this fine state of Wisconsin" to show the same, gaiashkibos spoke of
the historical generosity of the Lac du Flambeau people and their current patience with the non-Indians who were harassing their spearing.
Attempting to signal simultaneously a moral commitment to nonviolence and the potential of the use of force—thus locating the responsibility for future escalation of the conflict as that of the non-Indian
protesters—he noted the relationship between polity, tradition, and
subsistence: "We have always shared our resources. We have been pa-

tient, but our patience is wearing thin. We have our peace chiefs, ladies and gentlemen. And we also have our traditions and our rich culture to guide us. We don't look at these fish as something you put on a wall.[12] We've demonstrated over and over again, that the fish we take, we use for sustenance. We're a fishing people!"

After denouncing the state for not recognizing the economic contributions of Indians and for attempting to blame resource depletion on them, gaiashkibos drew attention to the prophetic aspect of the current conflict. "Let us not forget our traditional people, the people who belong to the drum, the people who carry the traditions of our tribe, because we are the generation that our grandfathers, in their wisdom, were thinking of when they reserved for us what [the land] we are standing on now today."

The newest participant in the spearfishing conflict, the American Indian Movement, was then heard. Edward Benton-Banai's daughter Sherole spoke for her father's old friend, Clyde Bellecourt. She read his message assuring everyone that AIM supported the effort and that no AIM member would be provoked into a violent response. Sherole then revealed that she had been told that many eagles were flying in the sky outside the hall. Those gathered inside broke out in whoops and applause. The presence of the eagles was a sign that a relationship between this world and the spirit world had been established, perhaps best thought of as the beginnings of a return gift for the pipe ceremony and unfolding rally.

Hilary Waukau (Menominee), the third vice president of the National Congress of American Indians and a U.S. Marine Corps veteran of the World War II Pacific campaign, was then introduced. Pointing out that most of the people on the speakers' stand were veterans, Waukau spoke as passionately about the effort that was currently required "to protect this land that our old people gave us to pass to our children" as he did about Indians' past contributions to fighting "the white man's wars" in defense "of this great country." Contributing some credibility to the capacity for force that lay behind the Lac du Flambeau band's commitment to nonviolence, he said that he had a white brother who fought by his side when taking the island of Saipan in 1944. "He told me that when the time comes, when you need some help for one last stand against oppression, you call me there and I'll be there to die with you." That time had not come yet but, Waukau ominously added, he could see that it was imminent.

William Means of AIM spoke last, setting the Walleye War within a national context. He began his remarks in Lakota, recalling the history of AIM's support for Indian rights: for Raymond Yellowthunder, who had been beaten to death by whites in South Dakota, and at Farmington, New Mexico, where AIM had uncovered a cult that required the finger of a Navajo child for membership. Means spoke of AIM's work in Oklahoma, where Indians were dying of suicide in the jails, and in Nevada to support the peyotists (members of the Native American Church harassed for their use of peyote in religious ceremonies). He mentioned Kentucky, where Indian burial grounds were being desecrated by the search for artifacts, and then moved on to remind listeners about the Wounded Knee occupation in 1973 and the novitiate takeover "just down the trail" at Menominee in 1974. "We took the power of the drum and we took the power of the pipe." When the first white had the privilege of seeing Turtle Island here, Means concluded, he saw spearfishing for the first time.

At the end of the speeches, those gathered were asked to clear the building so that the feast could be set up. Once outside, they were told that they would not be able to go into the community building next door because of a bomb threat; the sheriff's police were searching the premises. No anxiety greeted the news. Apparently, those at the rally had grown used to the presence of police and the threat of violence.

People instead visited outside on the lawn. Television crews from Chicago, Minneapolis, Milwaukee, Madison, and Wausau interviewed those leaders willing to speak. Young people gathered around the AIM drum, many wearing the brilliantly colored silk-like jackets decorated with neo-totemic emblems. Wa-Swa-Gon Treaty Association jackets worn by Flambeau tribal members were bright blue with a birch bark torch on the back; red AIM jackets marked with bold black and white lettering stood out in the crowd; Lac Courte Oreilles tribal members wore dazzling green jackets lettered with "Honor the Earth," their summer powwow.

Within an hour, everyone was invited back into the bingo hall to eat. Tables had been moved to accommodate scores of baking pans full of food. Corn soup, beans, potato salads, and deserts complemented numerous pans of walleye, wild rice, and venison that had been prepared in a few different ways in people's homes and in the kitchen of St. Anthony's Church, where three women active in the Wa-Swa-Gon Treaty Association worked. Elders and guests were invited to eat first. As is the custom at a feast, the hosts were asked to wait until all others were fed.

Fifteen hundred people were fed in less than an hour while telegrams of support from tribes around the United States were read aloud. Scott Smith, who had speared and then donated most of the walleye, was introduced by Tom Maulson and cheered by the feasters.

Tinker Schuman announced that there would be a pipe ceremony for women held outside; Sierra Powers of Witness for Non-Violence also called a meeting. By about 4:00 P.M., people were being encouraged to go back over to the gymnasium to dance as the bingo hall needed to be cleaned for Saturday night's business.

Edward Benton-Banai now assumed the role of powwow emcee. The altar from the prayer ceremony had been left in place in the gymnasium but the drum had been moved to center court. A few intertribal songs were sung and danced. The mood was happy, celebratory; people smiled and were confident. Nick Hockings and his wife led hundreds of couples in a round dance. Another intertribal song was sung. Nick Hockings took an active role in recruiting people to dance. "Come on!" he would say, gesturing, "this is for all nations."

Benton-Banai drew the dance to a close by directing everyone to go to Maulson's T&L, where a caravan of cars would be assembled before spearfishing that evening.

The Saturday pipe ceremony, feast, rally, and powwow at Flambeau brought more people to the reservation in one day than to any event since Dwight Eisenhower was adopted into the tribe in the mid-1960s. The speakers drew on multiple symbols of Ojibwe and pan-Indian identities, deeply rooting the conflict in local Indian culture and highlighting its significance for the intertribal Indian community. The sacrifice of tobacco and food, speeches, singing, drumming, and dancing were presentations to the spirits, gods, God. In traditional Ojibwe cosmology, the spirits of the walleye, deer, and wild rice that were consumed on that day were honored by this feast and now stood in a position to reestablish the balance with the Anishinaabes through blessings.

And the day was not over yet. Flambeau and its allies were returning to Butternut Lake.

WARFARE IN A REIMAGINED PAST

On an ordinary evening during the spearfishing season, the spearers would begin to arrive at T&L minimart an hour or so before sunset and gas up their vehicles. The cars, trucks, and vans that were gassing up on this late Saturday afternoon on May 6 were headed back toward the community center. A caravan that would stretch from St. Anthony's Church more than two miles back to T&L was being assembled for a drive to Butternut Lake. By the time the caravan was moving, over three hundred cars, most carrying at least four or five Indian people, began an hour-long journey north and west on Highway 47.

Non-Indians who lived along the route stood on the front lawns and porches of their homes, stores, and taverns as the procession made its way to Butternut Lake. Flambeau spearer Nick Hockings, who rode toward the front of the caravan, heard someone over the CB say, "Jesus Christ, the whole Chippewa nation is coming!" (Nesper 1989a).

That last night of spearfishing at Butternut Lake is remembered with great pride by Flambeau's tribal members as the only time that Indians outnumbered the protesters. It is recalled as the day that "we took Hamburger Hill," or "Butternut Hill," or "Walleye Summit"—all idioms of geographic repatriation. The significance of the event was not lost on some even as it was unfolding. A member of AIM as well as the father and son Flambeau team of Don and Scott Smith made videotapes of the assembling of the caravan and its arrival at Butternut Lake. Scott also made an audiocassette of the songs played by the AIM drum there.

The Smith videotape recording shows that the landing at Butternut Lake was very crowded that night. About six hundred non-Indian protesters and spectators were arrayed twenty or so deep along thirty yards of snow fence that the sheriff's police had stretched parallel to the landing. A few held signs denouncing spearing and treaty rights. Thirty "protester boats," alternatively referred to in a STA/W-made videotape as "the cavalry,"[13] lay in the shallow water off the landing preparing to make their "observation runs." Twenty-nine DNR boats patrolled the lake over the course of the evening. Two hundred and fifty sheriff's police separated the protesters from a narrow corridor of concrete that allowed access to the lake for the spearfishers. The protesters were in a good mood; the audio portion of the Smith tape is full of bits and pieces of genial conversation on the landing between protesters, punctuated only by Scott's quiet remark to his father: "We're gonna have them outnumbered."

AIM marshals in red jackets carrying walkie-talkies directed supporters through the darkness as they followed the AIM drum being played and accompanied by half a dozen singing men. The main body of more than a thousand mostly Indian people arrayed themselves alongside the protesters trailing the AIM drum.

The sight of a larger than usual number of supporters quieted the protesters for a short while. They became more active and vocal as more and more Indian supporters arrived, yelling taunts.

"Go back to where you fucking came from!"

"Go back to your fucking reservation!"

Supporters answered the chanting of "Equal rights! Equal rights!" with "Treaty rights! Treaty rights!" The spirit of General Custer was invoked by some protesters, who chanted, "Long live Custer!" until a supporter reminded them as the chant weakened, "He's dead. We killed him." Though the groups taunted each other and occasionally threw cigarette butts and small stones, most of the exchange was verbal. Individuals vocally sparred with anonymous opponents, displaying their wit to their surrounding confreres.

Part of the main body of protesters, perhaps a couple hundred, occupied a small hill no more than six feet high and fifty in circumference near the water at the landing. One man held a sign identifying himself as a Butternut Lake property owner; another waved an American flag. The AIM drum led the procession down to the landing, coming to rest just off the base of the hill. Supporters surrounded and stood facing the drum, their backs to the protesters.

Over the course of the evening, some of the larger treaty rights men interposed themselves as a first line between the supporters and protesters. Still facing the drum, they slowly began to step back and up the side of the hill. This undertaking was made up of numerous forceful acts, carefully calculated to stop short of the sheriff's definition of a violent act. During the next hour, the Indian supporters displaced the protesters from the hill, occupied it, and then called for the AIM drum to be placed on top.

While the supporters were slowly moving up the hill, the AIM anthem had given way to veterans' songs and finally to Round Dance or love songs with English lyrics, a twentieth-century innovation that preserved the "lub-dub" heartbeat drumbeat style of Woodlands women's dances.

> Whenever I am away from you, I always get those lovesick blues.
> Wayah hey hey heya. Wayah hey hay heya.

With the AIM flag unfurled, those surrounding and singing with the drum stood in place dancing, occasionally holding their hands above their heads in an ambiguous presentation of the "V" sign: for victory or for peace? In response, the protesters chanted a song often heard at professional baseball games: "Na-na-na-na. Na-na-na-na. Hey, hey, hey, Good bye." Before the hill had been completely occupied, a boat approached the shore with a spearer standing in the bow. He elevated his spear to reveal two walleye impaled on the tines. The men warwhooped and the women ululated as the singing grew louder.

Twenty-four spearers in eight boating parties were on the lake. Six of those parties carried permits for one walleye per spearer. The spearfishers would take sixty-three walleye, 18 percent of the tribal quota. Sixty to ninety permits were issued for one walleye each to provide an opportunity for as many spearers to fish as possible. The spearers finished by 11:00 P.M. Tom Maulson walked through the now mostly friendly crowd, telling people it was time to go home.

The following day, Mike Allen called a short press conference to announce that the season was temporarily over:

Yesterday we showed the State that there is strong support for us against racism and in support of the treaties. We showed that we can, if pressed, outnumber the racists at the landings. Earlier in the week, we showed that politicians can't take our right away with empty promises, and that the federal court will not be intimidated either. All season long, we have shown that racial violence can't bully us into surrendering the right. Having shown all of that, we have decided that it is time to stop for now.

I am announcing the end of the Lac du Flambeau spearing season. This was a decision made IN this community, BY this community, FOR this community.

It is a gesture of good will that neither the state officials nor the people of northern Wisconsin deserve, but that we are freely offering them anyway. (*Wausau Daily Herald* 1989j)

The depth of Flambeau's own conception of itself as autonomous and its disposition to construct and hold itself as separate are revealed in this hostile presentation of a gift—the closing of the season—to initiate a period of peace.

The experience at Butternut Lake in 1989 was a version and culmination of what had happened there twice before. The first time, in 1987, the spearfishers feared for their lives due to the inadequacy of local law enforcement. They had returned there three nights later with a few hundred supporters, spiritual leaders, and a drum, and fished ceremonially. The symbolic value of this action was compromised, though, because of the humiliation suffered a few nights before and the needed assistance of the county sheriff, whose officers had interdicted the landing to all but Indians and their supporters. In 1989 STA/W and PARR were defeated in their home territories and largely on Indian terms, with Indians deploying both spiritual and material resources to gain an unforgettable victory.

WAR PARTY

Ojibwe leaders who spoke and managed activities on that Saturday not only shared an implicit conception of leadership but also were inclined to incorporate people into their projects in similar ways. Instead of directly opposing each other, the leaders attempted to encompass and funnel each other's accumulated resources into their own agendas. Chairman Mike Allen sought to transform the conflict into a higher price for forbearance. Modern-day war chief Tom Maulson worked to transform the tribal council's negotiations with the state into a revaluation of the tribe's relationship with the federal government. AIM wanted to transform the fishing struggle into a broader, more national-based battle against racism, while the local leaders in turn sought to deploy AIM to further their own projects.

The outcome of these interactions on Saturday, May 6, 1989, was a social and ritual drama that bore a structural relationship to Ojibwe war parties of earlier times. This is not to say that the day's events had been consciously modeled on this knowledge of the bands' history. Rather, the activities that the different leaders sought to create were sequenced, or unfolded, in a certain way that made sense to everyone involved, an outcome resonating with their cultural history.

Like an Ojibwe war party, the day at Flambeau began with a pipe ceremony to which people had been invited as individuals. Like a war party, those who attended the pipe ceremony were not only feasted by the host but were offered more detailed explanations for the proposed course of action (see Densmore 1910:89). This information came at the rally, where Mike Allen, the official host, spoke first. The *ogimag*, tribal chairmen, and dignitaries from other reservations who were officially invited by Flambeau then spoke, and in doing so, rehearsed their own participation and deeds in different kinds of warfare. Those accounts recalled the rhetorical form of "striking the post," a traditional ritual retelling of war exploits that took place before men went off to war (see Densmore 1910:68; Johnston 1990:64–70; Warren 1984:332–334). Carrying the drum and the AIM flag to

Butternut Lake had its precedent in the drum and banner or flag that were carried on war expeditions. The colorful raiment worn by many that day evokes images of nineteenth-century "leaders arrayed . . . in brilliant trappings, bright feathers [which] rendered them conspicuous and showed their fearlessness" (Densmore 1910:91, 107).

The way in which the walleye were taken that night at Butternut Lake suggests that they were the symbolic equivalent of enemy body parts in all of their regenerative and reproductive power. The harvest was intentionally spread over as many spearers as possible that night, with many spearers interested in taking only one fish each. This meant that the spearfishers sought one large fish, a quest that became a kind of compensatory kidnapping, since a large fish would likely be female. With it widely recognized by Indian people that non-Indians were identifying with the walleye, fishing that evening was walleye warfare, as spearers took tokens of victory from this lake near what they called "PARR Falls." The fact that so many tribal members were interested in taking one fish further suggests that the speared walleye served as the symbolic equivalent of the scalps taken by their forebears. The most prominent of the spearers would later receive eagle feathers for their commitment to the off-reservation movement, and eagle feathers were historically signs of lives taken.

The singing of love songs, in English, by the allies and relatives of spearfishers while displacing non-Indian protesters from the land they occupied on a mock battlefield suggests the regenerativity of hunting and warfare. In Anishinaabemowin as in English the same terms can be used for both hunting and flirting. In the same way that warfare and the taking of scalps were regenerative of Ojibwe society before the practice was brought to an end in the treaty period, the conflation of hunting, warfare, and (songs about) sex at Butternut Lake signaled a deeply resonant, regenerative event for the modern Lac du Flambeau reservation.

7

Anishinaabe Summer

12. Carrying the AIM flag, members of the Wa-Swa-Gon Treaty Association march at the town of Minocqua's Fourth of July parade in 1989. Photo courtesy of the author.

Within days of the end of the 1989 season, the leaders of Wa-Swa-Gon Treaty Association were caught up in activities within and beyond the borders of Lac du Flambeau to gain more support for the treaty rights movement. Throughout the summer, they also intensified their efforts to shape the local revitalization of Ojibwe culture and prophecy that lay at the heart of the Walleye War. The broad-based coalition that had begun to develop that spring took root and blossomed. An alliance with the American Indian Movement and a host of non-Indian organizations helped the Wa-Swa-Gon Treaty Association to make a number of dramatic statements—including an epic walk across the state, a parade through Minocqua on the Fourth of July, and a showdown with the Flambeau tribal council at a reservation powwow. Such events worked to bolster the legitimacy of the WTA, mold tribal and public awareness of the spearfishing dispute, and further call into question the boundaries of cultural tradition the conflict evoked.

THE WAR AWAY FROM HOME

On May 11, four days after the Flambeau tribal council declared the spearing season temporarily over, four leaders of the spearfishing movement—Walter Bresette of the Red Cliff, and Nick Hockings, Scott Smith, and Tom Maulson of Lac du Flambeau—journeyed to Chicago to speak at a forum at the request of James Yellowbank of the Indian Treaty Rights Committee. The event was held at the United Church of Christ in Rogers Park on Chicago's far north side.

The importance of these four men seeing themselves and each other being listened to by a mostly unknown audience should not be underestimated. The City—meaning all cities—lies outside the known and significant reservation world, where the bonds of morality and accountability are perceived to be weakest. Indians occasionally will criticize those who represent themselves as super-Indians far away from home, where being an Indian is far easier than living up to the demanding moral standards of the reservation. Residents of reservations seem to recognize that identities simplify and essentialize with distance from the grounds of their original production. Representing the spearfishing conflict so far away from home, therefore, was a great risk for each of the leaders. What was said that night, then, became one of the operative histories of the 1989 season because it was communicated in that circumstance of trust.

About forty people attended the Treaty Rights Forum. Walter Bresette, as emcee, first introduced Scott Smith, who spoke about the value of spearing as a distinct Indian tradition and how he felt about seeing white high school acquaintances protesting at the boat landings. He presumed that the audience was more capable of recognizing the value of cultural distinctions than the local whites back in Wisconsin.

Of particular significance that night was Nick Hockings's stylized oratorical performance of what was one of the first public tellings of the events at Butternut Lake. Hockings drew connections between the current conflict, the Osh-ki-bi-ma-di-zeeg prophecy and revitalization of Ojibwa culture, and the importance of non-Indian interest and involvement in the struggle. The local conflict, he told those gathered, had global implications and their involvement in it had been prophesized.

Nick Hockings's comments are most comprehensive and revealing of the way in which the Walleye War was perceived and represented by the spearfishing leadership. Flambeau people were imagining and portraying themselves as the authoritative agents in an unfolding prophetic history. In transcribing his speech I choose a more poetic than prosaic style in order to foreground better his cadence, emphasis, and other rhetorical devices.[1]

> Boojoo!
> Biindigay Gezhick Giiwiitaakamikoaun indizhinikazh.
> Migizi nintotem.
> Waswaaganing nindoonjibah.
>
> I'm eagle clan and I come from Waswaaganing
>   what other Indians call Lac du Flambeau,
>   a long time ago it was called Waswaaganing
> Waswaaganing literally translates

"Waswa," means spearing, spearing with a torch.

"ganing," the locator, the place where it happens.

Waswaaganing, the place where they fish with a torch.

But spearing has been going on at Lac du Flambeau for many, many
hundreds of years, a long time before the non-Indians showed up.

I'm a teacher at the Lac du Flambeau grade school.

I teach culture. I tell *Winaboozhoo* stories.

I do many things that are really not in the school curriculum . . .

I teach the Ojibwe philosophy; I try to teach the Ojibwe philosophy.

Respect, love, humility, kindness,

 through stories, legends.

I use cedar, tobacco, sage, sweetgrass.

It's being done more and more on the reservations now. Because
 what they call

Neesh-wa-swi'ish-ko-day-kawn' literally translated means the Seven
 Fires Prophecy.

It talks about this time, this era that we're in.

Before I get into that I want to tell you about the spearing.

I been out there with Scott.

I been out there with Tom.

I been out there with many other, many other people.

I been out there with my wife, every night.

I been out there with a small young lady, about 115 pounds soaking
 wet.

Probably the bravest person I know.

Because these women, many of them non-Indian—and I see some
 of the women that were out there—at these landings,
 supporting us, I think they were very, very brave.

You can't imagine.

After a while you'd think you'd get immune to being swore at.

You'd think you would get immune to being told that you were,
 that you weren't going to get home that night,
 that you were going to get killed.

You'd think you'd get immune to being spit on.

You'd think you'd get immune to being . . . hit with rocks for a right
 that was granted by the Supreme Court of this land, their law.

You would think it would get easier . . .

Sometimes if we were to go out there by T&L,

it was kind of like a rallying point,
    Maulson's,
    a small grocery store and gas station where we would gather,
    kind of build ourselves up because here we were getting ready to
        go again.
We would go out there and talk amongst each other,
    trying to kind of joke around,
    make light of going out again,
    not knowing whether or not we were going to all come back.
Each night we would hear about maybe gunfire over a certain lake,
or somebody getting hit with a stone.
Definitely every night, every night that went on.

I talked with my brother, who was in the Air Force,
    101st Airborne, in Vietnam.
Him and his friends were describing the feeling that we would have
      before we would go.
How we would be joking around in, playing around as we were
going in these caravans wherever we were going.

Sometimes maybe no more than eight spearers were going to a
      certain lake,
    and others' cars would veer off going to another lake.
And as we were going,
you know, I would get this giddy feeling when we were driving
down the road,
feeling, joking, and laughing at just about anything and then all
of a sudden
once you got down to the landing, you begin to realize that
Jesus Christ, this is for real, you could get your,
you could get killed out here!

What the hell am I doing out here for ten fish?
Why am I jeopardizing my wife?
She wanted to go out, but why is this happening?
Then we'd be backing up the boat.
They would take our relatives,
    they would take them, our wives and our family,
    and they were put, mixed right in with this crowd,
    these people that were screaming and spitting at us,
    and that would be the last that you would see of them.
Maybe every once in a while you would catch a glimpse of them in

the lights with the generators going, police marching back and
    forth in front of you.
You never knew what in the hell was going on.
And you'd get down toward the water and start sliding the boat into
    the water
  and you knew,
    you knew you was gonna start getting hit with rocks at that time.
I don't know, I heard some people sometimes say that they were
    only rocks.
But you take a wrist rocket and you shoot somebody. It could kill ya.

And you never knew when you were going to get hit.
My friend got hit with a pretty good-sized rock in the back.
We're going along the lakeshore.
It's the easiest time for these people 'cause you're busy,
    you're fishing,
    you're going around with the motor going,
    you're looking,
    you've got a light on your head,
    you're watching . . .
I used to think about it the first couple of nights,
    about being blown off the bow of that boat,
    cause you're a real easy target.

And we're really lucky that it didn't happen to anybody.
Because, because I think there were a couple of things that
    happened.
Number one: We heard about some pipe ceremonies that were held
    here.
Believe me, these pipe ceremonies and these prayers that was
    happening here in this community, even though you couldn't
    be up there, were helpful.
Almost every night in Lac du Flambeau we'd have pipe ceremonies
    also.
And even before spearing we had a water ceremony.

These ceremonies are coming back to the reservation.
These water ceremonies haven't been held there for sixty, going on
    sixty-five years.
So they're beginning to come back to the Anishinaabe,
    because of that *Neesh-wa-swi'ish-ko-day-kawn'*,
that Seventh Fire Prophesy that I was telling you about.

These teachings are getting,
 getting stronger and stronger, and I think that spirit,
  that spirit of the Anishinaabe is returning.
It was always there but it's getting stronger and stronger.
It's being reinforced,
it's being reinforced by another part of the prophecy,
that talks about Osh-ki-bi-ma-di-zeeg.
That, translated, means New People.
It doesn't mean, it doesn't mean Ojibwe.
It means New People.
A New People will arise at this time.

And when we were going on these caravans,
 when we were going to these landings,
  each one of these cars had different people in it.
They weren't all Ojibwes.
There were blacks.
There were many whites.
There were Indians from different tribes.
They were supporting.
They were that New People that were acting with love and
  nonviolence.
That was the true Osh-ki-bi-ma-di-zeeg that that Seventh Fire
  Prophecy talks about. These were the people that were picking
  up, picking up this way.
This spirit, of the Anishinaabe Ojibwe.

And I remember this last place that we were going to be going to.
Butternut Lake. Right outside a town called Park Falls.
It's located, probably, right around thirty-five, forty miles from the
  reservation.
We had a big rally that afternoon there.
Some estimate, say that there were about fourteen, fifteen hundred
  people there. From all races, all four races were represented at
  that meeting there.
White, red, yellow, black.
Very powerful time there on that reservation.
After that rally ended,
 and all the cars were setting up,
  try to get lined up,
   try to get psyched up to travel again.

I don't think anybody realized how many people were there,
    started to get into their cars.
I was around the fifth or sixth car from the front of this caravan.
I happened to have a CB in my car.
Anyway, after quite a while, gassing up and getting ready,
we started off and as we'd go along we'd have the CB on and we were
    always being monitored by these anti-treaty people.
We were being monitored as we were going, and I remember
    hearing this one guy getting on and him saying,
"Holy Cuh-rist, the whole damn Ojibwe nation is on the move
    today!"
Cars were piling by.
This was the stand, this was the big stand that these people were
    going to make.

Park Falls.
This was the place that they were going to stop the Ojibwe.
This was the place that they were going to, hopefully, make them
    pay for all the other landings.
This was the place where they weren't going to be able to put their
    boats down and spear on that lake.

So these cars were filing down,
    they were going down to this landing.
What they would do . . .
A lot of us pulled down there.
There must have been eight hundred protesters down there with
    their cars,
and for the most part those public landings aren't any wider than
    this room.
So space is at a premium.
What they would do is park their cars down there and when
    we would get there we would have to park our cars sometimes
    half a mile away.
We'd put our boats down there and then we'd have to get out there
    and walk. And you always had a whole bunch of people.
And that's exactly what happened there that night.

I put my boat down there and then I had to go look for a parking
    space and I found one about a quarter-mile away.
And what would happen at that time, is generally,
something would happen to your car.

You would either get your tires slashed or scratched or your trim
    dented.
Things like that.
So we were waiting there and as we went down there,
    hundreds of screaming crazy people,
    hollering on the left side as we went down there.

Hundreds of them. You couldn't imagine, what it was like.
Right off in the distance you could see this rise where all of these
    protesters were waving their flags and screaming and hollering
    at the Indians that were down there putting their boat in.
These were all anti-treaty people.
So they were doing all their swearing and screaming and hollering,
waving their postcards, their flags, and whatnot.

Everybody was getting ready, all the spearers were getting down
    there, they were pushing off and you could hear,
back there in the distance,
    that this caravan, that was about three or four or five miles long.
I don't know how big it was, but it was taking that long for all these
    cars, all these pro-treaty people to park their cars and get out
    and start this march down to the landing.
You could hear that drum beat coming.
They didn't know what in the hell was going on.
More and more of these people kept coming along with that drum.

That hill became a symbol.
That hill became, they referred to as "Hamburger Hill."[2]
They had to take that hill. That was the objective.
So we were moving in a big wave.
People would say, "These protesters were around us spitting and
    throwing rocks . . ."

Each time we would rally before we would go out there,
    we'd have to talk to ourselves, to psyche ourselves up.
We're not going to do anything violent.
That's how we gotta win.
Everyone agreed,
everyone agreed that this was the way we were going to do it.
People moved down and were slowly moving in.
These protesters slowly backed up,
    pretty soon they were going down the other side.

They were moved out of the way.
There you could see those flags and those friendly faces,
and you knew that that hill was taken over.

So we pulled back in,
when we come back in with our boat and they called off the
    spearing,
all these people around there were friendly faces,
they were cheering, rather than being spit at and having rocks
    thrown at us.
One of the few times at any of the landings where the pro-treaty
    people outnumbered the anti-treaty people.
It was there. Butternut Lake.
They had upwards of eight, nine hundred people that came.
But when we, when they took a count, when they estimated how
    many we were, they said there were upwards of fifteen hundred
    . . . pro-treaty people.
And we owe it to these people . . . and I call these people,
Osh-ki-bi-ma-di-zeeg.

If you just read the history books, all the wars that have been fought,
    going far back in history. People are still killing each other . . .
And I would propose to the people that this is the true way . . .
That Ojibwes have shown how to really get things done.
You know the people that traveled in that caravan, they were all
    traveling in the spirit, they were all traveling as one people.
And I believe that that's the way that this world is going to be
    changed.
I have a good feeling that,
I have a good positive outlook on things, in general,
and I know that if could follow and keep to that,
that standard that those people up there kept to,
that night, on that lake,
that we might have hope for this time in general.

I want to leave you with one thought before I go.
We had a conference on one Saturday night in the middle of
    spearing.
A lot of religious people sitting in a big circle, about as big as this
    room.
There were ministers there with a lot of lay people, teachers.
We were told a lot of various and different things by a lot of people.

But the one thing that really struck me the most was
this little girl got up and she said,
"You know I really don't know too much about this treaty and what's
    been going on on the reservation, but my grandfather told my
    father and my father told me some very interesting things
    when I was younger.
My father told me that when we lived over in Germany,
my father is a Jew. We're Jewish. He said that when the Germans
    came after the Communists, we didn't do anything. When they
    came after the Polish people, they didn't do anything. When
    they came after other groups of people, my father said, they
    didn't do anything.
Finally when they came after us and we asked for help,
    there wasn't anybody to help us."
That's why Scott goes out in that boat.
That's why Tom goes out in that boat.
That's why I go out in that boat no matter what.
They're not going to keep us off those lakes . . .
Because we also know from all the people that showed up at that
    landing that there's a lot of people out here that care . . .

Hockings began his remarks in Anishinaabemowin, employing a stylized, neotraditional manner that conveys the linguistic competence embraced by so many contemporary Indian spiritual leaders. The rehearsal of the Osh-ki-bi-ma-di-zeeg prophecy was important in the context of the Indian Treaty Forum, since it was a diverse group listening. The prophecy helped explain the presence of that audience to themselves, to the other spearers, and to himself. Non-Indian people were being recruited to the Osh-ki-bi-ma-di-zeeg, and the prophecy was effectively coming true by virtue of its telling.

When referring to either the Weaving the Web conference or a meeting of witnesses at Treehaven, Wisconsin (the "Saturday afternoon meeting"), Hockings attempted to represent them as versions of the meeting that he was addressing. The little girl's story was designed to establish a common ground of sympathy and understanding with the audience. The story had been originally related by Sharon Metz of HONOR, who had worked more effectively than any other non-Indian to ally church groups to the Ojibwes' struggle (Whaley and Bresette 1994:113).

Much contemporary Ojibwe political rhetoric organizes action or space into fours as a sign of completeness; there is thus repetition in Hockings's oratory that builds to a climax, signaling that he is making an important point. He appeals throughout to the moral imaginations of the non-Indian audience, drawing upon analogies he imagines to fall within their experience. In representing the thoughts of other spearfishers, he indicates both their vulnerability to fear and their capacity to respond to the demands of the situation. There were also more women in the audience than men, and his narrative consequently honors his wife and the other women who came to the landing.

Hockings's emphasis on the spearfishers' commitment to nonviolence reflects their public position, despite some internal debate on the issue. He didn't entirely conceal the militaristic dimension of the movement, though, as indicated by his suggestion that the objective of spearfishing Butternut Lake was the seizure of a territory—"Hamburger Hill." The metaphor, perhaps learned from Hockings's brother in the 101st Airborne Division, which fought at that battle, helped elide the difference between service veterans and spearers.

Not only prophecy would be fulfilled by drawing more people into the treaty rights movement. In the bicultural political economy of the Northwoods, the ability of the four Ojibwe speakers in Chicago to attract metropolitan non-Indians would be regarded as a sign of power, on and off the reservations. The conflict would become further deracialized in the eyes of protesters, and more accommodating tribal members might question their position in the face of such outside support.

REDEFINITION AND REVITALIZATION

At the May 22, 1989, tribal council meeting, Nick Hockings, speaking on behalf of the Wa-Swa-Gon Treaty Association, asked the council for permission to set gill nets in lakes off the reservation in order to host a "spearing feast" on May 27 and to contribute walleye to the upcoming Three Fires Spring Midewiwin Ceremonies at Mole Lake (tribal council minutes, May 22, 1989). The decision to flatter the tribal council by "going through them," as is said, was strategic. It conveyed to the majority of the council membership that the value of the fish was understandable in the same terms that legitimized the very existence of the council—the walleye existed to help the people, to engender *pimada-ziwin*. Hockings's requests were granted.

At the Three Fires Spring Midewiwin Ceremonies at Mole Lake, Hockings asked to speak in the teaching lodge.[3] He requested that the summer ceremonies be held at Lac du Flambeau due to the spiritual need created by the deep hostility between Indians and whites. Hockings then asked the non-Indian supporters of the spearfishers who were present to stand in recognition of their efforts on behalf of the Anishinaabe people. Half a dozen stood. This act further galvanized the relationship between these supporters, Hockings (and, by association, the people of Lac du Flambeau), and the Three Fires Lodge, adding more credibility to the millenarian sensibility that was increasingly being expressed and lived out in the political and spiritual realms of local Ojibwe culture.

On Saturday, May 27, 1989, the Wa-Swa-Gon Treaty Association hosted a thanksgiving feast at the tribally owned Wa-Swa-Gon campground managed by Tom Maulson.[4] The event, a further shaping and unfolding of the concept of Osh-ki-bi-ma-di-zeeg, was held to acknowledge the non-Indians in the region who had supported or Witnessed at the landings during the 1989 season. Attending from Flambeau were a dozen or so tribal members, the most active core of the spearfishing faction, but none from the tribal council.

A pipe ceremony opened the event, conducted by Eugene Begay and Edward Benton-Banai in front of the campground's administrative building. Structurally very similar to the ritual preceding the rally held three weeks before, this pipe ceremony featured a more elaborate role for the sacrificer who distributed tobacco. Tinker Schuman again was asked to bless and distribute the water to all interested in this communion. Participants were asked to put their tobacco in nearby Flambeau Lake or at the base of a tree and then to return for a special ceremony that would be conducted by Benton-Banai. Such detailed instruction suggests an awareness by the leader that the event had an educational function.

Until the blessing, Tinker held the AIM flag with the Plains Indian on the Stars and Stripes, which was also hanging from the peak of the administrative building. This display of the flag in a ceremonial context facilitated its transformation from "the AIM flag," "the Indian flag," "the Plains Indian flag," or "Indian Joe" into what would be called "the banner of the treaty association," a pan-Indian symbol seen locally as evoking a reawakening of Ojibwe cultural consciousness.

Four *ogitchida* were presented with eagle feathers on behalf of the Wa-Swa-Gon Treaty Association. The first feather was given to Tom Maulson, honoring his willingness to fight for hunting and fishing rights and validating his leadership of the spearfishers. Neil Kmiecik of GLIWFC received a feather for his encouragement, research, and support of the exercise of the treaty rights. Kmiecik, a descendant of the Hunkpapa Sioux, was redefining his own identity during the spearing conflict. Honoring Kmiecik also acknowledged and strengthened the kinship between Flambeau and GLIWFC. Last, Flambeau tribal members Maggie Johnson and her sister Dorothy Thoms were called up together. In their sixties, they cried as they ambled up on their canes. Edwards and Thoms had stood on the boat landings for the last three seasons in support of spearers on the lakes.

Eagle feathers are intricately connected to Ojibwe warfare, their current use based on their traditional value as honors worn only by warriors who had taken or assisted in taking human life (McGee 1888).

Upon the receipt of a feather—a gesture that appeared to incorporate elements of contemporary knighting ceremonies—the *ogitchida* was touched on each shoulder with the feather and finally on the head. A drum then sounded four times. Benton-Banai asked the drum for an honor song. As the song started and the men removed their hats, the four *ogitchida* began to dance in a slow style typical of the Dream Dance from the early twentieth century, a dance often used in honor songs. An eagle was sighted overhead. The principals in the ceremony immediately responded, the presence of the eagle a confirmation that Gizhe Manido was observing "the doings." Benton-Banai explained the significance of the eagle as the major intermediary between Gizhe Manido and the Anishinaabe people, a gift for the people's faithfulness to his original instructions.

All were then invited to partake of a feast of wild rice, venison, walleye, and fry bread. At the same time, beneath a large pine tree on the shores of Flambeau Lake two hundred yards away, Tom Maulson, in his capacity as tribal judge—wearing both his judicial robe and his eagle feather in his "Walleye Warrior" baseball cap—married two spearers, Lisa Sorensen (one of a handful of women who speared) and Robert Martin. Eugene Begay then prayed over the couple and spoke to them about their responsibilities to each other and their families.

The linking of a thanksgiving feast mostly for nontribal members with the wedding ceremony of two spearers reflected the creativity of the middle ground between Indian and non-Indian civic ceremonial culture and expressed again the vital component of the struggle that had been dramatically manifested at Butternut Lake—the generativity of the spearfishing conflict. When the public wedding ceremony is placed in the context of the distribution of eagle feathers, traditional foods, music, and tobacco, and the sharing of thoughtful and thankful and prayerful words, the event effectively solidified the incorporation of tribal members, nontribal Indians, and non-Indians into an alliance grounded not only in the exercise of the off-reservation rights but also in a shared commitment to a more encompassing public morality that celebrated cultural diversity, grassroots democracy, and meaningful personal relationships.

At Flambeau, a powerful political and spiritual alliance for treaty rights was growing that included non-Indians and nontribal members in ceremonies and an expansive social life. AIM's recent visibility in the conflict provided an avenue to continue building and broadening this coalition by appealing to urban and other reservation Indians. For such an audience, the spearing conflict was a version of the oppression that whites visited on Indians in general. Mike Chosa was invited to speak by Clyde Bellecourt at an AIM meeting in Minneapolis a few weeks after the events at Butternut Lake. Chosa's affines were members of the St. Croix band, who first invited AIM into the spearfishing dispute. Aiming his remarks at the younger Indian listeners, Chosa first identified himself as Lac du Flambeau—"That means the torch. Where you spear." After reciting his qualifications to speak as a long-time leader of Indian protests, he drew on personal experiences of racism and abuse to sound pan-Indian themes of oppression:

> I can tell you some of the things that went on when we pulled our
>   boat down to the landing.
> And they (the sheriff's police) said, "You'll have to drive your
>   vehicle out, into that crowd.
> And you'll have to take your chances down there."
> So we did.
> And I took my grandchildren, Billy and Tanya,
> two young kids about ten, eleven years old.
> And we drove the van out and those vehicles followed us all around,
> for about three or four miles.

And they finally caught up to us.
And they started running after us.
And they started to tip the van,
and they were shooting and hitting the van with rocks.
They were trying to tip the van over.
Can you imagine the emotional things that these kids have gone
    through?
Looking at those people, hurling curses at them, insults?
Calling them little sluts, little timber niggers, they said.
"Go have another kid," they told that little girl, "Go have another
    kid."
Like that, that's how they talk, those people.

Chosa then leveled criticism against non-Indians in power. The governor was castigated for attempting to stop Indians from fishing, and for his failure to recognize that Indian people had suffered more than whites through this season. He also criticized the police and the Wisconsin Department of Natural Resources for failing to protect the spearfishers.

They don't have any care at all,
nothing in their hearts for our people in Wisconsin,
our Indian people.
They never will.

This moral characterization struck a resonant chord in the audience. In both the urban and the reservation experience, the whites in positions of power have no place for Indians "in their hearts." This is a metaphor for the love that ideally characterizes Indian kinship relationships on reservations and within urban, multitribal enclaves. Chosa concluded his speech in a rousing, almost militaristic fashion, emphasizing themes of struggle, leadership, and victories like Butternut Lake.

Those are the kinds of victories that we need.
Those are the kind of victories that we gotta strive for,
to bring our people together,
to fight to protect our rights, and not to sell them out, not to lease
    them to nobody.
Because these young people here are going to have to enjoy those
    rights in order to survive later on when we're gone.
And we have to be strong now amidst those insults and those rocks

and the ball bearings and the insults. And protect those rights
for our people.
And our tribal leaders have to stand up too and help us and we will
help them.
Because that's what needs to be done.

And you don't know how it felt when we were out on that lake,
and all that stuff was happening to us,
and we shut the motor off and we stopped and listened and there
was the drum.
It was AIM,
on our shoreline.
You don't know how good that felt.
And the only reason that they was able to be there was because of
leaders like Louie [Louis Taylor, the tribal chairman of the St.
Croix band]
was able to call them and they was able to come there and show
their support.
Flambeau called AIM and they showed up there, too.

You don't know how good that is to see Indian people come
together.
Our brothers and sisters from here, in the Cities, from Minnesota,
from all over and they come and they stood with us at the landings.

You don't know how good it was when we went to Butternut Lake on
Saturday,
and there was a line of Indian cars and supporters that stretched for
fifteen miles.
When we got there those protesters were on a hill,
they were already standing on a hill, and they took that hill,

and the Indian people and the white supporters,
they were down in the swamp.
And they just slowly edged up that hill and they took that hill.
[Applause]

Those are the kind of victories, that are small victories, few and far
between.
Those are the kind that count.
Those are the kind that these young people can understand.
They don't understand program money.
They don't understand delegations.

They don't understand nothing.
They do understand when their parents, and their grandparents,
     and their tribal leaders
stand up and say, "We're going to protect their rights."

In mid-June, twenty supporters of Ojibwe treaty rights undertook a six-day walk from Lac du Flambeau to the state capital at Madison, 220 miles away. Labeled "Walking Together for Justice and Peace," the event was another attempt to publicize the spearfishing dispute and attract supporters. The walk was organized by a coalition consisting of GLIFWC, HONOR, the Great Lakes Inter-tribal council, the Wisconsin Council of Churches, and a number of treaty rights support groups. Ending the walk in Madison was a good chance to attract more supporters to the treaty rights movement. The city is not only the legislative and governmental center of the state, but boasts a reputation as a center of political activism. Madison is an hour's drive from Milwaukee, the home of the founders of the Witness for Non-Violence and about a three-hour drive from Chicago, where the Indian Treaty Rights Committee had been organized.

The political objectives of the walk were announced in *News from Indian Country,* the nationally distributed Indian newspaper published at the Lac Courte Oreilles reservation: "This walk is a spiritual and symbolic joining of Indians and non-Indians to decry the racist outpouring against Chippewa Spearfishing. Selected participants will walk and carry a spiritual pipe from the Lac du Flambeau Reservation to the State Capital" (1989c). This symbolic political form had been learned in the civil rights movement.

Prominent among the walkers were Tom Maulson, James Schlender, the executive director of GLIFWC, and Nick and Charlotte Hockings. Accompanying them were members of AIM, non-Indian supporters, and other Wisconsin Ojibwes. The walkers carried a pipe that had been ceremonially filled with tobacco at the traditional Bear River powwow grounds near the Old Indian Village at Lac du Flambeau. Also taken and prominently displayed was what the June 23 issue of the *Lakeland Times* referred to as "a controversial American flag with a Native American superimposed on the Stars and Stripes."

The decision to carry a ceremonial pipe filled with tobacco along with the flag linked the concerns of an Ojibwe spiritual center in the Northwoods to the state's political center in Madison through the appropriation of an American political symbolic form for an Ojibwe ceremony. Approximately half the distance between Lac du Flambeau and Madison lies within the ceded territory; walking through it carrying the spiritual pipe and transformed flag represented another dimension of its repatriation. The specific form of protest—a walk between a spiritual and a political capital through hostile territory—had been used before by the Red Power movement of the previous decade. The Menominees in Wisconsin undertook such a walk in their successful effort to retribalize in the 1970s. "Walking Together for Justice and Peace" also recalled the "Trail of Broken Treaties"—in which Edward Benton-Banai had participated—that crossed the continent in 1972. The use of this form was an attempt to give credibility to an Ojibwe understanding of the conflict.

When threatened with arrest for displaying the "controversial" flag in Minocqua, the walkers acquiesced by wrapping the flag around the consecrated ceremonial pipe and then proceeded on their way. Their response simultaneously avoided arrest, honored the pipe, and, by physically associating the objects, further sacralized the flag. This gesture also reinforced the activists' ongoing efforts to remind non-Indians of the connection between the bands and the U.S. government and to help shape that relationship.

More walkers joined the group each day. By the time they reached East Washington Street near the center of Madison, five hundred supporters, about a dozen carrying the "controversial" flag, had joined them. The AIM flag was clearly gaining currency in the local struggle. Dorothy Thoms carried the pipe the last leg of the journey. On the steps of the capital building, Edward Benton-Banai completed the pipe ceremony that had begun six days before by praying in Anishinaabemowin, addressing Gizhe Manido, Tunkashila (a Lakota appellation that is becoming a pan-Indian term), Allah, and God. His prayer connected the spearfishing dispute to oppression against blacks, women, indigenous people all over the world, and the students who had just been attacked in Tiananmen Square in the People's Republic of China. Benton-Banai's use of multiple names for a monotheistic god and his references to injustices in many parts of the world continued a key theme initiated at the "Weave the Web" conference two and a half months earlier. The "racist outpouring against Chippewa spearfishing" was an incidence of a type; those who opposed any injustice could stand in solidarity with Ojibwes and do something about them all. Once again, an event sponsored by treaty rights advocates globalized local concerns and localized global ones.

Afterward, at a potluck feast hosted by the Madison Treaty Rights Support Group in a nearby park, Hockings and Maulson encouraged the hundreds of supporters to come to Lac du Flambeau on the Fourth of July to protest the tribal council's return to the bargaining table.

By "Walking Together for Justice and Peace," Indians and their supporters were not calling for respect of their understanding of fish biology, asking for acknowledgement of the value of separate collective rights, or even requesting recognition of their traditions. They were denouncing racism as Americans, and they hoped by doing so to gain some tolerance for the practice of spearing.

Many more outsiders were recruited to the treaty rights movement that afternoon in Madison.

INTO THE HEART OF ENEMY TERRITORY

The float and marchers of the Wa-Swa-Gon Treaty Association dominated the 1989 Fourth of July parade at the towns of Lac du Flambeau and Minocqua.[5] Organized yearly by Lac du Flambeau's chamber of commerce, which is mostly non-Indian, the parade usually features floats and marchers representing non-Indian civic, military, and youth organizations; summer camps; lake associations; and resort businesses as well as tribal social programs and a drum, singers, and dancers from the Indian Bowl, the site of the tourist powwow.

Nick Hockings led the treaty supporters in the Lac du Flambeau Fourth of July parade. His forehead painted red and wearing a traditional dance outfit of eagle feather bustle, breastplate, leggings, and moccasins, he carried a staff with thirty eagle feathers affixed to it.[6] Hockings led a pickup truck bearing a shield four feet in diameter, depicting a flaming birch bark torch and the words "Wa-Swa-Gon Treaty Assoc." lettered around the circumference. The AIM drum and singers sat in the back of the truck. Four smaller shields adorned Tom Maulson's pontoon boat, towed by the truck. A string of ten plastic American flags hung from each side of the boat, and red, yellow, and white ribbons stretched from the canopy to the railings. The Bear River powwow princess stood in the front of the boat while tribal elders, children, and one of the few African-American supporters of the spearfishers sat on the seats. The range of people on the float evoked images of the Osh-ki-bi-ma-di-zeeg. A few hundred non-Indian and Indian supporters walked behind, including AIM members from the Twin Cities and treaty support organizations from the cities of the region. They bore the banners of the United Tribes of Milwaukee, the Trail of Broken Treaties, Tourists for Treaty Rights, the Big Mountain (Navajo) Support Group, Witness for Non-Violence; some carried placards calling for diversity to be respected and thanking Judge Barbara Crabb.

The WTA's participation in the Lac du Flambeau parade was not welcomed by the members of the Flambeau tribal council. It did, however, serve as a useful rehearsal for the Minocqua Fourth of July parade that afternoon; there the effect was to further polarize opinion and deepen the political fault line among tribal members.

After the Lac du Flambeau parade, about two hundred participants, two-thirds of whom were non-Indians, came to the Wa-Swa-Gon campground at the reservation for a rally and pipe ceremony. It is a measure of the steadily widening effects of the spearfishing struggle that Verne Bellecourt of AIM and famed Menominee activist Ada Deer spoke there, both situating the conflict within a national context.

A much more hostile reception awaited the Wa-Swa-Gon Treaty Association's float and marchers in Minocqua that day. Nick Hockings led the float down Main Street, in full men's traditional dance regalia, making expansive and inclusive gestures with his arms. AIM flags were prominently visible around Tom Maulson, who wore a new ribbon shirt printed with American flags, given to him by AIM, and carried a fourteen-foot fishing spear. Two flags were affixed to the top of the spear: an ordinary American flag and above it, the AIM flag. It was estimated that more than four hundred people marched behind the Wa-Swa-Gon float, far more than all those in the rest of the parade. The imbalance disturbed the harmony of the civic parade, already rather fragile because of WTA's mere presence.

The reactions of non-Indian people lining the three-block parade route through the commercial downtown district echoed the treatment of the spearfishers at the boat landings. Though most of the hundreds of people standing on the sidewalks just stared—many were tourists—some booed, and others chanted, "Stop Treaty Abuse!" Non-Indian service veterans in uniform, holding American flags and black and white POW-MIA flags, turned their backs on the Wa-Swa-Gon float. One man stood silent, hands held over his head, middle fingers extended. Someone threw an empty pop can at an Indian flag bearer; another person threw half a bucket of ice cubes. Carrying a bullhorn, Clyde Bellecourt of AIM interpreted the significance of the parade for those watching, denouncing racism and extolling brotherly love. His remarks were as provocative as they were educational, especially since he responded directly to some of the protesters.

STA/W's parade contribution of half a dozen citizens dressed as loons festooned in a tennis net, a commentary on the putatively deleterious environmental effects of Indian gill netting, followed the Wa-Swa-Gon float and marchers at some distance and was welcome relief for the crowd. The STA/W marchers were cheered as conquering heroes.

Marching through Minocqua is remembered as a great day of victory at Lac du Flambeau by the spearfishers and their families. An unprecedented coalition of Indian and non-Indian groups had successfully protested at the local center of anti-treaty sentiment. No arrests were made. The Fourth of July parade is remembered with humor partially because it has some of the qualities of a successful violating foray beyond reservation borders. It is also humorous because of the way that the event effectively commented on the structure of elementary social, economic, and political life of the non-Indian residents of Minocqua-Woodruff. The last thing that the town fathers of Minocqua would have wanted in a celebration of a homogenizing American identity would be its domination by people who neither lived there nor were its lifeblood. At the same time, had the non-Indian leaders either refused to issue a parade permit to the Wa-Swa-Gon Treaty Association or attempted to arrest their flag bearers, they would have offended tourists and thus done far more damage to the image of the town than they did by allowing a pluralistic rain to fall on their parade.

THE FIGHT FOR LEGITIMACY

Such efforts to build and use a coalition by the treaty rights leaders at Lac du Flambeau intensified the disagreements between the tribal council and the Wa-Swa-Gon Treaty Association. Sensitive to the reservation's relations with the surrounding communities and responsive to Indian and non-Indian veterans' unhappiness over the display of the AIM flag on the Fourth of July, the Flambeau tribal council voted unanimously three days later in a telephone poll to ban "U.S. flags with an Indian figure superimposed on them from Lac du Flambeau tribal property and from official functions" (*Lakeland Times* 1989d). This resolution probably also reflects the council's attempt to regulate the Wa-Swa-Gon Treaty Association's presence at the tribally sponsored Seventh Annual Bear River Pow Wow, whose first Grand Entry would take place the next day.

The term powwow derives from the Algonquian *bawana* and the Cree *pamamiw* and has a complicated history. It has referred to a medicine man; the conjuring of a medicine man; a dance, feast, or celebration preceding a council, expedition, or hunt; a council and conference (Hodge 1959). Over the second half of the twentieth century, powwow has come to refer to a pan-Indian dance form usually accompanied by a feast. The modern powwow has its roots in three Plains ceremonial associations—the War Dance, also known as the Sioux, Grass, and Omaha Dances; the Squaw Dance; and the Dream Dance (see Barrett 1911; Densmore 1910; Slotkin 1957; Rynkiewich 1980; Vennum 1982). In a typical powwow, costumed dancers dance in various combinations in a circular arena, while groups of drummers sing at a large drum. Dancing to a drum is understood as form of prayer that reestablishes the dancer's relationship with the ultimate source of authority and power in the form of a *pawaganak* or dream visitor acquired as an adolescent. Powwows usually last for two or three days and are scheduled for weekends.

The Indian Bowl was built in 1951 on the site of the lumber mill at Lac du Flambeau for the explicit purpose of displaying powwow dancing as a tourist attraction. Shortly after the *Voigt* decision in January 1983, a small group of people began to organize in an effort to bring back what was argued to be a more traditional form of ceremonial expression to the Bear River dancing grounds, the site of Dream Dances and tourist powwows during the first half of the century. The Bear River powwow was said to be "traditional" as opposed to either "competitive" or "tourist": it was located on a site previously used for ceremonies; participants could camp there indefinitely; a sacred fire blazed at the eastern end of the dance arbor, prize money and competitive dancing were forbidden; the powwow featured giveaways, feasts, and an ongoing debate about whether an admission charge was acceptable.

An important element of both the War Dance and the Dream Dance that has been preserved in the Ojibwe powwow is the spontaneous speeches that are sometimes given by elders exhorting listeners to maintain their old ways. This is the basis of the use of modern powwows for political purposes (Avruch 1972:54), especially in Wisconsin Ojibwe country, where tribal powwow committees have superseded the custodianship of non-Indian entrepreneurs.

The political dimension of the powwow and the traditional Ojibwe manifestation of individualism were very much in evidence on Saturday afternoon, July 8, 1989.[7] At the Bear River Pow Wow, seven banned treaty flags waving from individual campsites and traders' stalls greeted Mike Allen as he welcomed everyone from the speaker's stand. The flags were ignored.

The next day, the leaders of the Wa-Swa-Gon Treaty Association took advantage of the general community commitment to individual liberty and made the powwow committee choose between upholding Ojibwe tradition and exercising the tribal sovereignty guaranteed by the federal government. On Sunday afternoon, in an action planned that morning at an open meeting of the Wa-Swa-Gon Treaty Association at the Outpost Cafe, Nick Hockings brought an Honor Song request to the powwow committee. He asked for a song for the spearfishers and their supporters for the work they were doing for peace and justice. The request was undertaken in the proper manner and so was acknowledged and made part of an Honor Song that was scheduled for 3:00 P.M.

As the song for the spearers started, Archie Mosay, a venerated elder, "traditional," and Mide lodge owner from the St. Croix area, danced into the arena. Kuno Blackhawk, a Ho-Chunk veteran of the Wounded Knee occupation and husband of a Flambeau tribal member, followed Mosay, carrying the treaty flag. Dozens of others began dancing into the arena.

Recognizing what was happening, the secretary-treasurer of the powwow committee walked into the arena, up to the drum, and stopped the song. A moment of stunned silence followed.

Walter Bresette, whose booth was displaying and selling treaty flags among other arts, crafts, and books, saw what was happening and began walking from drum to drum, asking who would sing for treaty rights. The leader from Mille Lacs in Minnesota—a drum that included a member of the Lac du Flambeau tribal council—took up and finished the song. The dancing began again; more and more people joined the dancers in the arena. When the song came near to its end, a veteran blew an eagle bone whistle over the drum and the song was repeated. This was done three more times, the maximum permitted by custom.

Members of both the tribal council and the Wa-Swa-Gon Treaty Association claimed that a number of people left the powwow grounds because of the incident. Council supporters declared that those who left were offended by the appearance of the forbidden treaty flag. WTA supporters argued that the exodus was due to the stopping of an Honor Song. Both groups sought to delegitimize the actions of the other by appealing to values that could be construed as traditional.

The flag dispute further polarized the Flambeau community over the meaning of the value of the treaty rights. In general, the generation in their sixties and early seventies who had fought in the Second World War did not like the treaty flag. The next generation, in their mid-forties, whose warriors had gone to Vietnam or were part of post–World War occupations, favored it. Both the tribal council and the WTA attempted to ally the more senior generation in the legitimization of their agendas.

The Flambeau tribal council scored a victory against the rebellious spearfishers on the following Thursday afternoon. They had requested of the Bear River Pow Wow committee that Nelson Sheppo (Potawatomi), a longtime resident, conduct a blessing at the powwow grounds. Sheppo had prayed at both the May 6 rally and in the Fourth of July parade at Lac du Flambeau. The blessing was accompanied by a feast and a mini-powwow. Among others, Dave Carufel sang and Chairman Mike Allen danced (*Lakeland Times* 1989e).

Sheppo prayed to the "Great Spirit," not Gizhe Manido, a significant difference. Different terms are used by different Ojibwe generations and mark different styles of inclusion, with the use of the "Great Spirit" generally signaling a more accommodationist attitude than Gizhe Manido. Sheppo concluded his prayer by saying that the Indian way was being lost, thus casting Wa-Swa-Gon's innovative ceremonialism as decadence rather than rebirth. Sheppo's remarks at the behest of the tribal council indicate that both factions at Flambeau were actively competing for traditional cultural legitimacy in the summer of 1989 by representing themselves as being or having access to the last "traditional" generation.

A reporter from the *Lakeland Times*, a newspaper invariably hostile to the spearfishers, was invited by the tribal council to the event. He reported that the blessing "reconsecrated the pow-wow grounds," which had been "dishonored after Tom Maulson breached etiquette and requested an honor song for the Wa-Swa-Gon Treaty Association's spearers and flew the controversial Indian flag though asked not to" (*Lakeland Times* 1989e). But the appearance of a flag that had been banned only a few days before cannot be the sole motivation for the complex ceremony that took place on that Thursday. Spiritual as well as political considerations guided the tribal council's actions, as they did the Wa-Swa-Gon Treaty Association. Interrupting an Honor Song is a serious matter, at least as powerful an act as violating a tribal council's resolution. To stop a song dishonors those who dance, drum, and sing, no matter the motivation. Interrupting a song is a willful violation of the autonomy of a number of others, a spiritually dangerous act since it invites spiritual retribution. The feast, blessing, and mini-powwow that Thursday in many ways were payment for that action. The event could also be used by the tribal council to promote its sensitivity to traditional spiritual matters; to impugn the spearfishers was an added benefit.

The leadership of the Wa-Swa-Gon Treaty Association did not have long to wait to continue legitimizing their agenda in a putatively traditional manner. "Honor the Earth," the oldest of the region's revitalized traditional powwows, was held the weekend following the Bear River powwow at the Lac Courte Oreilles reservation, two days after the Flambeau tribal council's "reconsecration." In a spectacular display of broad and deep support for treaty rights, a World War I–vintage Drum Dance society called "The Soldier's Drum" of Lac Courte Oreilles honored the contested AIM flag as the banner of the Wa-Swa-Gon Treaty Association at this powwow.

Shortly before the powwow was to begin early on Saturday afternoon, the main emcee, Edward Benton-Banai, announced that a special event would precede Grand Entry. Grand Entry, originally a form appropriated from rodeo, is usually the first event at a powwow. Indian U.S. Armed Service veterans (not necessarily dressed in dancing outfits) dance one and a half times around the dance arena to an Honor Song, bearing an eagle staff, American and often Canadian flags, and the POW-MIA flag. They are followed by the categories of dancers present—usually men's traditional, women's traditional, men's fancy, women's fancy shawl, Grass dancers, and Jingle dress dancers—then by age groups in the same categories, thus presenting a model of the social distinctions in contemporary Ojibwe society. The costumed dancers continue to circle the arena dancing while the staff and flag bearers dance in place 180 degrees opposite the arena entrance and facing the center of the arena.

Before the Grand Entry at the "Honor the Earth" powwow, Tom Maulson and Gilbert Chapman began to dance slowly around the arbor. Maulson held the now-shortened shaft of his fishing spear, and Chapman carried the treaty flag. They were then joined by hundreds of mostly Indian dancers from Lac Courte Oreilles and neighboring reservations. Some of the dancers were costumed, but most were not. When the dancers had made a full circle of the arena, the treaty flag was attached to the staff and Benton-Banai invited the crowd to honor the staff by attaching medicines to it. A man walked up and affixed a medal earned in Vietnam to the staff. Others advanced and attached items such as a hoop of sweetgrass, the shell of a turtle, a small leather bag of tobacco, and eagle feathers. While this took place, some excitement rippled through the dancers as eagles were sighted on the horizon. The appearance of these birds, proclaimed Benton-Banai, signaled the spiritual recognition and ratification of the Wa-Swa-Gon Treaty Association's goals. The arena was nearly completely filled with people dancing very hard in response to what was widely understood as a kind of epiphany.

The AIM flag had completed a further transformation. Because the honoring took place before Grand Entry, the treaty flag would be able to assume an equal place with the other flags for this and subsequent Grand Entries at powwows over the course of the summer. Through this ceremonial event, the flag became a more inclusive symbol of the willingness to fight for the distinction of remaining Ojibwe as realized in the practice of traditional subsistence practices. The gifts of medicine to the banner created a host of obligations to it. Those medicines were presented by veterans and elders, the most prestigious Ojibwe social categories today, thus weaving together "Walleye Warfare," armed service, and the WTA's interpretation of tradition. This action presumably helped to diffuse somewhat the Indian veterans' unhappiness with the WTA over the AIM flag and appropriation of the warrior term *ogitchida*.

Importantly, the Wa-Swa-Gon Treaty Association was now legitimated as an Ojibwe society by virtue of this ceremony and cast as a guardian of tradition. The Lac du Flambeau tribal council became increasingly isolated and under fire due to their continuing willingness to negotiate an arrangement with the state of Wisconsin, an exchange seen by a growing number as commodifying and compromising activities that were distinctly and irreducibly Ojibwe.

Indeed, the very day that the AIM flag became the banner of the WTA, the Lac Courte Oreilles tribal council voted that they would not negotiate with the state over the exercise of their treaty rights.

8

The Referendum

13. Flambeau tribal member Scott
Smith cleans walleyed pike. Photo
courtesy of the author.

Ojibwe society is made up of kindreds whose extensions and alliances are constantly shifting, contracting, and expanding (Smith 1974:9). People are related to each other in multiple ways, and kinship is typically manipulated for purposes of increasing and decreasing social distance and its attendant responsibilities and privileges. The combination of an egalitarian ethic, limited means, the high value placed on generosity, and the competition between families for prestige has resulted in factionalism on the reservations today. One of the ways in which these local groups are formed and maintained is through gossip, since it represents a moral consensus.

Characterizing Ojibwe psychology, Hallowell (1955:139) quotes Le Jeune's *Relation* describing the related Montagnais's penchant for backbiting: "The Savages are slanderous beyond all belief; I say, also among themselves, for they do not even spare their nearest relations, and with it all they are deceitful. For, if one speaks ill of another, they all jeer with loud laughter; if the other appears on the scene the first one will show him as much affection and treat him with as much love, as if he had elevated him to the third heaven by his praise" (Thwaites 1897, 6:247).

At Lac du Flambeau, when one "speaks ill of another" and that person is on the tribal council, it is called "being political";[1] there is little mystification of the process of negotiating the allocation of public goods. Backbiting and gossip as signs of factionalism are widely lamented by tribal members and have been studied extensively by scholars.[2] Gossip has its positive side, however. Not only does it maintain the unity of the kindreds (Smith 1974:9), factionalism on a reservation

operates to preserve and validate the great values placed upon equality and participatory, consensual democracy; it stresses the importance of the immediate kinsmen as a cooperative group and the potential significance of the more distant relatives of the major and maximal kindred as possible allies; and it prevents long term political dominance and economic exploitation by any single major kin group or faction. Above all, it is, given the limited arena of political activity a successful system for preserving an egalitarian ethic and society. The negative comment so often made by those of ability and ambition is that "they won't let anybody get ahead"; a positive restatement would be to the effect that the people believe that all should rise together, without any major disparities in terms of economic or political advantage. (Smith 1974:10–11)

At Lac du Flambeau, the goal of the Wa-Swa-Gon Treaty Association was to discount the tribal council's understanding of the value of the off-reservation hunting, fishing, and gathering rights and to halt negotiations with the state. The WTA also sought to represent itself as the legitimate guardians of Flambeau's Indian heritage. The key to accomplishing these objectives was to convince the membership that the tribal council was not adhering to traditional values.

At the powwow after the Fourth of July parades, Tom Maulson and Gilbert Chapman discussed how to use most effectively the coalition that had come together that afternoon. The tribe's attorney, James Jannetta, had just told Chapman that the Wa-Swa-Gon Treaty Association would lose if a referendum on treaty rights were to be held the next day. The tribal council had surveyed the membership about the negotiations and determined that tribal members favored the negotiation process by a nearly two-to-one margin.

Maulson and Chapman sharpened and energized their efforts by creating a political action group to work toward defeating the present tribal council's agenda of a lease of the rights. The political action group represented a compromise between Mike Chosa's recommendation that WTA remain an activist community organization and the inclination of others that it become a local political party and slate candidates for the tribal council.

Short newsletters and cartoons full of gossip and harsh criticism of the tribal council were soon produced by the Wa-Swa-Gon Treaty Association and distributed widely on the reservation in an attempt to sway the membership away from their support for negotiations. The newsletters typically thanked individuals and groups for their defense of the heritage of Chippewa people, a traditional past invoked by the elders and ancestors, two categories of persons synonymous with Anishinaabe moral and spiritual integrity. Tribal council members were criticized individually and collectively on a number of counts—greed, nepotism, and mismanagement of funds—all of which subvert traditional values of respect, generosity, and egalitarianism. Also made suspect were the relationships between members of the tribal council and non-Indians, indicating that the ability to manage the place of non-Indians in the reservation political process was a necessary measure of moral integrity (WTA 1989b).

On the issue of the leasing of off-reservation rights, the council was accused of proposing to lease or sell those rights for less than they were worth on the one hand; on the other, they were attacked for not understanding that such rights are integral to Ojibwe tradition and heritage and could not be sold at all. The Wa-Swa-Gon Treaty Association was basing its criticisms on the paradoxical assumption that treaty rights simultaneously are and are not commodities.

About three months after the WTA's initial petition to the tribal council, the council voted in mid-June to reopen negotiations with the state. Two days after AIM flags flew at two Fourth of July parades, the state and tribal negotiating teams met to discuss the future of the off-reservation treaty rights. Lac du Flambeau presented the state with its latest counterproposal.

The specifics of Flambeau's forbearance of the rights and the compensation it expected from the state were summarized in a memo written five days later by James Jannetta, who was increasingly regarded with suspicion by Maulson and other spearfishers that summer. He transmitted the following provisions demanded by the state's negotiator: The deer hunting agreement of the previous year would stand, but the tribe would forgo their interest in timber and gill netting and spear only 10 percent of safe harvest on two lakes per year. In exchange, the tribe wanted from the state 4.2 million dollars per year for the next ten years, earmarked for per capita payments; the payment of a debt incurred in acquiring Simpson Electric; 1 million dollars toward a new elementary school; monies for tribal higher education and improvements on the fish hatchery; and 1 million dollars to fund a joint "tribal–surrounding community committee to develop and fund projects to promote reconciliation, increase understanding and promote the area" (Taffora 1989). The tribal council also insisted on the retrocession of Public Law 280, which would permit tribal enforcement of state laws.

But the traditional ties of kinship and the value of egalitarianism at Flambeau are stronger than the modern forces that constitute exclusive, decision-making bodies. Jannetta's memo was leaked to a member of the Wa-Swa-Gon Treaty Association and to the *Lakeland Times* (which gave it headline coverage) and was widely disseminated on the reservation. Public disclosure of the proposed terms generated a flurry of media attention and debate on both the 42-million-dollar cost of settlement to state taxpayers and on the legality of closed meetings between the state and the tribe. In the editorial pages of the *Lakeland Times* that fall, the incessant themes of the morality of spearing and the actual distinctiveness of modern Indian polities were now joined by the reasons why Wisconsin taxpayers should not have to subsidize an agreement made between the federal government and Indian tribes.

The anti-treaty organizations quickly reacted to the news. Dean Crist of STA/W challenged and attempted to attend the closed meetings, was arrested, and won his case; the state in turn invoked a clause in its open meetings law that enabled it to go into closed session in deference to the tribe's desire to negotiate in private.

The town chairman of Boulder Junction, a Vilas County Circuit Court judge, and the mayor of Park Falls were invited to participate in the negotiations. PARR and STA/W sensed that the local figures were brought in at the last moment to use their influence to support an impending agreement. They responded by mounting campaigns against a settlement should a proposal emerge. STA/W also announced an effort to recall Jim Holperin, the state representative from the area, for his denunciations of both anti-treaty organizations.

At Lac du Flambeau, elections for the tribal council loomed in October. The Wa-Swa-Gon Treaty Association, through its shadow political action group, ran or endorsed six candidates. Claiming to be frustrated and angered by the abuses of power by tribal council members, Tom Maulson declared his candidacy as a write-in for the tribal council elections. He was promptly suspended from his position as tribal judge.

More tribal members voted in the October 3 elections—740—than had ever been recorded by the tribe's enrollment department. Maulson received 177 votes, not enough to join the eleven members of the tribal council. One WTA-supported candidate joined the council and one pro-negotiations incumbent lost. Betty Graveen and Tom Maulson, who rarely agreed, both acknowledged that the large voter turnout reflected a widely shared concern about the makeup and actions of the tribal council. The reason for their concern, however, was open to interpretation. According to Graveen, more people voted to prevent Maulson from being elected. Maulson regarded the 177 votes for him as a sign that Flambeau people were more closely scrutinizing the tribal council.

The numbers, though, speak for themselves. By nearly any reading, on October 3, 1989, a referendum on the tribal council's negotiations with the state gave the council a green light to continue.

CONFLICT BETWEEN THE BANDS

Traditionally autonomous and negotiating separately with the state, the other Ojibwe bands in theory would not be bound by a Flambeau-state agreement and could still spear any lake in the ceded territory they named. An unpublished addendum to Jannetta's leaked memo suggested to the contrary that the agreement being negotiated might very well have far-reaching consequences for the other bands.

NOTE: At the beginning we spent some time discussing the state's problem of not settling with all the tribes at once, since *theoretically the other tribes could step in to take what LdF forbears,* so [the] state would be no better off. I suggested in caucus that the Tribe could help meet this concern by continuing to designate lakes, etc., under the Voigt task force and just not spear them. We may wind up discussing this further at the table. (my emphasis)

Walter Bresette of the Red Cliff band annotated his copy of Jannetta's memo and sent it back to the WTA with a note that the addendum (circled in heavy marker) contained "the most dangerous of the concepts" (Bresette 1989).

Both supporters and opponents of treaty rights were distrustful of the possible implications of such an agreement, for different reasons. Larry Petersen, a paper mill worker and the president of PARR, was the first to point out publicly the significance of the restricted scope of the agreement; STA/W took up the issue shortly thereafter (*Lakeland Times* 1989f). Within three weeks, Minocqua's *Lakeland Times* ran editorials voicing concern that the state was about to spend fifty million dollars and would not be guaranteed that another Chippewa band wouldn't spear the lakes in the region. State senators Kincaid and Sensenbrenner both came out against a settlement for this same reason.

Members of the Ojibwe bands and the Wa-Swa-Gon Treaty Association were suspicious of the steps that Flambeau would take to enforce the terms of the agreement in order to receive its compensation. The infamous addendum suggested that the tribal council was open to working with the state to manipulate the Voigt Inter-tribal Task Force to demarcate a territorial hegemony for the reservation.

The idea of exclusive fishing territories did find some favor by council members at Lac du Flambeau.[3] It had been Lac du Flambeau that had interpreted the meaning of the *Voigt* decision by spearing the lakes in the Lakeland region, effectively affirming a de facto territoriality or hegemonic practice. The notion of territoriality could also have been deduced from the earlier dispute between the Lac Courte Oreilles and Lac du Flambeau bands over the latter's desire to spear the Chippewa Flowage. Lac Courte Oreilles considered Flambeau's request and turned them down. The presumption driving their actions points to a kind of territoriality that could make separate agreements between the state and the bands possible.

Decades of violating, however, worked against such a fractured perception of off-reservation space. Tribal members hunted on and off each other's reservations. Jim Pipe Mustache, an elder from Lac Courte Oreilles, gently summarized the sentiment in the region concerning tribal propriety: "It [recognition of the use rights by the different Ojibwe bands] was by mutual respect, but if they quit using a rice bed or hunting area, any other band had a right to enter that area and use it" (*News from Indian Country* 1989d:3). His interpretation of tribal autonomy seems to antedate the property customs that evolved with the fur trade, wherein resources used for subsistence had to be shared, but resources procured for exchange could be restricted. The idea of fishing territories also objectified and divided the reservations in a way that flew in the face of modern intertribal cooperation and the growing awareness of the meaning and value of a collective Anishinaabe identity in the upper Great Lakes.

The fears of treaty rights supporters were confirmed and heightened at an October 5, 1989, community meeting in Minocqua about the proposed agreement. James Holperin, a non-Indian state government official, assured those gathered that if other Chippewa band members should fish the off-reservation lakes traditionally speared by the Flambeau band, Flambeau would join the state in seeking an injunction against those bands (*Lakeland Times* 1989g). By doing so, Flambeau would effectively drop out of the GLIFWC coalition if another band attempted to harvest in their perceived resource use area, a departure that would severely compromise GLIFWC's capacity to seek operating funds every year from Congress.

The willingness of the Flambeau tribal council to join the state in a lawsuit against another band was unheard of in Ojibwe history— lawsuits had previously been used only between Anishinaabe and the Chamukaman (whites). Lac du Flambeau's tribal council members appeared greedy and prepared to disown their relatives on the other reservations in order to protect their own interests. The council appeared to be sending signals to some Ojibwe leaders that they were not sincerely and consistently operating within an Ojibwe system of value.

A swift response met the Flambeau tribal council's stance. Shortly after the October 5 community meeting, Donald Moore, president of the Bad River tribal council, issued fishing permits to tribal members from a number of bands to spearfish Round Lake and Lake Namekagan, both near Flambeau. The intertribal spearfishing group held a ceremony at both locations, planting the Wa-Swa-Gon banner on the shores. "We had to make our point," one spearfisher later told me dryly. The "point" was that those within the Lac du Flambeau tribal council who imagined that other band members would recognize some kind of territorial hegemony were wrong.

The Flambeau tribal council was further humbled and isolated at GLIFWC's sixth annual conference, which opened the following Thursday in Madison. The three-day conference focused on the relationship between treaty rights and racism and the potential for co-management of the natural resources of the ceded territory. It featured five Indian and non-Indian public and private officials who had crafted the coalition of state, sport, and tribal interests that was managing natural resources in the state of Washington.

Attending the meeting in his capacity as chairman of the Voigt Inter-tribal Task Force, Tom Maulson showed a videotape of the October 5 meeting in Minocqua to other task force members. After learning of the Flambeau tribal council's willingness to sue another band, the task force asked Mike Allen to resign his chairmanship of GLIFWC's board of commissioners; he was replaced by Donald Moore of the Bad River tribal council, who had been a driving force behind the intertribal spearfishing expeditions the previous week. Kathleen Tierney, lead counsel of the *Voigt* litigation for the past six years, had associated herself with Flambeau's strategy and so also stepped down after the meeting.

And so, as the fall of 1989 grew colder, Mike Allen and the Flambeau tribal council came increasingly under fire from without and within the reservation. The council faced isolation from the other

bands for its interpretation of its relationship with them. Allen continued seeking a way to allow the treaties to benefit everyone. He understood that the average person at Lac du Flambeau could barely afford
the investment in equipment to spear off the reservation, or was unin-
terested in expressing the right. Mike Allen and the tribal council were
concerned with the cost of the social conflict. They were pressured in-
ternally from people who wanted their kids to be safe at the high
school off the reservation, to get the canceled Little League games going again, and generally to restore social relations between the Indian
and non-Indian communities. They wanted to get out from under
the social conflict that was tearing at the community.[4] If inventing or
acquiescing in the invention of a traditional off-reservation use area
would entice the state to offer a more accessible value to a larger portion of the tribal membership, then so be it.

THE BATTLE OF TRIBAL COUNCIL RESOLUTION 369

On October 16, 1989, the tribal council of Lac du Flambeau unanimously approved an agreement between the band and the state of
Wisconsin and set a referendum for the membership to vote on the
agreement on Wednesday, October 25. A 38-page summary of the 160-
page agreement was made available at the tribal offices in the community center and a 5-page pamphlet outlining the proposed terms was
mailed by the council to all tribal members.

The summary set forth the general provisions of the agreement
—forbearance of the exercise of treaty rights, compensation for that
forbearance, and other significant provisions, perhaps the most important being a mutual pledge by both parties to enter into a gaming
compact that would permit the development of a casino. The tribe
also agreed to "take steps" to ensure that no other Chippewa tribes
would exploit these resources. Although it had no implications for the
federal court cases that were defining the scope of the treaty rights,
the agreement was to last for ten years and be renewable by mutual
agreement for additional five-year periods. Upon tribal membership
ratification, the agreement would next need to be approved by the
state legislature, the federal district court, the secretary of the interior,
and Congress, all within two and one-half months.

The proposed agreement stipulated that 29.2 million dollars would
be appropriated for per capita payments that would be neither taxed
nor included in state or federal means-tested programs to determine

eligibility for other transfer payments. The payments amounted to 1,800 dollars for every adult the first year and 1,250 for each year thereafter; per capita payments to minors would be held in trust by a third party. The 1 million dollars' allocation for a new elementary school was retained, but the state's contribution to retire the tribe's debt on the purchase of Simpson's Electric was reduced to 1.8 million dollars. Monies for law enforcement and the joint tribal-community relations committee would be halved from what had been proposed that summer, but forty-two tribal development initiatives and programs in the areas of education, general government, transportation, health, social services, economic development, and natural resources would be funded at 3.5 million dollars per year. The agreement also permitted the tribal regulation of nonmember fishing on the reservation, tribal enforcement of state laws and, as yet another measure of the continuing value of hunting, a procedure to allow tribal felons to hunt (Taffora 1989).

In a seemingly democratic but also self-serving tactic, the tribal council announced that it would allow absentee balloting for this referendum. Apparently, the council assumed that a per capita check for 1,800 dollars would be more valuable for Flambeau tribal members "staying" in the cities—as people tend to say—than the opportunity to hunt and spear on their occasional trips home to the reservation. The council announced that it would hold an informational meeting to discuss the agreement on Tuesday evening, October 24, the night before the referendum vote.

With eight days remaining until the referendum, the Wa-Swa-Gon Treaty Association intensified its campaign to derail the tribal council's momentum and undermine the membership's confidence in its leadership. They raised concerns about the per capita payments and about tribal sovereignty and renewed their efforts to portray the tribal council as antiegalitarian and dependent on non-Indians for direction. The Wa-Swa-Gon Treaty Association also enlisted the aid of Lew Gurwitz, a non-Indian lawyer who had worked for many years on Indian issues. Middle-aged with shoulder-length white hair, Gurwitz had been attracted to Flambeau from Massachusetts and was working for a very small amount of money.

The Wa-Swa-Gon Treaty Association scheduled two meetings—the first on Monday evening, October 24, their usual meeting time, and the second for Tuesday, the night before the referendum, at the same time as the council meeting. In their advertisement for the Monday night meeting, the WTA challenged the per capita payments: they might be reduced by future enrollments or attorney and bank fees or diverted to the tribe's general fund. The bank that was to manage the per capita trust fund for minors was claimed to have handled Menominee termination. Half the money to Flambeau's children would be disbursed when they reached the age of eighteen and the rest at twenty-one. The advertisement concluded with a warning that the state might make further incursions onto the reservation at the expense of "your Sovereignty" and sounded an ominous note: "There will be no further tribal involvement in our lifetime" (WTA 1989a).

Many of the concerns raised in the advertisement were voiced at the Monday night meeting. Referring to the issue of tribal territorial propriety, Tom Maulson criticized the council's attempt to find advantage for Flambeau in a treaty that was signed by and intended to benefit all, "the whole Chippewa nation." Indian rights lawyer Lew Gurwitz gave a passionate speech, remembered years later by attendees. Gurwitz spoke of the usual irreversibility of losses of Indian sovereignty and, invoking Flambeau's honor, noted that such an agreement would be used against the other Ojibwe tribes. Jerry Maulson remembers that Gurwitz argued that the settlement was written by and for lawyers; the information released by the tribe thus far was inadequate; and no council members were present to answer the audience's questions. Gurwitz recommended that those present spend the next thirty-six hours "telling people to vote against the referendum" (*Lakeland Times* 1989h).

Some people took his advice very seriously. On Tuesday, October 24, Wa-Swa-Gon Treaty Association members traveled across the reservation, attempting to convince people of the value of the treaties and explaining what their ancestors had given up for them. The five sisters of spearfisher Don Smith, one who returned from the state of Washington to vote, went from door to door, either talking with people or leaving a copy of WTA's Tuesday meeting announcement under their doors. The returning sister's presence on the reservation at this time signaled to a number of people the gravity of the circumstances, in her brother Don's judgment. Also returning was Denise Wildcat, the daughter of the previous tribal chairman, who was a student at the University of Wisconsin at Stout at that time. She had sent in her absentee ballot, voting against the agreement, but came back to the reservation in response to her mother's request. Wildcat was angry that the council was rushing through the process. "They worked on this [the agreement] for two years and now they wanted us to vote on this in less than two weeks. That set me against it."

Apparently expecting a large turnout, the tribal council held their informational meeting on the referendum in the gymnasium of the community center. In order to ask questions and directly confront those who negotiated the agreement, the Wa-Swa-Gon Treaty Association moved their meeting to the gymnasium as well and attended as a block. The leaders of the WTA and attorney Lew Gurwitz walked into the meeting. As customary, the tribal council announced that the information meeting was restricted to tribal members. According to Jerry Maulson, someone on the council requested that nontribal members leave, noticed the "lawyer with the white hair," and asked specifically for Gurwitz to depart. Gilbert Chapman stood and said that if Gurwitz had to leave then the non-Indian tribal attorney, James Jannetta, could not be present either. Unlike the tribal council, the Wa-Swa-Gon Treaty Association could credibly represent itself and its agenda as endogenous, since it was willing to exclude Gurwitz if the council would part with James Jannetta.

Tom Maulson, the modern war chief, then asked Mike Allen, effectively the modern civic chief, a key question: "Can you explain the agreement without Jannetta at your side?" This question reflected ongoing criticism of outsiders' influence on the council's policies and direction. A member of the tribal council replied to the rough interchange, "If it's going to be like this, I think I'm going to go." He got up to leave. Jerry Maulson later recalled that Chairman Allen also rose, and the rest of the council followed, walking out of the meeting and never returning.

Most people went home. Some were confused, others angry, a few disappointed, and some fearful.

The following day, October 25, the polls at Lac du Flambeau opened at 10:00 A.M. Mike Allen was threatened; the Vilas County sheriff's police searched the community building in response to a bomb threat and locked all doors save the main entrance. As a measure of his grace at this moment of crisis, Mike Allen decided not to press charges against those who had made threats to his safety.

Wa-Swa-Gon Treaty Association supporters gathered around a fire and drum across Highway 47 over the course of the day, singing for hours. Tom Maulson told a reporter, "I feel really good. This is what it's all about. People here wanting to be Indians again" (*Lakeland Times* 1989i).

Shortly after the polls closed at 6:00 P.M., Scott Smith was singing at the drum when Goldie Larsen burst out of the community center. The treaty rights supporters had won: 439 tribal members had voted against ratifying the settlement with the state; 366 voted in favor (*Lakeland Times* 1989i).

More and more people gathered in front of the community building. In the memories of some who were there, it was not always clear who had voted on what side, but a celebratory atmosphere began to develop. Tom Maulson asked the drum for a victory song, offering tobacco. Assembling a caravan of cars, the treaty rights supporters drove through the reservation and Minocqua-Woodruff for hours, honking their horns in a kind of hybrid vehicular wedding dance.

There is an ambivalence in Ojibwe community members about their tribal councils that is rooted in egalitarian ideology and practice. This ambivalence was revealed when the membership of the Lac du Flambeau reservation essentially voted to retain the council in the fall of 1989 yet shortly afterward voted down the main project that the council had been working on for over two years.

There is also an ongoing ambivalence about the treaties themselves. On the one hand, they are remembered as sacred covenants between the government of the United States and the *ogimag*, the legitimate, civic leadership (sometimes seen as spiritual leaders of the Mide- wiwin) of the most important Ojibwe villages. In this view, both the United States and the Ojibwes were equally committed to the separate existence of Ojibwe society and culture. The current conception of the *rights* to hunt, fish, and gather—a sign of sovereignty—is deduced from this memory. There is, however, a prominent spiritual dimension to treaty rights. As noted earlier, a long-standing Ojibwe sensibility acknowledges that the productive activities themselves are reproductive of both human and nonhuman persons. This is accomplished by virtue of the debt incurred by the spirits through feasts and generous gift giving. Consequently, the exercise of the rights itself becomes a spiritual activity and, more importantly, a responsibility. Emphasis on this meaning of spearfishing supersedes the modern conception of treaty rights—the treaties from a spiritual perspective tend to be remembered as compromises made with civic leaders who had slowly usurped the leadership of the spiritual leaders over the course of the fur trade period.

Regardless of one's interpretation of the value of the treaties, their meaningfulness and intimate connection to modern Ojibwe identity is clear. Exercising the rights and being an Indian converge. Edward Chosa recalled, "That was the greatest day in the history of this reservation. We turned down 50 million dollars. 1,800 dollars per person in a trust fund. Paid every year. That's a lot of money. I don't know why. It's hard to explain. I wish I could . . . We wouldn't be able to call ourselves Indians . . . At Grand Entry time during a powwow, that's what I thought of. When all the tribes come in. Would we have to sit down?"

Scott Smith thought about why he took the position that he did.

Before the treaty, the question was what did it mean to be an Indian. I hunted and fished all my life. It was what I looked forward to as a kid after school. I thought hard about the sellout and there was two reasons I was against it. Pride. What would it be like to go to Minocqua and have people say, "My tax money bought him his truck"? I wouldn't be able to hold my head up.

Second, the youth. I want for them to be able to go off and hunt and know what it is to be Indian. I see them doing nothing and I want for them to have that opportunity.

Denise Wildcat, when telling the story of that monumental referendum vote, begins to cry when she recalls Goldie Larsen coming out with the announcement. "We didn't know what we had," she admits.

Conclusion

14. A spearfisher searching for
walleye. Photo courtesy of Tom
Maulson.

As among the Hopi (Geertz 1994), millenarian prophecy has a long history in the social thought of the Anishinaabeg. In the nineteenth century, historian William Whipple Warren noted an Ojibwe belief that the coming of the white race and the demise of the red had been foreseen by their forebears (Warren 1984:117). In the first decades of the nineteenth century, the Shawano prophet "prophesied that the day was nigh, when, if the red race listened to and obeyed his words, the Great Spirit would deliver them from their dependence on the whites, and prevent their being finally down-trodden and exterminated by them" (Warren 1984:322). A series of prophecies swept the Indian communities of the old Northwest from the 1840s to the 1860s (Peers 1994:171). The prophecy set forth by Edward Benton-Banai in *The Mishomis Book* incorporated whites into the emergence of the New People, Osh-ki-bi-ma-di-zeeg, but was no less millenarian and hinging on a revitalization of cultural practices.

The reappearance of totalizing, revitalizing prophecy in the 1980s indicates that the Ojibwes in northern Wisconsin were reimagining themselves and their relationship to others. The prophecy functioned to legitimize and exalt contemporary political concerns for Anishinaabe people. Current events represented the unfolding of a sacred history and were sweeping into its wake other Indian people as well as non-Indians. The prophecy emerged, circulated, and motivated people because its main link to current practices, spearfishing, was widely regarded as customary and inherently Ojibwe despite changes in its cultural value and technology over the centuries.

The revitalization movement (Wallace 1956) and ethnic reorganization (Nagel and Snipp 1993) that accompanied the prophecy initially sprung from the imagination and desire of a small group of indigenous people who wanted to take greater control of the conditions of their collective existence. One of the reasons that goal became credible is due to global transformations in the value of indigenous cultures in the world-system (Friedman 1994). A social evolutionary narrative that emanates from the city—say, Chicago, New York, or London—and represents the metropolis as the center and places like the Lac du Flambeau reservation as peripheries, is less compelling now than it was in the middle of the twentieth century. At that time, both Indians and their ethnographers agreed and coproduced a narrative that regarded the Indian past as glorious, the present as disorganization, and the future as assimilation. Increasingly since that time, the narrative is being rewritten: the past is revalued as exploitation, the present as resistance, and the future as ethnic resurgence (Bruner 1986:139).

It was the *Voigt* decision that originally challenged the Ojibwe Indians of Lac du Flambeau to articulate, confront, and weigh different paradigms of their history and identity. Tribal attorney James Jannetta recalls that the community was "closely and deeply divided" and that the eventual referendum in the agreement was "for the soul of the tribe." Such a paradigmatic transformation of historical consciousness and identity in recent years also helps explain the involvement in the Walleye War of non-Indians who were sympathetic, willing, and interested in identifying with a revitalized Indian cause—they were seen by some and came to imagine themselves as "Walleye Warriors," as Whaley and Bresette (1994) designated them, or as Osh-ki-bi-ma-di-zeeg in Edward Benton-Banai's Seventh Fire Prophesy (1988:89–93). The emergence of revalued practices, ideas, and objects—spearfishing, prophecy, the WTA banner, *ogitchida* ideology, the Walleye Warrior caps—became multivocal symbols of a people's aspirations for recognition.

The conflict within the Lac du Flambeau community over the meaning of the off-reservation rights and the dispute among the tribal communities over the meaning of Indian identity in a liberal democracy energized all parties, regardless of viewpoint. The internal debates revolved around the extent to which the Indian community should assume responsibility for authoring the terms of mutual accommodation. Did the community imagine that it had the resources to assert itself as something more than a flexible labor pool in the region's economy? Flambeau, as vortex and nexus of regional and state forces, was seen differently by its members.

For the most part, members of the oldest living and active generation at Lac du Flambeau in the 1980s were political realists and accommodationists; they sought and counseled cooperative relations with the surrounding non-Indian communities. A number of these elders came of age in the early years of the Indian Reorganization Act in the 1930s and are the first generation to have worked full forty-year careers at Simpson Electric. They are the last generation to have grown up speaking Anishinaabemowin as children in their homes, and some are practicing Christians. Their strategy of accommodation over the decades has permitted them to do well enough economically to allow their children to leave the reservation, at least for a while. Some members of this elder generation have assumed positions of leadership within the tribe. They and some of their children have attracted federal and state money for tribal projects—first the fish hatchery, then Office of Economic Opportunity monies for social and cultural development in the 1960s, contracts under the Indian Self-Determination and Education Act of 1975 and, finally, drug abuse prevention programs in the 1980s and the Indian Gaming and Regulatory Act in 1990s. This group also acceded to the reshaping and representation of certain signs of Indian identity, beginning with the tourist powwows in the Indian Bowl in the 1950s, arts and crafts shows in the 1960s and, most recently, a museum and heritage tourism project. All the while, this generation has inclined toward individualizing the meaning of Flambeau Ojibwe cultural identity. Their accommodation did not resist the loss of some significant cultural forms, such as fluency in the Ojibwe language, the Midewiwin, fasting, and the Big Drum. Their strategy, however, has also permitted the continual redefinition and endurance of other aspects of Ojibwe culture, like hunting and fishing, and it has fostered a social coherence and continuity that made a cultural revival thinkable in the late 1980s.

It was some of the children of the eldest living generation who formed the core of those at Flambeau who actively criticized the accommodation strategy of their parents and peers. This younger generation was relatively cosmopolitan, having served in the armed services or made their homes away from the reservation for extended periods of time. They were cultural brokers, investing in the maximizing of cultural differences between the enclave at Lac du Flambeau and the surrounding society. Most were within a few years of fifty years old and so had seen a great deal of change on the reservations during their lives. They had come of age when the dominant culture's assimilative forces were at their peak in the termination era. They had become young adults when a worldwide cultural revolution began to challenge long-standing power relations between the dominant and the dominated.

Both generations bitterly resented, occasionally confronted, but more typically just suffered injustices, marginalization, and misrepresentation by outsiders—outsiders defining Indians in their postcards and billboards, outsiders projecting images of the Indian community at Lac du Flambeau in newspapers and telecasts. Whites also over time transformed the landscape of Flambeau's Indians at the reservation's expense. Flambeau people tell stories about the cutting of pines, the disappearance of rice beds, shoreline degradation, and the appearance of game wardens and vacation homes at favorite hunting and fishing spots. Some part of Lac du Flambeau's rage was increasingly poured into the issue of spearing off the reservation.

As the surrounding non-Indian communities recoiled and began harassing fishermen, spearfishers became militant. When they had the opportunity, the people of Flambeau struck back, and they struck back at night, the time they had always hunted and fished. They speared the whites' precious, pristine, and pure lakes in small motorized boats, using harvest tools they knew offended the sensibility of outsiders, who had come to define nature as a sphere of leisurely, sporting interaction between man and beast.

The Walleye War foregrounded cosmological differences between local Indians and whites that became realized as a political and social conflict. The spearing of spawning walleyed pike represents the nexus of opposed theories of reproduction. For polytheistic Indians, humans are weak and gain the spiritual power they need to live meaningfully and effectively in the world through reciprocal exchange with the spirit world. People achieve such reciprocity through gifts of their human capacities, like drumming, singing, dancing, and smoking, as well as the sacrifice of animals and subsequent distribution of their bodies as food. Harvesting is a link in a reproductive chain, because the animal spirit or master of the game is placed in debt through the honor received in feasts, a debt paid by reincarnating more animal bodies. This view presumes and produces abundance. For monotheistic whites, spiritual power in the form of grace is procured by action in a social realm; nature is a separate domain and is appropriated to build culture. Nature reproduces in spite of human appropriation and needs to be protected from graceless human intention and excess since it can be easily depleted. This perspective is predicated on the presumption of an eventual scarcity, even as actions taken based on this perspective produce that scarcity.

Lac du Flambeau can best be understood by viewing the reservation as an emerging center within a local system that in turn articulates with global forces, rather than as a reactive, peripheral, and dependent component in the hinterland of the modern world-system. Ojibwe cultural and social identity emerged in a seventeenth-century caldron of interacting global forces. To refer to the Anishinaabe people as forest proletarians during that time (Hickerson 1973; see also Wolf 1982) ignores elaborate ethnogenetic, authorial, and articulatory processes. Flambeau people have continually improvised their collective relationship to larger forces since their emergence in this region. Their very ability to move between a range of modes and styles of articulation and interaction with outsiders—accommodation, opposition, distancing, separate development, collusion, or cultural distinctiveness (Sider 1993:109)—is one of the qualities they identify as most Indian about themselves. The continuing existence and transformation of a disposition to improvise and manage the meaning of the inexorably invasive forces of the city is a definitive sign of a total and local system of the world.

The movement over time between different modes of articulation is a crucial dynamic in the cultural history of Flambeau. Access to European guns and exotic trade goods enabled the Ojibwes to advance into the northern highland region of what would become northern Wisconsin and to drive out the Dakotas. Acquiescing to the policy of allotment toward the end of the nineteenth century and the development of a lumber mill at Flambeau created the conditions for lucrative commercial and subsistence hunting because the regrowth of forest attracted deer that could be hunted and marketed both locally and regionally. Similarly, for the first half of the twentieth century, the guiding of affluent whites by Indians in conjunction with the appearance of a fish hatchery on the reservation yielded an infrastructure of practices that underpinned the confrontation over off-reservation hunting and fishing rights in the last decades of the twentieth century. The treaty rights recognized by a non-Indian government became a cornerstone of a revitalized Anishinaabe cultural movement as the millennium drew to a close.

Though a capacity, and even perhaps an inclination, to fight with one's neighbors under various circumstances was, no doubt, traditional, the rewards for this complex of values and behavior was considerably enhanced with the coming of the Europeans and access to their goods. So, too, a version of these forces converging in the late twentieth century, with the federal recognition of treaty rights, engendered the elaboration of a subethnic identity during the 1980s described as Flambeau Ojibwe, Flambeau Anishinaabeg or, among some neotraditionals, Waswaaganan, the Torch Lake People. It was a revival of a term that originated in the eighteenth century at the peak of the cultural efflorescence that brought the Ojibwes into being and onto the world stage.

The changing nature of Flambeau local autonomy and the long-standing and valued ability of its members to shift their modes of articulation with outsiders help account for the deep and seismic division that nearly tore the reservation apart during the spearfishing conflict. Tribal members did not agree about the meaning and value of their identity and relations to non-Indians; they appreciated the meaning of spearfishing, and thus of themselves, in different ways. The referendum vote had been close. Given the individualism and factionalism of Ojibwe communities, another outcome would have been unexpected.

The vote itself more than the outcome signaled another victory in a longer and more profound conflict—Flambeau's ceaseless and successful struggle to resist, endure, and thrive in a changing world.

Epilogue

15. Spearing at Mille Lacs,
1998. Photo courtesy of Charles
Rasmussen, GLIFWC staff.

sion to hunt deer in the summer and established a season from Labor Day to December 31. Deer could not be hunted at night, and they could not be hunted on private land, with some minor exceptions (*LCO et al. v. Wisconsin* 1990a).

In October of 1990, Judge Crabb (*LCO et al. v. Wisconsin* 1990b) ruled that the tribes could not pursue their claim for damages against the state of Wisconsin for deprivation of off-reservation treaty rights from the time shortly after the signing of the treaties until 1983. The value of the damages in the form of involuntary forbearance had been estimated at between 250 and 300 million dollars.

On August 14 of that year, the Mille Lacs Band of Minnesota Chippewas, signatories of the same 1837 treaty upheld in the *Voigt* decision, filed suit in federal court against the state of Minnesota and the Minnesota Department of Natural Resources, seeking to enjoin the state from enforcing laws infringing on treaty usufructuary rights.

Lac du Flambeau became more actively involved on the legal front in 1990. It attempted to capitalize on the newly passed Hunter Harassment Law (protecting the state's lucrative deer hunting season from the increasingly powerful animal rights movement) by seeking remedy against four leaders of the protests arrested during the spearing season. In July, a Langlade County judge dropped the charges against the defendants. The leadership of the Wa-Swa-Gon Treaty Organization responded by enlisting the aid of the legal firm of Cherne, Clancy, and Taitelman and the Wisconsin chapter of the American Civil Liberties Union; on February 1, 1991, they filed suit in federal court under section 1982 of the Civil Rights Act of 1866, which forbids infringement on civil rights motivated by racial animus. The Lac du Flambeau band and its diverse leaders—tribal council chairman Mike Allen, Tom Maulson, Robert Martin, Nick Hockings, and Gilbert Chapman —sought an injunction to prevent Dean Crist of STA/W, fifteen other named individuals, and unnamed others from interfering with any tribal member's treaty rights. The suit also named three county sheriffs as defendants in a racially motivated conspiracy to deny the Indians their treaty-guaranteed rights. On March 15, 1991, a week after a day-long hearing of the evidence presented by Tom Maulson, spiritual leader Edward Benton-Banai, and Nick Hockings, Judge Crabb (*Lac du Flambeau v. Stop Treaty Abuse/Wisconsin* 1991) issued a temporary injunction against the protesters but not against the sheriffs. The tribe reproduced the one-page court order as a full-page advertisement in the *Lakeland Times,* and the Wa-swa-gon Treaty Association made it into a three-foot by five-foot poster that spearfishers brought to the boat landings and prominently displayed.

News of the injunction decreased the numbers of protesters and observers during the 1991 season; the display of the court order at the boat landings quieted the ones who remained. With the exception of the lakes in the center of Vilas County—Big Arbor Vitae and Big St. Germaine—the protesters left the landings to spearers' families and their non-Indian supporters.

The protests may have also cooled as a response to Crabb's finding that the Ojibwe bands did not have a right to the commercial harvest of timber on public lands (*LCO et al. v. Wisconsin* 1991), her final ruling in the regulatory phase of the *Voigt* decision. The judge set May 20, 1991, as the last day on which an appeal by either the tribes or the state could be filed. Much to the dismay of the protest organizations, the state and the tribes agreed to let that day pass without taking action. The tribes did, however, come together and issue the following statement, signed by all six tribal chairs of Lake Superior Chippewa Indians on that day:

TO THE PEOPLE OF WISCONSIN:
The six bands of Lake Superior Chippewa, allied for many years in litigation against the State of Wisconsin in order to confirm and uphold their treaty right to hunt, fish and gather, and now secure in the conviction that they have preserved these rights for the generations to come, have this day foregone their right to further appeal and dispute adverse rulings in this case, including a district court ruling barring them from damages. They do this, knowing that the subject of the latter ruling is currently before the United States Supreme Court, and has been decided in favor of Indian tribes in the Ninth Circuit Court of Appeals and other federal courts. They do this as a gesture of peace and friendship towards the people of Wisconsin, in a spirit they hope may someday be reciprocated on the part of the general citizenry and officials of this state. (Satz 1991:193)

After winning a decision in district court (*Lac du Flambeau v. State of Wisconsin* 1991) that further limited the state's power to define the kinds of games tribal casinos could offer, Lac du Flambeau signed a gaming compact with the state of Wisconsin in June of 1992 to establish a casino.

In October of that same year, Tom Maulson was elected president of the band, a position he held until the fall of 2000 when he, too, suc-

tribal governments to suspend the 1918 federal law that prohibited Indians from consuming alcohol on their reservations (1984:77).

3. This aspect of Flambeau Indian identity was nuanced with a connection to Depression-era urban gangsters. Baby Face Nelson hid out in the home of Flambeau tribal member Ollie Catfish for three days in 1934 and the story circulated for years (Hollatz 1989:62–62).

4. Working at Lac Courte Oreilles in the mid-1940s, Victor Barnouw elicited the following about hunting: "We're wards of the government. We live on reservation land, and there's no violation there. That's under the old treaty law, and it's higher than Wisconsin State law" (Barnouw 1950:87).

5. In the summer of 1999, I saw deer on the reservation for the first time in more than ten years. I joked with tribal members that these sightings were the local Dow Jones Industrial Average, as they indexed the numbers of people who were employed.

6. This principle generates ethnic markers in multiple domains. In a conversation with an elementary school administrator at Lac du Flambeau, I was told that when Indian students fail, "at least they can't be accused of being white."

7. See Thomas Buckley's article on Yurok teaching and learning (1979).

4. THE WAR BEGINS

1. The Lac Courte Oreilles band has a long history of actions supporting their treaty rights. By the early 1970s Lac Courte Oreilles's tribal council, unlike Lac du Flambeau's, was dominated by neotraditionalist activists with a variety of ties beyond the local community.

2. Session on the Chippewa Treaty Rights case in the Indian Law Section of the 1994 Annual Convention of the State Bar of Wisconsin held in Milwaukee, on Thursday, June 23, 1994.

3. Ed Chosa was also part of the Chicago Indian Village occupation.

4. These conclusions are drawn from the remarks of staff counsel Michael Lutz, speaking at the Indian Law Section at the 1994 Annual Convention of the State Bar of Wisconsin.

5. According to Greg Guthrie, who was on the tribal council at the time of the *Voigt* decision.

6. For an extensive discussion of the national history of anti-Indian movements in the late twentieth century, see Ryser 1995.

7. This belief and practice echoes Levi-Strauss's concept of bricolage (Levi-Strauss 1966:16–36).

8. Vera Lawrence's claim that treaties were made with the full-bloods,

eliding the difference between politics and genetics, was repeated in the area until at least 1992. She was one of a few Indian people nationwide to join with non-Indians in calling for the abrogation of treaties and the termination of the trust relationship between the bands and the federal government. For a history of this movement, see Ryser 1995.

9. This hostility emerges in a variety of ways. A non-Indian eighth-grade student at the Lac du Flambeau grammar school occasionally wore a commercially produced T-shirt that asked the question on the front side, "What's the difference between a FIB and a cheesehead?" and answered on the back: "The Wisconsin State Line." I asked him what FIB meant. He laughed and answered, "fucking Illinois bastard." Note the projection of a state identity on people who invariably identify themselves as "from Chicago" whether they reside within the city limits or not. The fact that there would be a market for T-shirts bearing this message and that teachers would tacitly pretend ignorance of the meaning of the "F" in "FIB" are measures of the consensus on the moral valence of the Chicagoland tourists who make the Northwoods residents' continued existence above the "tension zone" possible.

10. Its alloform "Save a Deer, Shoot an Indian," though more rare, was formally equivalent. Like a number of other tropes, "Save a Fish, Spear an Indian" first appeared nearly ten years before when the Michigan Ottawas and Chippewas were asserting their rights to fish in Lake Superior under treaties signed with the federal government. A videotape made by Flambeau spearers recorded a white answering an Indian by declaring, "We won't kill your women if you won't kill our walleye"—apparently they had been discussing another variation, "Spear a Pregnant Squaw, Save Two Walleye." Testifying to the power of the equivalence, the version "Save a Whale, Harpoon a Makah" has appeared in the conflict over Makah whaling in Washington (Erikson 1999:562).

11. A non-Indian protester wrapped himself in the American flag and stood knee-deep in his waders in the 45 degree water at the boat landing on Catfish Lake near Eagle River.

12. According to Nick Van Der Puy, a non-Indian hunting and fishing guide based in Eagle River, the May sports fishing season has been in decline since at least the mid-1980s, and it is this loss that motivates protests against treaty rights. There are a number of reasons for the decline. There are fewer walleye to take compared to the 1950s and 1960s, partly the result of greater fishing pressure and also due to the overall environmental degradation. The more affluent sportfishers who used to take a few days off to fish in the area now either travel to Canada on fly-in vacations or go to Lake Erie—or can no longer afford to take time off (a legacy of down-

sizing, perhaps). There have been shifts in what constitutes a vacation in some of the urban areas. Furthermore, a 1981 Wisconsin Department of Development report on the tourism industry indicates that 60 percent of the resorts in the area have not been improved since they were built and that most of them require the same one-week stay commitment as fifty years ago (Strickland 1990:13). None of these reasons for the decline are very tangible, however, and rapidly recede in the perception of many local people when they witness Indian spearers carrying off the bread and butter of resort owners.

5. THE WAR WITHIN

1. LaVeen 1978 examines this event in detail. For a full citation of newspaper coverage, see Beck 1988:185, 231.

2. "No people reverence old age more than the Indians," the Ojibwe historian Peter Jones wrote of his people (1861:68).

3. In 1994, Rick Whaley and Walt Bresette, as cofounders of Witness for Non-Violence, published *Walleye Warriors: An Effective Alliance against Racism and for the Earth,* an account of the organization's activities through this conflict. A number of spearfishers objected to the misrepresentation of Walleye Warriors as an "alliance," suggesting the complexity of the competition to represent this conflict.

4. It was originally planned that Benton-Banai would conduct the ceremony. I was told much later that Benton-Banai had been called in the middle of the night by one of his sons, who had dreamed that he would be in danger if he led the sunrise ceremony in Minocqua. The warning, his absence, and the improvised delayed ceremony were measures of the danger perceived to exist in Minocqua and the mythopoeic way in which the unfolding events were being understood by some.

5. Wind is the spiritual father of Winaboozhoo (Barnouw 1970:14).

6. The same motivation informed the actions of Charcoal, the nineteenth-century Algonquian-speaking Canadian Blood Indian when he realized that he would die for killing another Indian (Dempsey 1978). Discussing the idea of killing a man in this life to create for oneself a servant in the next, Hall (1986:65) notes: "The concept of spiritual servants was widespread in the Mississippi Valley and Great Lakes."

7. Note the similarity between this prophecy and that of Greenpeace: "An ancient North American Indian legend predicts that when the Earth has been ravaged and the animals killed, a tribe of people from all races, creeds and colours would put their faith in deeds, not words, to make the land green again. They would be called 'The Warriors of the Rainbow,' protectors of the environment" (quoted in Wenzel 1991:41). As in the Hopi

prophecies, which have an important place for the "White Brother" (Geertz 1994), non-Indians play a crucial role in this Anishinaabe prophecy. The motif of the Seventh Fire parallels the concern for the Seventh Generation in Iroquoian political action.

8. The rank of Ojibwe men is partially determined by displays of inclination and ability to fight. This willingness to fight is a descendent of historical forms of conflict resolution wherein dreams were the only final authorities that determined whether and how physical violence might be deployed.

6. SPEARING IN THE FOUR DIRECTIONS

1. With the exception of Friday, May 5, I was on the landings during the 10 P.M. local news broadcast, so this analysis does not include electronic coverage, though I have viewed some of it subsequently. The content was not qualitatively different from that of the print media.

2. I made this trip with the caravan and was present that night for the activities described.

3. That first night at Big Eau Pleine, tribal member David Valliere crossed the police line after being taunted all evening. The event revealed the status of the line, as he was pushed back by the protesters but was not arrested. When protesters crossed the line the next day, however, they were arrested, indicating that the line was drawn to exclude non-Indians. Valliere admitted that the purpose of his action was to demonstrate that he was not afraid of the throng of protesters (*Milwaukee Sentinel* 1989).

4. In actuality, tribal members were relatively safe on the landings in the presence of scores of sheriff's police. They were most vulnerable driving back to the reservation as protesters attempted to run them off the road.

5. I attended this meeting.

6. Judge Barbara Crabb wrote, in granting an injunction to the tribe against the protesters (*LCO v. Wisconsin* 1990b), that they "yelled, 'Dead Indian, dead Indian' and sang, 'A half breed here; a half breed there,' to the tune of 'Old McDonald Had a Farm.' At Eau Pleine Reservoir, they referred to Indian women as squaws and bitches and said, 'The only good Indian is a dead Indian' and that 'Custer had the right idea' and 'Tom Maulson is nothing but a fucking Jew. We need another Hitler to take care of him.'"

7. I attended the rally, feast, dance, and doings at Butternut Lake that day.

8. The drum belonged to Nick Hockings. I say "Dream Dance style" because, although the painting of the drumhead suggests it was commonly used for spiritual purposes, Dream Dance drums are painted much differ-

ently. See Vennum 1982, the most thorough discussion of this ritual complex available.

9. As one of the founders of the American Indian Movement, Benton-Banai might have had good reason to be anxious about the FBI (Churchill and Vanderwall 1988).

10. Carufel spoke extemporaneously but had written out what he intended to say a couple of days before at the home of Nick Van Der Puy in Eagle River, forty miles east of Lac du Flambeau, where I was staying at the time. Carufel spoke while Van Der Puy typed on a word processor. The piece was subsequently published in *News from Indian Country* in three parts over the summer of 1989.

11. He uses the lowercase "g," translating "Barber" back into Anishinaabemowin from which it came (see Ritzenthaler 1945).

12. Though gaiashkibos had insisted that "We don't put these fish on our walls," implying that "we" referred to Ojibwes, a number of the leaders of this movement do in fact contract the services of local taxidermists to stuff and mount some of the bigger fish they take for display purposes, rather like the non-Indians in the area. In many cases, however, the fish that have been mounted have been speared and not taken with hook and line.

13. The tape was not commercially made and came into the possession of Tom and Laura Maulson, who made a copy for me. There are no credits of any kind identifying it.

7. ANISHINAABE SUMMER

1. I attended this event and made an audiotape of the speakers' remarks (Nesper 1989a).

2. The original "Hamburger Hill" was a ten-day battle in 1967 in Vietnam, the subject of a film made in 1987.

3. Nick Hockings had invited me to these ceremonies while at the Treaty Rights Forum in Chicago, so I attended them.

4. I attended this feast.

5. I watched the Flambeau parade and marched with the WTA in the Minocqua parade.

6. According to Gerald Vizenor, "the signs of moccasins, canoes, feathers, leathers" constitute a "reversal of the striptease" that results in disempowerment (Vizenor 1987:181). However, because that context in this case was effectively controlled and manipulated by the Wa-Swa-Gon Treaty Association's agenda, the confusion of cultural images served to reverse the reversal, as it were, and empower their efforts in a Bahktinian, carnivalesque way.

7. I attended this powwow and witnessed the events described.

8. THE REFERENDUM

1. Writing about the White Earth reservation in Minnesota in the 1960s, James G. E. Smith noted: "Those men of standing who successfully compete for elective office expose themselves to severe criticism. Discussion of individuals is often critical and destructive, and those holding public office are the most obvious targets" (Smith 1973:27).

2. Rebecca Kugel (1985) cites the relevant studies of factionalism in her second footnote.

3. Because the *Boldt* decision of 1974 in Washington State had allocated 50 percent of the salmon fishing to thirteen different tribes of Indians, they found it necessary to reinvent the idea of separate and traditional fishing grounds (see Boxberger 1989). This process may have been the basis of the failed attempt to import the idea to northern Wisconsin.

The idea had other roots as well. Lac du Flambeau's attorney, James Jannetta, had not only worked as attorney-advisor in the Office of the Solicitor, Division of Indian Affairs in the Department of the Interior, but also assisted attorney Bruce Greene after the Sault Ste Marie tribe of Chippewa Indians, and the Bay Mills and Grand Traverse bands sued the state of Michigan over their fishing rights in the Great Lakes in 1973 in what became *United States v. Michigan.* One of the elements of the settlement that was worked out after the Indians won that case in 1979 was the concept of fishing zones, i.e., sections of the Great Lakes earmarked for Indian commercial fishing, Indian trap net fishing, sports fishing, lake trout refuge (Doherty 1990:69, 112, 118).

4. These concerns rose to the level of legislation. In July of 1989, the tribal council passed Resolution 230, which was critical of the Wa-Swa-Gon Treaty Association's recent actions, pointing out that the WTA "has no connection with the Tribe," that it "does not speak for the Tribe, which firmly supports treaty rights, but represents the interests of *all* members with regard to their rights, and not just a faction" (Lac du Flambeau 1989; original emphasis). The resolution was sent to Jim Schlender, executive director of GLIFWC, asking that it be distributed to treaty support groups.

Bibliography

Adams, Arthur T. 1961. *The Explorations of Pierre Radisson*. Minneapolis: Ross and Haines.

Alinsky, Saul D. 1971. *Rules for Radicals: A Pragmatic Primer for Realistic Radicals*. New York: Vintage Books.

Avruch, Kevin. 1972. "Politics and Pow Wows in Lac Courte Oreilles." Bachelor's thesis, University of Chicago.

Baraga, Frederic. [1878, 1880] 1992. *A Dictionary of the Ojibwa Language*. St. Paul: Minnesota Historical Society Press.

Barnouw, Victor. 1950. *Acculturation and Personality among the Wisconsin Chippewa*. Memoirs of the American Anthropological Association 52, no. 4, pt. 2, memoir 72.

———. 1961. "Chippewa Social Atomism." *American Anthropologist* 63:1006–1013.

———. 1970. *Wisconsin Chippewa Myths and Tales and their Relations to Chippewa Life*. Madison: University of Wisconsin Press.

Barret, S. A. 1911. "The Dream Dance of the Chippewa and Menominee Indians of Northern Wisconsin." *Bulletin of the Public Museum of the City of Milwaukee* 1, article 4.

Beck, David. 1988. *The Chicago American Indian Community, 1893–1988: Annotated Bibliography and Guide to Sources*. Chicago: NAES College Press.

Becker, George C. 1983. *Fishes of Wisconsin*. Madison: University of Wisconsin Press.

Benton-Banai, Edward. 1988. *The Mishomis Book: The Voice of the Ojibway*. St. Paul MN: Red School House.

Bird-David, Nurit. 1992. "Beyond 'The Original Affluent Society': A Culturalist Reformulation." *Current Anthropology* 33, no. 1 (February):25–47.

Black-Rogers, Mary. 1977a. "Ojibwa Power-Belief System." In *The Anthropology of Power: Ethnographic Studies from Asian, Oceania, and the New World*, ed. R. D. Fogelson and R. N. Adams, 142–152. New York: Academic Press.

Blu, Karen. 1980. *The Lumbee Problem: The Making of an American Indian People*. Cambridge: Cambridge University Press.

Boggs, Stephen T. 1954. "Ojibwa Socialization." Ph.D dissertation, Washington University.

———. 1956. "An Interactional Study of Ojibwa Socialization." *American Sociological Review* 21:191–198.

———. 1958. "Culture Change and the Personality of Ojibwa Children." *American Anthropologist* 60:47–58.

Bokern, James K. 1987. "The History of Primary Canoe Routes of the Six Chippewa Bands from the Lac du Flambeau Region." Master's thesis, University of Wisconsin–Steven's Point.

Bourdieu, Pierre. 1977. *Outline of a Theory of Practice*. Cambridge: Cambridge University Press.

Boxberger, Daniel L. 1989. *To Fish in Common: The Ethnohistory of Lummi Indian Salmon Fishing*. Lincoln: University of Nebraska.

Bresette, Walter. 1989. *Memo to the Waswagon Treaty Association*.

Brightman, Robert. 1976. "The Montagnais Naskapi 'Eat-All' Feast: Ritual Gluttony and the Hunter-Prey Relationship." Master's thesis, University of Chicago.

———. 1983. "Animal and Human in Rock Cree Religion and Subsistence." Ph.D. dissertation, University of Chicago.

———. 1993. *Grateful Prey: Rock Cree Human-Animal Relationships*. Berkeley: University of California Press.

Bruner, Edward. 1986. "Ethnography as Narrative." In *The Anthropology of Experience*, ed. Victor W. Turner and Edward M. Bruner, 135–154. Urbana: University of Illinois Press.

Buckley, Thomas. 1979. "Doing Your Thinking: Aspects of Traditional Yurok Education." *Parabola* 4, no. 4:29–37.

Caudill, William. 1949. "Psychological Characteristics of Acculturated Wisconsin Ojibwa Children." *American Anthropologist* 51:409–427.

Champagne, Duane. 1989. *American Indian Societies: Strategies and Conditions of Political and Cultural Survival*. Cultural Survival Report 32. Cambridge MA: Cultural Survival.

Chicago and Northwestern. 1924. "Summer Outings." Chicago and Northwestern railroad map. Joseph Regenstein Library map collection. University of Chicago.

Churchill, Ward, and Jim Vanderwall. 1988. *Agents of Repression: The FBI's Secret Wars against the Black Panthers and the American Indian Movement*. Boston: South End Press.

Cleland, Charles. 1982. "The Inland Shore Fishery of the Northern Great

Lakes: Its Development and Importance in Prehistory." *American Antiquity* 47, no. 4:761–784.

Clifton, James. 1978. "Potawatomi." In *The Northeast,* ed. Bruce Trigger. Vol. 15, *Handbook of North American Indians,* gen. ed. William Sturtevant, 725–742. Washington DC: Smithsonian Institution Press.

———. 1987. "Wisconsin Death March: Explaining the Extremes in Old Northwest Indian Removal." *Transactions of the Wisconsin Academy of Sciences, Arts, and Letters* 75:1–39.

Cohen, Fay G., et al. 1986. *Treaties on Trial: The Continuing Controversy over Northwest Indian Fishing Rights.* Seattle: University of Washington Press.

Copway, George. 1850. *The Traditional History and Characteristic Sketches of the Ojibway Nation.* London: Charles Gilpin.

Cornell, Stephen. 1988. *The Return of the Native: American Indian Political Resurgence.* New York: Oxford University Press.

Day, Gordon M., and Bruce G. Trigger. "Algonquin." In *The Northeast,* ed. Bruce Trigger. Vol. 15, *Handbook of North American Indians,* gen. ed. William Sturtevant, 792–797. Washington DC: Smithsonian Institution Press.

Dempsey, Hugh A. 1978. *Charcoal's World.* Lincoln: University of Nebraska Press.

Densmore, Frances. 1910. *Chippewa Music.* Smithsonian Institution, Bureau of American Ethnology, bulletin 45. Washington DC: Government Printing Office.

———. [1929] 1979. *Chippewa Customs.* St. Paul: Minnesota Historical Society.

Dewdney, Selwyn. 1975. *The Sacred Scrolls of the Southern Ojibway.* Toronto: University of Toronto.

Doherty, Robert. 1990. *Disputed Waters: Native Americans and the Great Lakes Fishery.* Lexington: University Press of Kentucky.

Dunning, R. W. 1959. *Social and Economic Change among the Northern Ojibwa.* Toronto: University of Toronto.

Erikson, Patricia Pierce. 1999. "A-Whaling We Will Go: Encounters of Knowledge and Memory at the Makah Cultural and Research Center." *Cultural Anthropology* 14, no.4:556–583.

Faiman-Silvaa, S. L. 1997. *Choctaws at the Crossroads: The Political Economy of Class and Culture in the Oklahoma Timber Region.* Lincoln: University of Nebraska Press.

Fixico, Donald. 1987. "Chippewa Fishing and Hunting Rights and the Voigt Decision." In *An Anthology of Great Lakes American Indian History,* ed. Donald L. Fixico, 481–519. Milwaukee: University of Wisconsin–Milwaukee, American Indian Studies.

Fotsch, David. 1989. Spearfishing Coverage: Multiple Reports. WUHM public radio audiotape. Milwaukee.

Fowler, Loretta. 1987. *Shared Symbols, Contested Meanings: Gros Ventre Culture and History, 1778–1984.* Ithaca: Cornell University Press.

Friedman, Jonathan. 1994. *Cultural Identity and Global Process.* London: Sage Publications.

———. 1999. "Indigenous Stuggles and the Discreet Charm of the Bourgeoisie." *Journal of World Systems Research* 5, no. 2:391–412.

Geertz, A.W. 1994. *The Invention of Prophesy: Continuity and Meaning in Hopi Indian Religion.* Berkeley: University of California Press.

Gillan, John. 1942. "Acquired Drives in Culture Contact." *American Anthropologist* 44:545–554.

Gillan, John, and Victor Raimy. 1940. "Acculturation and Personality." *American Sociological Review* 5:371–380.

GLIFWC. 1988. *Great Lakes Indian Fish and Wildlife Commission 1988 Annual Report.* Odanah WI.

Gough, Robert. 1997. *Farming the Cutover: A Social History of Northern Wisconsin, 1900–1940.* Lawrence: University Press of Kansas.

Greenberg, Adolf M., and James Morrison. 1982. "Group Identities in the Boreal Forest: The Origin of the Northern Ojibwa." *Ethnohistory* 29, no. 2:75–102.

Habeck, J.R., and J.T. Curtis. 1959. "Forest Cover and Deer Population and Densities in Early Northern Wisconsin." *Transactions of the Wisconsin Academy of Sciences, Arts and Letters* 48:49–56.

Hall, Robert L. 1997. *An Archaeology of the Soul: North American Indian Belief and Ritual.* Urbana: University of Illinois Press.

Hall, Thomas D. 1986. "Incorporation in the World-System: Toward a Critique." *American Sociological Review* 51:390–402.

Hallowell, A. Irving. 1955. *Culture and Experience.* Philadelphia: University of Pennsylvania Press.

———. 1992. *The Ojibwa of Berens River, Manitoba: Ethnography into History.* Ed. Jennifer S. H. Brown. Harcourt Brace Jovanovich, Case Studies in Cultural Anthropology.

Hamell, George. 1983. "Trading in Metaphors: The Magic of Beads." In *Proceedings of the 1982 Glass Trade Bead Conference.* Research Records no. 16, gen. ed. Charles F. Hayes III, 5–28. Rochester NY: Rochester Museum and Science Division, Research Division.

Hanaway, Donald. 1990. "History of the Treaty Rights Controversy." Madison WI. Typescript.

Hay, Thomas. n.d. "The Dynamics of the Development of Ojibwa Emotional Restraint." Ph.D. dissertation, Michigan State University.

Hickerson, Harold. 1962. *The Southwestern Chippewa: An Ethnohistorical Study.* Memoirs of the American Anthropological Association 64, no. 3, pt. 2, memoir 92.

———. 1963. "The Socio-Historical Significance of Two Chippewa Ceremonials." *American Anthropologist* 65:67–85.

———. 1970. *The Chippewa and Their Neighbors: A Study in Ethnohistory.* Prospect Heights IL: Waveland Press.

———. 1973. "Fur Trade Colonialism and the North American Indian." *Journal of Ethnic Studies* 1:15–44.

Hodge, Frederic. 1959. *Handbook of American Indians North of Mexico.* New York: Pageant Books.

Hoffman, W. J. 1891. "The Mid'wiwin or Grand Medicine Society, of the Ojibwe." In *Bureau of American Ethnology Seventh Annual Report,* 143–300. Washington DC.

Hollatz, Tom. 1984. *Louis No. 1: The Life and Legend of Louis St. Germaine, Native American.* Neshkoro WI: Laranmark Press.

———. 1989. *Gangster Holidays: The Lore and Legends of the Bad Guys.* St. Cloud MN: North Star Press.

Huber, Albert. 1936. "Meeting at Lac du Flambeau." *Indians at Work* 4 (October):26–27. Washington DC: Government Printing Office.

James, Bernard. 1954a. "Some Critical Observations Concerning Analysis of Chippewa 'Atomism' and Chippewa Personality." *American Anthropologist* 56:283–286.

———. 1954b. "A Study of an American Indian Village." Ph.D. dissertation, University of Wisconsin–Madison.

———. 1961. "Social-Psychological Dimensions of Ojibwa Acculturation." *American Anthropologist* 63:721–746.

———. 1970. "Continuity and Emergence in Indian Poverty Culture." *Current Anthropology* 11, nos. 4–5:435–452.

Jenness, Diamond. 1935. *The Ojibwa of Parry Island: Their Social and Religious Life.* National Museum of Canada, bulletin 78, Anthropology Series. Ottawa: Department of Mines.

Johnston, Basil. 1976. *Ojibway Heritage.* New York: Columbia University Press.

———. 1990. *Ojibway Ceremonies.* Lincoln: University of Nebraska Press.

Jones, George O., et al. 1924. *History of Lincoln, Oneida, and Vilas Counties, Wisconsin.* Minneapolis: H. C. Cooper Jr.

Jones, Reverend Peter. 1861. *History of the Ojibway Indians; with Especial Reference to Their Conversion to Christianity.* London: A. W. Bennett.

Kappler, Charles J., ed. 1904–41. *Indian Affairs: Laws and Treaties.* Vol. 2. Washington DC: Government Printing Office.

Kinietz, Vernon, ed. 1991. *The Indians of the Western Great Lakes, 1615–1760*. Ann Arbor: University of Michigan Press.

Kmiecik, Neil. 1987. *Results of Spearing during Spring 1986: Data Summaries*. Administrative report 87-3. Odanah WI: Great Lakes Indian Fish and Wildlife Commission, Biological Services Division.

———. 1991. *Spearfishery of the Lake Superior Tribes of Chippewa Indians: Spring 1990 Summary Report*. Administrative report 91-4. Odanah WI: Great Lakes Indian Fish and Wildlife Commission, Biological Services Division.

Kmiecik, Neil, and Dale Shively. 1990. *Open Water Spearing and Netting in Northern Wisconsin by Chippewa Indians during 1989*. Administrative report 90-1. Odanah WI: Great Lakes Indian Fish and Wildlife Commission, Biological Services Division.

Kohl, Johann Georg. [1860] 1985. *Kitchi-Gumi: Life among the Lake Superior Ojibway*. St. Paul: Minnesota Historical Society Press.

Kugel, Rebecca. 1985. "Factional Alignment among the Minnesota Ojibwe, 1850–1880." *American Indian Culture and Research Journal* 9, no. 4:23–47.

Lac Courte Oreilles Band, Etc. v. Voigt. 1983. 700 F.2d 341.

Lac Courte Oreilles Band of Lake Superior Chippewa Indians et al. v. State of Wisconsin et al. 1987a. 653 Federal Supplement 1420–1435.

———. 1987b. 668 Federal Supplement 1233–42.

———. 1989. 707 Federal Supplement 1034–1062.

———. 1990a. 740 Federal Supplement 1400–1427.

———. 1990b. 749 Federal Supplement 913–923.

———. 1991. 74-C-313-C:1–39.

Lac du Flambeau. 1989. Tribal Council Resolution No. 230.

Lac du Flambeau Band of Lake Superior Chippewa Indians et al. v. Stop Treaty Abuse/Wisconsin, Incorporated et al. 1991. 91-C-117-C:1–39.

Lac du Flambeau Band of Lake Superior Chippewa Indians v. State of Wisconsin. 1991. 770 Federal Supplement 480, 485.

Lakeland Times (Minocqua WI). 1983a. "Ruling Allows Chippewa Indians Off-Reservation Hunting Anytime." February 3:1.

———. 1983b. "Tribes Say Taking Steps on Hunting Rights." February 10:1.

———. 1986a. "Chippewa Also Invite Confrontation." March 14:10.

———. 1986b. "Spearfishing Positions Outlined at Forum." March 14:1.

———. 1986c. Letter to the Editor. March 25:12.

———. 1986d. "Protest Peacefully at PARR Rally." April 18:9.

———. 1986e. "PARR Rally-March Draws 100 Protesters." April 29:1.

———. 1986f. Letter to the Editor. May 6:9.

———. 1986g. "Obey Won't Support Tribal Fishery: Angry about Harvest." May 6:1.

———. 1987a. "State to Appeal Doyle Decision." February 24:1.

———. 1987b. "Thompson Tells PARR He Supports Change." March 10:1.

———. 1987c. "Two Sides of the Treaty Coin." March 31:1.

———. 1987d. "Tribe Condemns PARR as Racist." May 1:1.

———. 1987e. "Chippewas Hold Unification Ceremony at Butternut Landing." May 5:1.

———. 1988a. Letter to the Editor: "Stop Sucking Your Thumb and Act!" April 8:10.

———. 1988b. "Permit Granted PARR for Rally." April 8:2.

———. 1988c. Treaty Beer Advertisement. April 19:2.

———. 1988d. Letter to the Editor: "At What Price Heritage?" April 26:8.

———. 1988e. Letter to the Editor "Rape of Precious Resource." May 6:6.

———. 1988f. Letter to the Editor "Speared Fish Left." May 13:7.

———. 1988g. "New Anti-Treaty Organization Brewing." May 20:1.

———. 1989a. "Mole Lake Rejects Offer." January 13:1.

———. 1989b. "Spearing under Fire by Governor." May 5:1.

———. 1989c. "Spearing Season Ends Quietly in North." May 6:2.

———. 1989d. "Tribal Council Restricts Use of Altered U.S. Flag." July 11:1.

———. 1989e. "Blessing: Sacred Grounds Cleansed of Tribal Etiquette Breach." July 18:4.

———. 1989f. "State Reportedly Ups Treaty Ante." September 26:1.

———. 1989g. "Let Feds Handle Spearfishing: Crowd." October 10:1.

———. 1989h. "Agreement Needs More Study, Says Group." October 27:1.

———. 1989i. "LdF Vote: Members say 'No.'" October 27:1.

———. 1991. "Education: Truth Must Be Taught in Class." March 1:14.

Landes, Ruth. 1937. *Ojibwa Sociology.* Columbia University Contributions to Anthropology, vol. 29. New York: Columbia University Press.

LaVeen, Deborah. 1978. "Hustlers and Heroes: Portrait and Analysis of the Chicago Indian Village." Ph.D. dissertation, University of Chicago.

Leacock, Eleanor B. 1954. *The Montagnais Hunting Territory and the Fur Trade.* Memoirs of the American Anthropological Association, 56, no. 5, pt. 2, memoir 78.

Les, Betty. 1988. "Summary: History of Fishing in Wisconsin." Wisconsin Department of Natural Resources, Bureau of Research. Typescript.

Levi-Strauss, Claude. 1966. *The Savage Mind.* London: Weidenfeld and Nicolson.

Loew, Patty. 1996. "People of the Seventh Fire: A History of Chippewa Treaty Rights in Wisconsin." Typescript.

Mahliot, François. 1910. "A Wisconsin Fur Trader's Journal, 1804–05." *Collections of the State Historical Society of Wisconsin,* ed. Rueben Gold Thwaites, 19:163–233.

Marcus, George E., and Michael M. J. Fisher. 1986. *Anthropology as Cultural Critique: An Experimental Moment in the Human Sciences.* Chicago: University of Chicago Press.

Masinaigan. 1987. "Spring 1987 in Review." (Summer):1–3.

———. 1990. (Spring).

McGee, W. J. 1898. "Ojibwa Feather Symbolism." *American Anthropologist* 11:177–180.

Meyer, George. 1985. "Statement of the Department of Natural Resources at Joint Press Conference on the 1985 Chippewa Spring Spearing Season—May 9, 1985." Typescript.

Milwaukee Journal. 1986a. "Chippewa Spearers Overharvest Star Lake." May 1:7A.

———. 1986b. "Thompson, Watts Hit Indian Treaty Rights." June 20, pt. 2:3.

———. 1989a. "DNR Cuts Walleye Limits." April 28:1.

———. 1989b. "Chippewa Stays Calm Amid Storm." April 30:1B.

———. 1989c. "Revised Bag Limits for Anglers." April 30:3B.

Milwaukee Sentinel. 1989. "'Bitter' Anti-Spearing Protests Spread, Are Deplored as Racist." April 27:9.

Minnesota v. Mille Lacs Band of Chippewa Indians. 1999. 124 F.3d 904, 97–1337.

Nagel, Joane, and C. Matthew Snipp. 1993. "Ethnic Reorganization: American Indian Social, Economic, Political, and Cultural Strategies for Survival." *Ethnic and Racial Studies* 16, no. 2 (April):203–235.

Nesper, Larry. 1989a. Audiorecording of the Chicago Indian Treaty Rights Committee Forum on Treaty Rights. United Church of Christ of Rogers Park, May 11.

———. 1989b. "Contemporary Anishinaabe Spirituality and Politics: Preliminary Soundings on the 1989 Lac du Flambeau Chippewa Spearfishing Season," *Chicago Anthropology Exchange* 18 (autumn).

News from Indian Country. 1989a. "Judge Crabb Not Afraid of Controversy." Vol. 4, no. 6 (June):4.

———. 1989b. "Supporters Take Lead: Hot Words, No Violence at Spearfishing Protest." Vol. 4, no. 6 (June):8.

———. 1989c. "Walking Together for Peace and Justice." Vol. 4, no. 6 (June):27.

———. 1989d. "Flambeau Membership Rejects State Pact 439-366." Vol. 3, no. 11 (November):1.

Oberly, James. 1991. "The Lake Superior Chippewas and Treaty Rights in the Ceded Territory of Wisconsin: Population, Prices, Land, Natural Resources, and Regulation, 1837–1983." Typescript prepared for the Great Lakes Indian Fish and Wildlife Commission.

Obey, David. 1989. Letter to Lake Superior Chippewa Tribal Chairmen. April 18.

Ojibwa General Council. 1931. Minutes. November 3–6. Manuscript collection. State Historical Society of Wisconsin, Madison.

Overholt, Thomas W., and J. Baird Callicott. 1982. *Clothed-In-Fur and Other Tales: An Introduction to Ojibwa Worldview.* New York: University Press of America.

Peers, Laura L. 1994. *The Ojibwa of Western Canada, 1780 to 1870.* Winnipeg: University of Manitoba Press.

Perrot, Nicholas. 1911. "Memoir of the Manners, Customs, and Religion of the Savages of North America." In *The Indian Tribes of the Upper Mississippi Valley and Region of the Great Lakes,* ed. Emma Helen Blair, 1:23–272.

Pickering, Kathleen. 2000. *Lakota Culture, World Economy.* Lincoln: University of Nebraska Press.

Pope, Captain John. 1849. "Map of the Territory of Minnesota Exhibiting the Route of the Expedition to the Red River of the North, in the Summer of 1849." Joseph Regenstein Library map collection. University of Chicago.

Quaife, Milo Milton, ed. 1921. *Alexander Henry's Travels and Adventures in the Years 1760–1776.* Chicago: Lakeside Press.

Rasmussen, Charlie Otto. 1998. *Where the River Is Wide: Pahquahwong and the Chippewa Flowage.* Odanah WI: Great Lakes Indian Fish and Wildlife Press.

RCIA. 1840–1906. *Reports of the Commissioner of Indian Affairs to the Secretary of the Interior, 1840–1906.* Washington DC: Government Printing Office.

Rhinelander Daily News (Rhinelander WI). 1989a. "35 Arrested at the Boat-landings." April 27:1.

———. 1989b. "Crabb Rejects Spearing Limits, To Hear Argument Friday about Ending Season." May 4:1.

Ritzenthaler, Robert. 1945. "The Acquisition of Surnames by the Chippewa Indians." *American Anthropologist* 47:175–177.

———. 1950. "The Building of a Chippewa Indian Birch-Bark Canoe." *Milwaukee Public Museum Bulletin* 19, no. 2 (November):53–99.

———. 1978. "Southwestern Chippewa." In *The Northeast,* ed. Bruce Trigger. Vol. 15, *Handbook of North American Indians,* gen. ed. William Sturtevant, 760–771. Washington DC: Smithsonian Institution Press.

Rogers, E. S. 1962. *The Round Lake Ojibwa.* Toronto: Royal Ontario Museum, Royal Ontario Museum, Art and Archeology Division.

Rostlund, Erhard. 1952. *Fresh Water Fish and Fishing in Native North America.* University of California Publications in Geography 9. Berkeley: University of California Press.

Rynkiewich, Michael A. 1980. "Chippewa Powwows." In *Anishinabe: 6 Studies of Modern Chippewa,* ed. Anthony J. Paredes, 31–100. Gainesville: University Press of Florida.

Ryser, Rudolf C. 1995. *Anti-Indian Movement on the Tribal Frontier.* Occasional Paper 16-3. Olympia WA: Center for World Indigenous Studies.

Sahlins, Marshall. 1985. *Islands of History.* Chicago: University of Chicago Press.

———. 1988. "Cosmologies of Capitalism: The Trans-Pacific Sector of 'The World System.'" *Proceedings of the British Academy* 74:1–51.

St. Germaine, Ernie. 1990. *Winaboozhoo Adisokan: 24 Traditional Ojibwe Stories and Legends.* Lac du Flambeau WI: Lac du Flambeau Family Resource Center.

Satz, Ronald. 1991. *Chippewa Treaty Rights: The Reserved Rights of Wisconsin's Chippewa Indians in Historical Perspective.* Transactions of the Wisconsin Academy of Sciences, Arts and Letters 79, no. 1.

———. 1994. "Tell Those Gray Haired Men What They Should Know: The Hayward Indian Congress of 1934." *Wisconsin Magazine of History* 77 (spring):196–224.

Schenk, Theresa M. 1997. *The Voice of the Crane Echoes Far: The Sociopolitical Organization of the Lake Superior Ojibwa, 1640–1855.* New York: Garland Publishing.

Schlender, James. 1991. "Treaty Rights in Wisconsin: A Review." *Northeast Indian Quarterly* (spring):4–16.

Schlesier, Karl. 1990. "Rethinking the Midewiwin and the Plains Ceremonial Called the Sun Dance." *Plains Anthropologist* 35:1–27.

Schoolcraft, Henry Rowe. 1847. *Historical and Statistical Information respecting the History, Condition, and Prospects of the Indian Tribes of the United States; Collected and Prepared under the Direction of the Bureau of Indian Affairs per Act of Congress of March 3rd, 1847.* Philadelphia: Lippincott, Grambo.

Schorger, A. W. 1953. "The White-tailed Deer in Early Wisconsin." *Transactions of the Wisconsin Academy of Sciences, Arts and Letters* 42:197–247.

Schwimmer, Erik G. 1972. "Symbolic Competition." *Anthropologica*, n.s., 14, no. 2:117–55.

Scrobell, Daniel D. 1988. *Early Times*. Minocqua WI: Heritage House.

Shifferd, Patricia. 1976. "A Study in Economic Change: The Chippewa of Northern Wisconsin: 1854–1900." *Western Canadian Journal of Anthropology* 6, no. 4:16–41.

Sider, Gerald. 1993. *Lumbee Indian Histories: Race, Ethnicity, and Indian Identity in the Southern United States*. New York: Cambridge University Press.

Silvern, Steven. 1997. "The Geography of Ojibwe Treaty Rights in Northern Wisconsin." In *Wisconsin Land and Life*, ed. Robert C. Ostergren and Thomas R. Vale, 489–504. Madison: University of Wisconsin Press.

Slotkin, James S. 1957. *The Menominee Pow Wow: A Study in Cultural Decay*. Milwaukee Public Museum Publications in Anthropology.

Smith, Huron. 1932. "Ethnobotany of the Ojibwe Indians." *Bulletin of the Public of the City of Milwaukee* 4:327–525.

Smith, James G. E. 1973. *Leadership among the Southwestern Ojibwa*. Publications in Ethnology, no. 7. Ottawa: National Museum of Canada.

———. 1974. "Kindred, Clan, and Conflict: Continuity and Change among the Southwestern Ojibwa." Typescript, University of Waterloo.

Spicer, Edward H. 1971. "Persistent Cultural Systems." *Science* 174, no. 4011:795–800.

Spindler, George, and Louise Spindler. 1984. *Dreamers with Power: The Menominee*. Prospect Heights IL: Waveland Press.

Spindler, Louise. 1978. "Menominee." In *The Northeast*, ed. Bruce Trigger. Vol. 15, *Handbook of North American Indians*, gen. ed. William Sturtevant, 708–724. Washington DC: Smithsonian Institution Press.

Strickland, Rennard. 1990. "Keeping Our Word: Indian Treaty Rights and Public Responsibilities." Report on a recommended federal role following Wisconsin's request for federal assistance. Manuscript, University of Wisconsin–Madison, School of Law.

Taffora, Raymond P. 1989. Memorandum regarding the Lac du Flambeau Agreement. October 2.

Tanner, J., and E. James. 1830. *A Narrative of the Captivity and Adventures of John Tanner (U.S. Interpreter at the Sault de Ste. Marie): During Thirty Years' Residence among the Indians in the Interior of North America*. New York: G. & C. & H. Carvill.

Thompson, David. 1916. *David Thompson's Narrative of His Expeditions in Western America, 1784–1842*, ed. J. B Tyrell. Toronto: Champlain Society.

Thwaites, R. G., ed. 1896–1901. *The Jesuit Relations and Allied Documents:*

Travels and Explorations of the Jesuit Missionaries in New France, 1610–1791. 73 vols. Cleveland: Burrows Brothers.

Valaskakis, Gail Guthrie. 1988. "The Chippewa and the Other: Living the Heritage of Lac du Flambeau." *Cultural Studies* 2, no. 3:267–293.

Vennum, Thomas. 1982. *The Ojibwa Dance Drum: Its History and Construction*. Smithsonian Folklife Studies, no 2. Washington DC: Smithsonian Institution Press.

Vine, Fred. 1897. Vine to Scott, July 30, 1897. Bureau of Indian Affairs, Field Office Records, LaPointe Agency, Letters Received. Federal Records Center–Chicago.

Vizenor, Gerald. 1987. "Socioacupuncture: Mythic Reversals and the Striptease in Four Scenes." In *The American Indian and the Problem of History*, ed. Calvin Martin, 180–191. New York: Oxford University Press.

Wallace, Anthony F. C. 1956. "Revitalization Movements." *American Anthropologist* 58:264–281.

Warren, William Whipple. [1885] 1984. *History of the Ojibway People*. St. Paul: Minnesota Historical Society Press.

Wausau Daily Herald. 1989a. "State Talks Put Tribal Head, Group at Odds." April 28:1A.

———. 1989b. "Rumors of Hit Men Circulate." April 29:1A.

———. 1989c. "Police Officers Injured in Boatlanding Scuffle." May 2:1A.

———. 1989d. "Flambeau Threatens Full Harvest." May 3:1A.

———. 1989e. "For Chippewa Spearers, [It's] Time to Clean Fish." May 3:1A.

———. 1989f. "Obey Bill Would Limit Spearfishing." May 4:1A.

———. 1989g. "One Parent's Concern." May 4:4A.

———. 1989h. "Spearing Limits Denied." May 4:2A.

———. 1989i. "Dozens Arrested at Trout Lake." May 6:1A.

———. 1989j. "Spearfishing Ends; 2 Sides Claim Victory." May 8:1.

Wausau Sunday Herald. 1989. "Chippewa, Supporters Gather." April 9:1A.

WDNR. *See* Wisconsin Department of Natural Resources

Wenzel, G. W. 1991. *Animal Rights, Human Rights: Ecology, Economy, and Ideology in the Canadian Arctic*. Toronto: University of Toronto Press.

Whaley, Rick, and Walt Bresette. 1994. *Walleye Warriors: An Effective Alliance against Racism and for the Earth*. Philadelphia: New Society Publishers.

White, Richard. 1992. *The Middle Ground: Indians, Empires, and Republics in the Great Lakes Region, 1650–1815*. Cambridge University Press, Cambridge Studies in North American History.

Wilkinson, Charles F. 1990. "Treaty and Fishing Rights of the Wisconsin

Chippewa." The Oliver Randall Lecture. Occasional Paper from the University of Wisconsin Law School. Madison, April 19.

Winn, Vetal. 1923. "The Minocqua Lake Region." *Wisconsin Archeologist,* n.s., 3, no. 2:41–51.

Wisconsin Conservation Commission. 1938. "Deer Bootleg Trail Ends." *Wisconsin Conservation Commission Bulletin* (December):6–9.

Wisconsin Department of Natural Resources (WDNR). n.d. "License Chronology History." Typescript.

Wolf, Eric. 1982. *Europe and the People without History.* Berkeley: University of California Press.

———. 1999. *Envisioning Power: Ideologies of Dominance and Crisis.* Berkeley: University of California Press.

WTA (Wa-Swa-Gon Treaty Association). 1989a. "Come to the 'Treaty Agreement' Town Hall Forum Tonight 5:00–8:00." Poster.

———. 1989b. "Tell It Like It Is." Typescript.

Index

Italicized numbers refer to illustrations.